MOLLY
Child Number 583

by

MARY KEENAN

Published by

 GENERAL STORE
GSPH PUBLISHING HOUSE

Box 28, 1694 Burnstown, Ontario, Canada K0J 1G0
Telephone (613) 432-7697 or 1-800-465-6072

ISBN 1-894263-27-8
Printed and bound in Canada

Copyright 2000
Family photo on back cover by *Sam*.

Layout and Design by Derek McEwen
Printing by Custom Printers of Renfrew Ltd.
General Store Publishing House
Burnstown, Ontario, Canada

Canadian Cataloguing in Publication Data

Keenan, Mary, 1925-
    Molly : child number 583

ISBN 1-894263-27-8

    1. Keenan, Mary, 1925- 2. Orphans–New Brunswick–
Saint John–Biography. I. Title.

HV1010.S232K43 2000   362.7'3'092   C00-900927-2

This book is for my children - Mary - Frankie - Paddy and Molly
and for their children - Julie - Jenny - Tommy - Brennan - Katie - Marion
and Jack
and for their children - Genny - Liam ~ ~ ~ ~ ~ ~ ~
for Paul who insisted
for Jim who assisted

and my Mother ~~ for life

ACKNOWLEDGEMENT

This work was inspired by an orphan's life. The backgrounds are authentic. Some characters are composites. Most situations do portray actual events and facts selected and arranged with purpose. I have used the fabric of life to make this book. It's an amalgam of what I've seen, heard and felt. If good people find themselves in my pages, I'm flattered. If villains do, would they admit it? Generally, if the name of any person is used it could be coincidence, but loved names have spilled from the tumbling box of my mind and were used when the feeling was right.

An experience is never finished until it is written.
Anne Morrow Lindbergh

INDEX

FOREWORD

To Be is to belong to someone.
            Jean-Paul Sartre

When I was growing up my only dream was to belong to somebody. I remember my foster mother, Doris McGlyn, putting me outside in a new red snowsuit, a woollen scarf tied around my face, warm mittens and stiff rubbers. There was a bright red runner for me to pull around the yard. I couldn't have been four. I knew my sled would go farther on the street so I just walked out the gate, towing it behind. I met a little boy and swapped my runner for his wad of gum and kept walking. The gum tasted good, my nose was running, I felt happy being out. I didn't know I was lost until Doris came running towards me, crying out with relief. "Molly, you ran away! You bad girl. What's in your mouth? Where is your sled?" After that she locked the gate and I was lonely in the yard. Strange men walked by and I wanted to say: Take me home, be my father, give me a nickel.

Thirty-three years later, the loneliness of longing was the same, and walking still the reliever. It eased the condition, made the psyche come alive, stirred the emotions and in the late autumn stillness of the Rosedale avenues a shameless little voice still wanted to call out to unfamiliar, handsome men: Take me home, be my love, give me security.

Walking intently, faster, I remembered the powerlessness of our failure. We had entered each other's lives too soon, before Julian or I had become the persons we could be. Now I missed him. I always did. I hustled around a corner into the brisk breeze off Bloor Street and was startled by the sudden pungent smell of starch and steam from the Chinese laundry. It took my breath away, evoking a long-ago memory of captivity—but being free, I savoured it. Kipling's words went round in my head, sing-song and insistent. "Smells are surer than sounds or sights to make your heartstrings crack." And then the other inevitable sing-song cadence began while I marched to its monotonous rhythm: Where is my mother and what is her name?

There is no fire like passion,
There is no shark like hatred,
There is no snare like folly,
There is no torrent like greed.

Gautama Buddha

BOSTON ➤ 1987

*I*F A GOD THERE BE I expect my mother is sitting at His right hand, amazed at the tableau unfolding in Judge Leahy's court. She might be saying, "I did my best, Lord, You know that. But boys will be boys!" That image sustained me and I allowed myself to find it amusing.

I had filed a petition in a Boston court of law to amend administration of my half-brother's estate by including my name as heir to the decedent. Not for the money entailed but to affirm that I was Molly Shannon McBeath, my mother's daughter, illegitimate human being. I was represented in court by Geoff Stall, a young Boston lawyer. At this point in the trial my identity was being challenged by the defendant's lawyer in an American court, using a Canadian document that I had tried for years to drag from an intractable Canadian justice system. I was born, my birth recorded, but I had never seen a copy of Particulars of Registration of Birth. Yet a strange lawyer in another country brought forward as evidence that proof, sent to him by the very person who had told me repeatedly for years that I was not entitled to it. My stomach heaved as he waved the paper in the air, disputing my identity and my mother's signature with unqualified prejudice, but I kept my anger inside, knowing my mother would approve as I struggled to tolerate the legal process.

My fourth appeal to the registrar general of vital statistics had asked if my lawyer might have access to the document or ". . . is there a higher authority I should petition?" The reply was: "Neither I nor anyone else can authorize release of a photocopy of your birth record, to you, your lawyer

1

or to anyone else. Under the Vital Statistics Act you are not entitled to a copy of Particulars of Registration of Birth."

Dogs had papers. I did not. I was *not entitled*. Putting it bluntly, Revenue Canada and the RCMP could know all about me. I was not allowed to know about myself. Over a period of thirty-five years, I had a file bulging with pleas for information and refusals from the Department of Health & Community Services, Vital Statistics, Privacy Commissioners, Children's Aid Coordinators, Catholic Charities, The Human Rights Commission, priests and nuns. It seemed a simple request, but my mother had been unmarried and legislation did not permit the release of the copy I requested. A human rights officer wrote, "The kind of information you are looking for is beyond the scope of the Canadian Human Rights Act." Should I have tried the Humane Society?

My own mother tried to reclaim me from St. Vincent's Orphanage in New Brunswick when I was twelve years old. When I was an infant, a couple had fostered me for three years. Whatever my name had been, they changed it to theirs—McGlyn. After a few years they divorced and sent me back to the orphanage bearing that name. They never adopted me.

My half-brothers' lawyer waved my birth registration in the air, dismissing the handwriting and signature. It was not *their* mother's writing. "This woman just latched onto *this* Kathleen Shannon to satisfy her need. The sons saw no harm in the relationship. They didn't stop it for it did amuse their mother. 'Twas nothing more than wishful thinking on Molly McBeath's part." I wanted to snatch the paper from him and ask the judge, *How did they get this? Could anybody get it? Anybody except me?*

I had the courage to fight my brothers; this was my choice, my doing. Still at this stage I thought it possible to shake the grudge. Foolish wishful thinking. There was no hope that we would ever continue as before. When hatred and malice and bitterness explode in a family, the rift is monstrous.

Paul, my son-in-law, was with me in court. Could he see any logic in this mess? He said of course he could. Understanding my quest, he said it was a daunting experience to hear the vicious fabrication of events suggested by their lawyer, attested to by my seven half-brothers, while their legal counsel, a person named Fox, sat red-faced and leering during my testimony and cross-examination.

The white-haired Judge Leahy showed annoyance with their procedure. His voice, charged with authority, cautioned counsel: "The only issue in this court is whether Molly Shannon McBeath is the daughter of Kathleen

Shannon O'Connor and the half-sister of Sean O'Connor. Argue the facts, please."

Stunned silence followed that reprimand.

After four days in court, Paul and I were thoughtful during the flight home. He grasped the true nature of my quarrel with my brothers and said he believed I had fought the good fight. *He was there and now he knows them.* My comfort and my pride in his presence were indescribable. In a quiet moment I merely said, "You know, Paul, my joy at finding my mother was sufficient. Siblings were secondary. I wanted to know about them but had no intention of compelling them to know me. They all came forward. It was amusing in a way. There was fun and teasing and sharing. It was good while it lasted."

"I know. I do know." Paul nodded with emphasis. "I'm glad I was there with you."

In Toronto the airport was lost in a teeming rain and for all its pouring, it had a softening effect. Earth and air were fresh, renewing a childhood love I'd always had for the sound and feel of water. Memories came roaring back. Little murmurings of guttered water in the lane at St. Vincent's where I would stoop, fascinated by the soughing. The flutter of wet leaves astir and shimmering during a warm fall rain so utterly captivating, I wished I could waft away with them, away from an orphan's life. The warming comfort of walloping rains on the long dormitory windows at night and no one with whom to share that lonely warmth, or the drips long after the rain had stopped. And the times the nuns had allowed the orphans to run under the eavespipe after a sudden summer storm. We'd squeal and push each other under the drain spouts, our little cotton dresses clinging to our bodies while we stomped barefoot in the puddles and sometimes the nun would smile a bit. Then, all too soon, at the height of our fun, she'd spoil it. "Enough," and point silently to the heap of little shoes. She'd turn away, contemplative, walking with her God, knowing we would do what she indicated. Her unspoken command was the rule.

Paul and I moved along the queue to a taxi and though I felt used up, spent, I was lighthearted and satisfied that this trial had ended. Judge Leahy had told the court he would write his decision on the weekend. How would I ever put in the time until my lawyer, Geoff Stall, phoned with news?

Crystal eddies of water doused the taxicab windows and took me back in time to the night I ran away from the orphanage. I felt as if I were thirteen again and as smug and satisfied as I felt on that wet October night. Then too the rain had pelted down, warm and muttering, singing happily with me because I was running away from abandonment and loneliness; running for freedom. Running away to find my life.

*I wish I could somehow erase a single word
that has needlessly, unfairly caused more searing human
anguish, more pain than any other.
That word is 'illegitimate'.*

Alex Haley

SAINT JOHN ➣ 1938

*A*UNT ELSA meant well when she tugged me by the hand, I could tell. But I dragged my feet, reluctant to leave the comfort of mist falling on my face, petrified of the unknown in my struggle for existence. On this ordinary day in the Maritimes I was certain my life was ending before it had hardly begun. The fog hung dark and thick, beads of water clung like a rosary to the clotheslines and the foghorn croaked its mournful, singsong wail. Always there, constant in my life, a deep, loud, friendly voice I trusted. Suddenly a fearful apparition of the old familiar building with iron bars on the windows loomed ghostly from the fog and there in front of me were five long steps I must take to lock-up. It might as well be doomsday!

"Come along Molly. Please darling. I understand. This is hard for me too."

I couldn't blame Aunt Elsa for hurrying, but I could not rush. Pausing on each step to stretch my freedom by a second or two, pain in the hollow pit of my stomach. Five . . . four . . . three . . . two . . . I stepped slowly towards the heavy Gothic door with its pointed arch and black wrought iron hinges. In the vestibule Aunt Elsa tried to be light-hearted when she said goodbye, but the sadness in her soft gray eyes filled me with terror.

"Don't give up darling, you're only thirteen. You can't look after yourself yet. Soon you'll be old enough to do the things you want to do. Time is on your side. You must never give up. Don't forget that, never give up."

All the same, she sounded scary and serious. *I'll never get out now.* I wanted to cling to Aunt Elsa and go right back outside with her but in the cloistered parlor of the Good Shepherd Convent, the solemn porter

5

intoned piously, *"Nil desperandum, Deo Gratias,"* and closed the heavy Gothic door with such finality it seemed like it could be forever. A definite religious smell of incense, polish or a stale locked-up odor of sanctity or something did nothing to calm my nerves. *Just like St. Vincent's, only gloomier.* Three short peals of a bell summoned a white-clad nun, beautiful in the frame of her black veil.

"I'm Mother Monica, mistress of the penitent's class where you'll be. Follow me."

She led the way through long halls and up dark stairways. I had to stop for breath. The nun smiled and waited decorously. *I don't think she hates me. Maybe she knows I had pneumonia when I was small and I cough a lot. Maybe she knows I was in the TB hospital.* I wanted to tell the nun right there all about myself and how much I believed I would find my mother someday. But the silence was foreboding; I knew I mustn't speak. Selecting a key from a large ring, the nun stooped to unlock a huge door. I resented locks. *Locked in, locked out. No place to run to, no way to fight back. Oh God, just let it work this time.*

The nun faced me. "We've decided to call you Magdalen," she said merrily as though her words should cause great joy. "Do not use your own name or give it to anyone." Desperate, I cried to myself, Why? *Is it required? I prefer my own name. I'm Molly, changing my name won't help. I'm Me. You can't take away my right to be me.* My head pounded with anger and frustration, but in the sacrosanct stillness argument was out of place. Besides, behind the bright face, the pretty smile, there was a steely look that told me I had no choice.

I was thirteen and determined to summon the strength to accept whoever it was I had to be. I'd wait to know why I had to be called Magdalen. I'd do everything right, from the beginning. I'd be so good they wouldn't judge me before they even knew me. So what if they had called me bold at the orphanage; a ringleader, they said. They were wrong, for I meant well. Anyway, they didn't know that here. Running away from the orphanage to find my mother was the end of my hard childhood. That hadn't worked and now my search would have to wait. This journey through dim halls with the nun was strange. I wanted to cry so that maybe someone would help me know who I was instead of always punishing me for being a nuisance. But I had learned that tears didn't help, they just made you more of a nuisance, so I practiced smiling behind the nun's back. *I'm determined. In the end I'll find my mother. This place is spooky. There's high fences, even bars on the windows, worse than St. Vincent's. The doors are all locked and who knows what else. Anyway I'll find my mother someday; it's just going to take longer than I thought.* Curious and apprehensive, I followed the nun into a long room past sewing machines and tables to a smaller room.

"Undress," she ordered. "Put your street clothes in your little trunk. Knock on the door when you have changed into this clothing."

I looked around the small room with benches, a sink and a toilet, overhead cupboards with locks. There was a curious door with a small window and hand-lettered words, *St. Peter's Room*. I didn't look inside; some ritual or sorcery might pull me through the Pearly Gates. I'd just do everything the right way, right from the start. The new clothes felt strange. A coarse gray cotton dress almost to my ankles, black woollen stockings and handmade, thin-soled shoes. Underneath, the stiff cotton chemise scratched my skin and the tight cotton band with straps and hooks to flatten my growing breasts was not comfortable; cotton bloomers with a button at the waist were coarse and the petticoat heavy with a deep pocket in which I found a black chapel veil. *Is this what being a penitent is like? Why am I a penitent?* I was glad the others at St. Vincent's couldn't see me. But I wasn't one of them any more so what did it matter? They wouldn't know me now. I hardly know myself. Molly was gone. Head to heels, top to toe, old-fashioned clothes completed her displacement—except maybe deep inside where fright and dismay or hope and daring still crouched. Pretending I was playing a part on stage might make a difference; playacting was fun.

Presently another nun, with a sheet tied around her waist, fine-combed my long, dark hair while I knelt with my back to her, the sheet around my shoulders. *They're looking for lice.* They always did that to new kids at St. Vincent's. *Well, they won't find any.* One thing you could say about St. Vincent's, we all had clean heads. If they ever found bugs on the new kids they just rubbed kerosene into their heads and wrapped a rag around them. It smelled bad and it burned your head and the poor kid had to walk around with that smell and that rag for everyone to know. I pretended I didn't know what was happening.

"It's too long," the nun whispered solemnly.

"I'll braid it, Sister."

I was given a toothbrush and a comb and put into the care of a head girl named Myriam who just said, "Come."

During playtime in the lane at St. Vincent's we used to wonder about the Good Shepherd girls on the other side of the fence at the high, rocky bank in the lane. I followed Myriam self-consciously into a large recreation room where these girls sat in groups at round tables. Mother Monica presided at the front of the room on a raised platform, a table and a bell in front of her. She nodded assent and Myriam took me directly to the rear of the room into the dormitory. It could have been St. Vincent's for it was nearly the same: rows and rows of beds facing a wide aisle down the middle of the room, an oak prie-dieu, a stoup of holy water for sprinkling on everyone after prayers and a big, black-handled brass bell. Myriam put my toothbrush in a tin mug, showed me my nightgown under the pillow and pointed to the towel and basin, the deep sink where I would get water. She explained that everyone bathed sometime Friday or Saturday and shampooed once a month and " . . . always, you must sign in with Stella when you do these things. She's in charge in the dormitory. Oh yes, you must wear your chemise in the tub." The tub was in a dark room in a corner of the dorm with a backless chair and a rubber mat on the wooden floor. The only light came from a transom. We went to the outer room and Mother Monica rang the bell. The group stared in absolute silence.

"I want you all to meet our new girl, Magdalen." Her eyes sparkled; she appeared to enjoy her function. Tired faces stared at me; overhead lights seemed brighter. The heavy clothes felt like an uncomfortable costume, my scalp went damp and a prickly sensation under my arms made me want to scratch. Myriam led me to a chair and we sat together in a small group. When conversation started around the room I felt better, no longer at centre stage. But it was awkward sitting with strangers. No one asked me where I came from or how old I was or wanted to know my name. No one used a surname. They didn't talk about anything interesting as they all sat with hands above the table. *They're all older than me. They don't talk to each other, just sit. Seems strict, are they criminals with changed names? Is that why my name is changed? Some girls from the orphanage are here, they know my name and I know them, so it's no secret. There's a woman wearing a black dress like Myriam's in every group . . . there's one younger, there's another.* I was startled when Myriam leaned forward and whispered, "You mustn't cross your legs."

Presently Mother Monica rang the bell again and the sudden pushing of chairs along the floor was deafening. I watched. Within seconds the head women had moved the tables to either side of the room and the chairs were in neat rows, the strange group of women and girls stood with heads bowed. One could have heard a feather fall. Again the nun tinkled the bell and they all knelt with a great thud. I knelt where I was, my hands folded on the seat of the chair until I noticed all the others knelt behind their chairs. The nun smiled and that was a release to the women to turn and stare. I could actually hear their smiles by the change in their collective breathing. I was assigned a place near the front of the assembly and moved my chair self-consciously. That place would be mine from now on. The bell tinkled again and night prayers began.

The acts of faith, hope and love were said by rote. A sonorous voice above the others reiterated the tedious forms of confession, supplication and contrition, nearly the same as St. Vincent's except the examination of conscience was longer with more quiet time to ponder what evil one might have done that day. After prayers, one of the head girls led a woman into the room. She knelt in front of the mistress and said something about begging pardon. She kissed the floor. The nun responded, "All right, Germaine. We'll see if you mean what you say this time. Just remember that." The bell rang again and the women moved in orderly rows to the dormitory. Some of them left by another door. Later I found out they went to the French dormitory. More loud prayers in bed and a wide sprinkling of holy water and I wondered if it was the same in Catholic places all over the world.

Sleep wouldn't come. Cold walls of deprivation closed around me. Walls I had knocked down a short time ago, higher now, boundaries tighter. Was this the beginning of a better life or was it the end of life? I fancied myself a person named Magdalen and though I was drained of emotion and energy, sleep wouldn't come. A stale dormitory smell and strange noises emanating from tired bodies invaded my senses. Faces loomed in my mind and, as always, there was that yearning to know the face without a name, the mother without a face. *It's not like St. Vincent's. They're not small girls and big girls; they're nearly all women. I thought growing up would be kind of different. It isn't so different being a woman, except it's stricter. I wish my mother knew I was a woman now.*

That sense of maturity became more complicated. In the days that followed I had to act like an adult while working but was treated as a child with no choice or inclination. Just give up, surrender, follow. There was no option, no passion, no compassion. At the Good Shepherd *you* weren't *you* any more. Such a distressing feeling of being unwhole, unconnected, of living on the other side of Being. I'd known nothing of family life. At St. Vincent's the orphans were all homeless, we had that in common, there was a connection. Here there was nothing. Communication was not allowed, but it appeared that some problem or misdemeanor, as in my case, had brought these women to the Good Shepherd. We had no other place to go. We were unwanted. Some were not very bright and probably couldn't function on their own; a few of us were underage and had to be governed. Being friends with the girls my own age was impossible. They were scattered deliberately, a few to each group of older women. Ethel, for instance, could have been seventy years old. The majority were thirty or forty. Ethel reminded me of a witch in a fairy tale. She had snow-white hair, a pointed chin and a long nose. She had no teeth and her gums were always in motion as though she talked to herself, or maybe she was praying. On Friday I was summoned to the infirmary to see a doctor, which seemed normal to me. I was used to doctors listening to my chest, saying "ahh" and "ninety-nine," giving little coughs and being fluoroscoped; having Dr. Cooper lift one little breast and then the other to see what he had to see through the machine. This day I was examined internally, *down there* we'd say at St. Vincent's. I objected but the doctor said I had no choice and the nun in charge of the infirmary stood watch on the other side of a screen, so I had to lie down and spread my knees.

I tried, oh God I tried not to be downhearted. I was rejected. I was frustrated. That grew worse each day and I couldn't pretend it didn't matter. Even though everyone had a saint's name, I resented being called Magdalen. What was the nun driving at? I knew from the gospels that Mary Magdalen was called the *penitent*, the bad woman converted by Jesus. It was in the scriptures that she met Jesus on his Galilean ministry. St. Luke called her a "notorious public sinner" but there was nothing else in the gospels to tell me what she had done wrong. She had bathed His feet with her tears, anointed them with ointment from an alabaster box and dried them with her red hair. That was daring, especially doing it to Jesus. I kind of admired her. I had no idea what made a woman public or what the word meant but the inference was bad. I had nothing to be ashamed of. My only passion was to know my mother or father and for that I'd be brazen, I'd never repent. I wasn't able to begin life on my own when I ran away from the orphanage but that didn't mean I should give up now. Anyway Elsa said I must never. *It's going to take a bit longer than I thought, that's all. I'm only thirteen and they can't do this to me for long.*

At the Good Shepherd the inmates were separated into three classes: the Preservates, the Penitents and the Prisoners. The Preservates, a group of children called the Guardian Angel's class, had a short school routine. They were protected and never encountered women from the Penitents and Prisoners as they came from and went to their quarters. They were favored with first place in the chapel. Very often the Penitents were obliged to stop abruptly on the stairs or along the dark hallway and wait until the patter of little feet coming from another direction had ceased. The Penitents, my group, were called St. Mary Magdalen's class. We entered the candlelit chapel next in holy silence and never saw the Prisoners, St. Barbara's class, who knelt in assigned places at the rear. There would be a secretive shuffling noise from behind while the last two rows filled up with female prisoners. There was an occasional alarming disturbance but no one dared turn a head. Mother Monica knelt high on her prie-dieu serenely praying, beautiful dark eyes on every one of her charges. If there was pushing, commotion or swearing from the back rows the priest simply intoned the Mass louder. "*Introibo ad altare Dei.*" I will go unto the altar of God, he boomed. "*Ad Deum qui laetificat juventutem meam.*" Unto God who giveth joy to my youth, we responded loudly in Latin, pretending nothing was going on behind. *Joy to my youth*, I implored. *Please God, give joy to my youth!*

The Penitents were the backbone of the commercial laundry operated at the Good Shepherd. They staffed the counting room, machine room, ironing room and packing room. A nun presided in each place. The washing was done by the Prisoners, who boiled and scrubbed in a hot, steamy area filled with enormous drum washers, massive hand extractors and the acute smell of lye and bluing.

The steamy, starchy smell of the machine room was different. Clean. Strong buxom women worked the big mangles and presses. I was sent to the ironing room to work, a room with a long counter down the centre and twenty or more ironing boards built into both sides of it. Though this group seemed less robust, the work was demanding and hot. The old iron implement was heavy and there was pressure to iron the greatest number of items. Nevertheless, I did my best each day, ironing the satin step-ins, slips and peignoirs of the well-to-do, their maids' uniforms, their linens. It was mortifying to be given back any piece of work with a crease or a rough spot. Mother Celestine would peer over her spectacles while two red annoyance spots appeared on her cheeks and she approached your ironing board holding the item high for all to see. The look on her face made you feel you had done something wicked. When an alb or a surplice was to be ironed, the nun smiled over her spectacles while deciding who was worthy to iron this piece of altar linen. We all hoped for the honour even if the starched pieces were difficult and scorched easily; great care had to be taken to not tear the delicate lace with the pointed iron.

Each time the clock struck the hour, the nun would intone loudly, "In the name of the Father," and make the sign of the cross. Then the workers recited the rosary aloud while continuing to work. The droning responses helped pass the time. The nuns never allowed that once in a while we workers had monthly cramps and didn't feel well. No consideration was allowed for times like that. Then, I just made trips to the toilet and bolted the door to sit for a while and to loosen the band that bound my tender breasts, being careful not to stay too long. The nuns recognized I was good at what I did, so more was expected of me. In time I was moved to the second ironing board in the first row, behind Gladys, the head girl. Gladys and I became a team. I was surprised that the nuns allowed even a working relationship. She did the poky puffed sleeves, collar and shoulders, then I would take over the waist and large skirt area. Gladys worked fast, I had to move at breakneck speed to keep up and not let the starched skirt dry, making it harder to iron. If I moved too fast, the iron sometimes tipped and wrist burns were commonplace. I pretended I was a servant, ironing maid's uniforms for those who worked for the lucky rich people. Thinking that way also helped pass the time. The heavy iron had a big wooden handle; it caused blisters and after a day's work it was hard to hold. But then, in a few months the blisters became calluses and I was broken in.

The routine was severe. Mother Monica rang the big bell at five-thirty and everyone jumped from bed to kneel for loud morning prayers. We dressed quickly under tentlike nightgowns and were in the laundry by eight after daily Mass, more morning prayers and breakfast. The first break came at eleven-thirty when we returned to the recreation room for religious instruction from *Butler's Catechism*, a little book easily kept in a pocket, eighty-six questions and answers memorized by heart from a very early age. *Who made the world? God made the world. Who is God? God is the Creator and Sovereign Being of heaven and earth and all things. How many Gods are there? There is but one God Who will reward the good and punish the wicked. How many persons are there in God?* Repetitious rote. I knew it since age five and some words we strung together making strange made-up words, like "He suffered under bunch-a-spiders," instead of Pontius Pilate, or "God is great and God is good, let us spank Him for our food."

After dinner we often walked outside in groups or in a large circle, but by one o'clock we were all back at work. Midafternoon there was a break for tea, bread and molasses. Sometimes in the evening we returned to the high fenced yard, but most often were marched to the recreation room to sit in the groups where conversation, the only time during the day that talking was permitted, was limited and tiresome. Talking with anyone was a sin and that's where I failed most. All my confessions admitted, *I talked during holy silence, I talked on the stairs, I talked in the laundry, I talked to another girl, I talked to myself, I talked to Germaine.* Talking to Germaine was the biggest sin of all.

When spring came, the cool air wafting through the barred windows in the ironing room brought a terrible longing to be free. Ironing was routine; too much time to think. I craved some justification for the state of my life; I wanted to go to school and was frantic to have some authority over myself. Unhinging myself from Molly was impossible. Magdalen was a stranger. I could not agree to be someone else and never responded to the very thought of it even when Molly seemed a dispassionate observer urging me to sustain those qualities of trying to please, wanting to belong, needing to be important. Recreation time was depressing—just a time to sit down, exhausted from the long hours in the laundry. At St. Vincent's there had been a semblance of childhood. To amuse ourselves we learned to knit with sucker sticks and twine. We made doll clothes out of rags, dolls' knickers with a running drawstring stitch through the waist and a knot at each end. Or, in a big circle we'd "pull wool" into small pieces to stuff the ticks so there'd be a mattress for everyone. But any semblance of childhood had vanished now. I wanted so much to know my mother, to be important on that basis, to gladden someone with my endeavours, to think that someone cared about me.

Mother Monica sensed my restlessness. Twice she summoned me from the ranks on the way to chapel and gave me a whispered homily by the sisters' elevator. "Magdalen, we make the most of a situation whether it is a happy one or not. We become stronger by accepting what God has sent us." She smoothed her veil, betraying a vestige of femininity that was appealing, like smoothing long hair. "Pray for courage, Magdalen. God wants you to belong to Him. Be careful." She smiled.

I walked to my place in the chapel and genuflected. I felt important because I had been singled out. Two days later, again on the way to the chapel, the nun plucked my sleeve, pinching my arm. The terse words stung more than the pinch.

"You've been warned once, Magdalen." She rocked back and dug in her heels, arms folded tight up the big sleeves under her white scapular, head inclined and eyebrow arched in annoyance. "You be careful miss, I'm warning you one last time. You will not continue your disgraceful conduct with Germaine."

Humility and acceptance of reproof were absolute. I wasn't permitted to speak and went to my place in chapel bewildered, this time not feeling the pride of having been singled out. Indeed not knowing where I had failed. While ironing I decided to ask the nun what was wrong. I knew about decorum in her presence. One knelt and spoke only when permitted. The women often went to kneel a step lower on Mother Monica's dais during recreation and while she listened her dark eyes would scan the room. Ironing rapidly, I felt some determination while my mind raced over the things I would say. *If she thinks I'm not good I'll tell her I'm trying to fit in but I'd rather be going to school. If she loathes self-pity, I'll let her know I need my mother.* Would she understand that? Sometimes the nun mentioned her family life complacently and spoke to the group about her resolution to be a nun. Her vocation had "come with a bang" she would say, on that day in 1917 when the *Mont Blanc*, with its cargo of explosives, collided with the *Imo* in Halifax harbour. Windows shattered over her classmates, nearly two thousand people were killed, nine hundred injured and hundreds left completely blind. "It was the world's worst man-made disaster," she told us. "So much terrible tragedy, so much of Halifax and Dartmouth were devastated. At that exact moment I knew I would give my life to God and become a nun." The words were always the same. It was a meager sharing of her life that we all seized upon. We wanted more and tensed eagerly, but the intimacy ended there.

That night during recreation time I waited my turn to kneel before Mother Monica. Myriam was kneeling before her now. My heart raced, my hands sweated. Did I imagine all eyes were on me? Germaine sat a little apart from her group. Black piercing eyes, stark, watery whites; imbecile or witch? I wanted to escape the unflinching stare. Her frizzy hair stuck out. She was brazenly defiant, arms folded, legs crossed, inviting trouble. Her bouts with authority always started that way, a moving away from the rules. I pitied her need to flare up regularly and I smiled sadly at Germaine and immediately wished I hadn't. Germaine looked at me as though we were alone in the room. I turned away self-consciously. Mother Monica sounded the bell and began to speak.

"We are proud of the spirit in this class. We will not put up with a sneak." She was deliberate and calm. "You all know we do not tolerate particular friendships. Anyone daring to break this rule will be taught a lesson." Her glance swept round the room and her indignant brown eyes rested on me. Muffled agreement from a mass of eighty up-turned faces, crafty faces and cruel, bored and weary, fleshy and wrinkled. Expectant. Stella, a head girl, sat aloof and melancholy. Sometimes I saw beauty in Stella's piety. Tonight I saw madness as she began to sing to herself, *O sight of shame, and pain, and dole* . . . .

"That's enough, Stella," cautioned the mistress as she adjusted the folds of her deep, white sleeves and tossed the black veil behind her shoulder. Stella started weeping and the nun sat tall and presumptive looking towards me.

"We will not put up with a sneak. I want to make it perfectly clear that particular friendships are forbidden. You all know that."

"We'll show her!" One ugly voice goaded the others.

Germaine sat, smug and daring, inviting trouble. Bewildered, I watched her.

The nun's further words about virtue were lost when a woman named Agatha lunged at me, shouting, "She'll learn her lesson!" and clawed at my face. I jumped to protect myself and caught a kick in the stomach and a punch in the nose. Blood spurted all over. Belligerent faces closed in on me, twisting my arms, kicking my shins and wrenching my braids. In the chaos I saw Stella excitedly working her toothless gums and brandishing a crucifix, but that ancient remedy did not shrivel my attackers.

"Fucking brutes leave her alone, goddamn you all to hell!" screamed Germaine. "Fucking whores, get away from her!" she hollered as she pushed someone aside. "You Christ almighty bitches, stinkin' bloody beasts." As the words spewed out, some of the leaders tried to wrestle Germaine from the room. I longed to hear the bell that would restore order. But then someone pulled my collar from behind and, choking on my own blood, I fell limp to the floor and lay in a web of black woolen legs and menstrual stench. I heard the nun step from the platform. Her long sleeves rustled and her beads rattled as she wound the Victrola and the strains of "Colonel Bogey's March" filled the room to drown out Germaine's profanity.

"Be careful now. She's weak you know. She's been in hospital. Back to your places. Everyone." They obeyed at once, breathing loudly. ——

"Get up Magdalen," she ordered.

Why should I?

"That shouldn't have happened. It won't happen again. Now get up."

I didn't care what she said. I couldn't be in worse trouble. I stayed on the floor, face down, sobbing, not caring at all that I was the centre of everyone's attention. She prodded me with her shoe. "Get up this instant! What's the matter with you?"

"I want my mother," the child in me cried. I was surprised by the plea in the words that often hummed in my heart but I didn't remember ever saying them out loud. The women groaned in unison.

"Magdalen, stop your foolishness and stand on your feet this minute. Do you hear?" I heard. I didn't care. I was in deep trouble; it couldn't get any worse. I'd stay on the floor and see how it all ended. I cried harder than before and turned my face away from the hateful group and pressed my hot cheek to the cool polished floor.

"I'm asking you once more, control yourself. Now get up. If you don't we'll carry you to St. Peter's room for the night. You obey when you're spoken to, or else." Without a scrap of dignity I lay there. They could carry me back to St. Vincent's for all I cared. I wasn't going to get up if I stayed there until I died.

Locked in St. Peter's cell, there was some comfort from the pillow and blanket; the wooden shelf was hard. Sobbing myself into exhaustion seemed best right now. Maybe the mistress could hear me while she lurked outside to satisfy herself that I wasn't hurt. I cried louder, a door slammed and the lock turned. *She started it all, she wanted it to happen.* I wondered about the feelings of a child who hoped its mother would hear and come to comfort. A wistful thought because I didn't know the feeling. *The real me is in prison. Now they've locked this stranger called Magdalen up for some unknown reason. Shit! I don't care one bit about them but I have to know about myself. Who knows who I am. Who I will be?* I moved my battered body and stood up, feeling around the four small walls for a light switch. There wasn't one. There wasn't a sound in the black night. I pressed my hot face against the cool wall and wished it was my mother's cheek. I slid to the floor with a wail of defeat and despair and cried again. *Where had they taken Germaine? Maybe there's another room, even worse. Those bad words will get her in lots of trouble. Whatever was wrong? I don't even like Germaine. Particular friendship? What did they mean?* In the pitch blackness the questions went on and on. *What happened? What will happen to me?* Up to now all my physical hurt had come from those in charge. I hated the lunatic bunch who had jumped on me. Were they insane? They were an angry lot by circumstance, not allowed to be offensive and they lost control when incited. *Now I'm really a prisoner. Well, they can lock me up but they can't take away my ability to think, I have privacy in my head. And they can't take pictures of my thoughts or know what I'm thinking. My mind is my own. I'm safe in there for there's no such thing as a mind-reader.*

*O*nce upon a time, and a very bad time it was, I had accepted the conditions of my life over which I had no control. In the beginning I knew that my mother, Doris McGlyn, lived in Boston. My father, Harry McGlyn, had a food store in the old City Market in Saint John not far from St.   . Vincent's orphanage. It would turn out all right someday because I belonged to them. I didn't know why my parents didn't live in the same house, or why I was in the orphanage. I didn't blame them but I was sad and thought my father was sorry too. I loved him and I'd risk stealing out on any occasion to see him in his shop. I'd just stand there for a while until he noticed. He always pretended to be surprised and said quite happily, "Well, well, how are you today?" It was the same every time. Then he'd put his hand behind his white apron for a shiny half-dollar and press it into my hand. Every time. I wanted to be loved by this kind papa with the white silken hair, white mustache and white apron. He treated me like his little girl. He never came to see me though. I watched the gate on Sundays, hoping he would come, and stared for hours out the long, high windows through glass that distorted things. My mother would come from Boston during the summer and we'd visit in the sisters' parlour or the sisters' music room. I was shy when my mother spoke a lot about movie stars and her pride in being a Yankee because Sister Juda was always there beside me. Then my mother would take me out overnight to visit her widowed sister, Aunt Bertha, and when I was put to bed I'd listen to them talk about life as long as I could stay awake.

Then I learned they weren't my real parents.

*T*here were nearly a hundred girls at St. Vincent's Orphanage. Some were from broken homes and one parent would visit, some were there temporarily, some were real orphans; most were illegitimate. I thought I was special. I had parents. Someday it would all be better for me. The others used to say, "You think you're somebody, Molly McGlyn," and they never really knew how much I did believe that *I was* somebody because I had parents.

The May I turned thirteen was a desolate birthday. Being thirteen was important. You were one of the big girls and you were treated better. But

Sister Juda said I was twelve! At first I thought Sister forgot then it dawned on me she meant it. *She doesn't want me to be older, so she said I was twelve. She hates me.* Anyway, on my thirteenth-twelfth birthday I knew there'd be a letter from my mother in Boston with maybe an American dollar in it, and certainly a parcel with a dress or some candy or a book. The parcels from Boston were special, all tied up in brown paper and twine and customs labels in my mother's swirly handwriting telling me beforehand what I'd find inside. But Sister Juda opened all the mail and when I would be given that letter or parcel would be up to her.

Sister Juda was a big person with a round, red face. Her black habit and wooden rosary hanging from her cincture stressed the authority all the children understood. She wore a starched coif, crimped on the extended sides and a wide, stiff *guimpe*. When she was irritated her teeth clicked. I didn't have good feelings for her. Some of the orphans said she was motherly, but that was kind of wishful thinking. Some were forever begging for attention, waving their hands and calling, "s'ter, s'ter!" I knew they were afraid of Sister Juda. Some of them were afraid of her strap and pretended to like her. At mealtime she wore a large blue-and-white checkered apron over her bulky black habit. She spread molasses on bread from a blue enameled basin at the front of the refectory and continued this for as long as the big girls carried tin plates full of it to the tables where all hands reached hungrily for bread at the same time. We got awful cocoa at every meal, dark and bitter, made with water. There was no milk. Some kids threw their burnt crusts under the table, slyly heaving them away from their own place; if a crust was found under your chair on the dirty floor you were made to eat it. "I didn't put it there," was my only defense.

"Eat it!" Sister Juda commanded.

"I won't," I said brazenly, knowing I'd get it! Some of the others looked up to me to defy her so I had to stand up for myself because I thought I was helping them. They were glad someone had the nerve to do it.

"I won't," I insisted, feeling brave enough while others watched. The result was getting the crust rammed down my throat or getting the strap again. I could not please this nun, even if I half-tried. My aversion to mealtime worsened because, while Sister Juda dipped the knife into the basin of molasses, she'd look at me stirring the lumpy porridge or moving the cold hash around the tin plate. When the light hit the nun's gold-rimmed glasses it was hard to know for sure if she was watching me, but I knew she was exasperated when her lips parted and a bubble grew in front of a shiny gold tooth. I'd stare back defiantly, then the nun would drop the knife, come to my place at the table, hold my nose, stuff three spoonfuls into my mouth and slap my mouth with the back of the spoon. This happened all the time. Sometimes I hoped the stuff in my mouth would spurt all over the gold glasses and gold tooth and the red face. I secretly wished I had the nerve to spit it there. Some of the others got into trouble too, but I would stand up for them, be the leader. I had a mother and some family. I could take Sister Juda's attention away from them. They said I was brave. Then I was bold more often. I earned and lived up to my reputation.

On my birthday, I waited for Sister Juda to beckon and give me the birthday letter but nothing happened. Next morning, when the others had gone to school Sister did say, "Your mother's letter is here, but first I have to tell you a story."

I didn't want the old nun to tell me any stories. *Just give me my letter, please.* I was distracted while Sister Juda talked about a young girl who had come to Canada from Ireland.

"She came by boat and settled in Saint John. She was in trouble and she couldn't keep the baby. You are the baby, your mother left you here."

That didn't make any difference to me. I supposed it had something to do with the time in my mother's life kept secret from me. I knew I was Irish and I was proud to be something. Many of the orphans were French, a few were Indian. I'd never heard the boat story before and hearing that my mother had come by boat from Ireland made me happy and curious. *Maybe I should ask my mother about the boat next time she comes.* Sister Juda wouldn't know anyway and there was no point looking for pity from this cold-hearted nun.

When I finally read the birthday letter my head began to whirl. Bewildered, stunned, I ran to the basement where I could be alone in the coal bin and no one else would see the awful words.

> *My darling daughter Molly* [her letters always started that way],
> *Now that your thirteen I might as well tell you I am not your mother
> . . . the sisters found you on the doorstep at the infants' home with
> only one bootie on. Mr. McGlyn and I took you when you were a year
> old and when I left him I had to take you back. You were nearly four
> and too old to go back to the infants' home so I had to take you to the
> orphanage. I wanted a baby so badly and when I saw you standing in
> your crib I knew right away you were the baby I wanted. I want you*

to know most off all you were a good baby and I was sorry to give you up. [I laughed when she wrote *off* in her letters; even I knew the difference.] *The nun told me there is a family who might take you and it was time to tell you the truth. Most off all I want you to be happy. With God's help you'll get along wonderful. Love, from your mother.*

I wanted to tear those words into shreds and bury them in the coal where they would be blasted by the flames of the furnace. Insecure as I had been before my birthday, my world was now a bottomless black hole. There had always been that fact that my mother lived in Boston and someday I'd be taken home. But now? *Is she writing this because she doesn't want to have anything to do with me? If a family wants to take me would that be good?* The others often hoped for adoption, but I didn't think about it; I had my parents. I cried until my whole body hurt inside and out. My head, my eyes and ears and nose, my throat, lungs and stomach all hurt. "Who *is* my mother?" I wailed.

The hollow hush was despairing but better for thinking. I remembered the times St. Vincent's kids would peek through knotholes and cracks in the fence in the lane to watch the babies at the infants' home, especially in the spring when the new babies were out. I couldn't believe I'd been an infants' home baby! I didn't even come from a family!

My first vague memories of the Sisters of Charity came back: the day I arrived at St. Vincent's, wearing a white lacy dress, white stockings and shiny black boots. The only thing I remembered before that was trading my sled for gum to a boy on the street. Nuns stood around me that first day, hands buried in great big sleeves like blackbird's wings. I was small and I waited to be hugged. Instead one nun whispered out loud, "I think she soiled herself." The hopelessness that started when I first stood in that circle of blackbird nuns just grew and grew every day and on this birthday I knew I'd drown in my tears in the dark coal bin. A novice nun brought some garbage in a colander and dumped it into a pail. I held my breath and licked the salty tears away. The sound of the nun's rattling beads faded and I went to the pail to look for lemon or banana peel. We always ate it. I shook hot tea leaves from the used lemon and took it back to my hideaway and chewed it without a grimace. I had hoped for so long about the ever-coming new day. Ever dreaming that sooner or later, one of these days, I could go to live with my mother. *Tomorrow will be better,* I'd tell myself. *Tomorrow I'll live in her home.* Now, tomorrow would not come. Tomorrow's dream was impossible.

Sister Juda didn't punish me for the coal dirt on my clothes or scold me for crying. She ignored me as I sat alone in the rec room, hunched in a corner, and she didn't insist that I join the others. Next day she told me there was a family named O'Connor in Boston inquiring about taking me to live with them. "Your real mother was nursing Mrs. O'Connor and they started talking about you. Write and tell Mrs. O'Connor if you want to go or not."

I couldn't believe I was given a choice and that I might go to live in somebody's home, especially someone who knew my own mother. That overwhelmed me. My formal little letter to Mrs. O'Connor didn't beg to be given a home and I don't know why I felt honour bound to say, "I already have a mother in Boston and I'll always love her." Maybe I'd said everything wrong, there was too much to think about all at once but I was writing what I thought Sister Juda wanted me to say, for she read all our mail. I lived in breathless expectation that each day might be my last at the orphanage, a condition I couldn't imagine. After a long time I began to hang around Sister Juda's door, wanting to ask if the O'Connors had answered my letter. When the nun found me there one day she tugged me by the ear and thrust me into a dark closet.

"For snooping," she said.

Little by little I gave up, for I never heard about the O'Connors again.

Doris McGlyn came to visit that summer in the sisters' parlour with its big armchairs and lace antimacassars. Not one word was said about her shocking letter. I wanted to go on liking her, after all she had been the centre of my life, but it was different now. There was a time I'd burst with pride when my mother came. Though she was plump, her face was pretty. She had big brown eyes and she dressed like a movie star. I liked her red-gold hair and delicate scent. She said it was Coty's Emeraude. I hoped the smell would stay on me when I went back to my place amongst the orphans. I did adore her, but now it was different. We weren't alike at all. I felt paler than usual. I was certain I was not pretty and hated my ugly black bangs. I resented that Doris would visit, then go away again and leave me there, especially when I heard her telling Aunt Bertha one night that she had a new husband and he had a little girl. This haunted me night and day for years.

Aunt Bertha's son, Peter, was allowed to visit me at the orphanage because his mother now cooked for the bishop and he was an altar boy on his way to the priesthood. He was gawky with a pile of curls combed forward but in the sanctuary he knew what to do and looked very important. I was allowed out of the orphanage once to go to a movie with Peter; Deanna Durbin in *That Certain Age*. It was said at the hospital that I looked like Deanna Durbin and there was a secret pleasure knowing I looked like someone else in the world. I watched Deanna Durbin on the screen and felt so much love for her because people said we were alike. Imagine! Anyway, I told Peter I wanted to run away, far from the strap and punishment in dark halls, having my mouth taped shut for talking; run away from all manner of cruel things. He and his brothers had been sent to the boys' orphanage at Silver Falls when their father died. I knew he could tell me what to do. After the movie he kissed me and said running away was a good idea. He kissed me again in the vestibule at St. Vincent's and asked me to promise not to let anyone else do that, which was funny because I didn't know another boy in the world, except perhaps that one named Billy McCarthy who wrote in my autograph book at the orphans' picnic once. The next day I sneaked out to his rooming house across from the cathedral, hoping he would help me. Peter hugged me and said it was a good plan to run away. I liked standing there being hugged by his warm body. I wanted to stay near him.

He seemed upset that I was not happy. He was out of breath; I was surprised that he cared so much about me. All at once he gasped and his heart was pounding then he told me running away wasn't such a good idea after all. He said I should go back. At least that venture had been a good rehearsal. It was easy to get out; I hadn't been missed, Peter cared about me and, best of all, it felt good being out.

The idea never left me and then I talked it over with Maggie Murphy one night in the bathroom. She just offhandedly said humph! The nuns said Maggie Murphy was bad. The ringleader, they called her. That was drilled into our heads like so many other things: The last day, Judgment Day, the end of the world. Threats of hell for all eternity, no food or water after midnight, no meat on Friday. Pray for General Franco, he is a good man, a good Catholic; Maggie Murphy is evil. Singsong litanies heard without attention to meaning but retained, making a lasting impact. Maggie usually took my part, so it was taken for granted that I was bad too. The worst thing we ever did was climb over a partition in a laundry room looking for food in the sisters' kitchen for something to eat one night. We only found stewed prunes and filled a cardboard box and left it on the chair by Maggie's bed, hidden under her nightie. We'd eat them later in the dark. How could we know that Sister Patrick would sit on the prunes while she was supervising night prayers? We all thought Sister Patrick would laugh; all the girls at prayers laughed. But she was cross and made us say the long prayers three times that night. Each time we began praying, someone would snicker and we'd all burst out laughing again. If one or two of us laughed, they'd be in trouble, but what could Sister Patrick do to all of us? I knew I shouldn't have laughed. I was every bit as guilty as Maggie was, but it wasn't my chair. Maggie'd never tell. She was like that. She just sat back on her heels during prayers, defiant, like we all did when we were in trouble. Anyway, I was surprised Maggie didn't encourage me to run away. We were forever ready to risk the challenge of a dare "They'll send you to the Good Shepherd, that might be worse than here."

"I don't know. Some say it's better. Besides, they won't send me anywhere because they won't catch me,"

We tiptoed back to the dorm and Maggie whispered, "There are prisoners over there. You might never get out."

I shuffled past Maggie's bed, the first in the row, and Maggie Murphy cupped her hand around her mouth and whispered, "I double dare you!"

I loved a dare and couldn't wait to tell Olive O'Leary and some of the others that I was running away. They'd heard it before and scoffed, "You're so highfalutin'."

"Oh, dry up and blow away, Olive. You'll see. Wait till this time tomorrow. You'll see then."

Too excited to want supper, I was forced to eat my hash. I wrapped two slices of molasses bread in a handkerchief and tucked them into my bloomer leg for later. Then, while the others were moving upstairs from the basement refectory, I slipped away to the cellar where my doll's trunk, stuffed with a few clothes, letters and pictures, my diary and autograph book, was hidden. I was sorry to leave behind the scrapbooks I'd made at the hospital. All coloured pictures from the weekend rotogravure papers about the royal family, Princess Lilibut and Margaret Rose, their father and mother, the new king and queen, and all about King Edward the Eighth and the woman he gave up his throne to marry. Maybe someone else would take care of my scrapbooks. I might not be missed until bedtime, I thought. I hurried from the basement, for the scariest part was the dark. Someone might touch me and if I screamed my plan would be spoiled.

Outside on Cliff Street I stole a last look at the weather-beaten edifice with the word ASYLUM in stone above the door. The orphans hated that word and looked the other way to avoid seeing it. We knew the asylum was a place for crazy people, not a home for orphans. We'd heard it said "she's from the asylum," not meaning the orphans but maybe some poor creature who rocked or twisted her hair or shrieked and looked frightened. *Asylum.* The word didn't bother me now. I wouldn't belong there any more so I looked squarely at the word again then at the gold letters on the Gothic glass door, 31-35 Cliff Street and the statue of St. Vincent de Paul. The patron saint of orphans rested his ever-so-gentle gentle hand on an orphaned child's head that had big stone tears on her cheeks. The symbolism of his caring hand was quite different from Sister Juda's feared middle finger. She'd often thump away on the top of our heads with her tin thimble to wrest any admission of wrongdoing from frightened little girls. It really hurt. I winced at the memory, for I had a tender spot to remind me of that hard-hearted habit.

The evening Angelus bell was pealing as I walked down Cliff Street. I crossed myself and bowed my head and listened to the muted sounds until the triple bells faded. I loved the Angelus and the significance of that omen at the beginning of my search filled me with hope and anticipation.

"Mother of God," I prayed, "lead me to my own mother for surely you know the way." I lifted my face to Heaven and a warm October rain washed the orphanage away from my skin and out of my life. *I'm old enough to do something important. I'll find her. I'll be loved and I'll love back. I'll do anything I want to do, Sister Juda said that once. Molly McGlyn could do anything she put her mind to if she would only listen.*

I hummed "Pennies from Heaven." I had no umbrella to turn upside down, no coat either. But I was warm enough in this new, dark, shimmering world of streetlights and puddles. The coalman's horse turned the corner, thumping into Cliff Street with a late delivery. Steamy breath flowed from its nostrils and the clippity-clop on the pavement made a lovely rhythm with the bells on the harness. "Git up," sang the driver with a flourish of the reins and it looked as if the horse was laughing.

I made the sign of the cross as I hurried past the chapel and ran down Waterloo Street past the Sugar Bowl candy store. The trays in the window were empty, but I peered in to see mounds of candies in the glass counter covered with cellophane; hard hats, huge pieces of fudge and great big suckers, green, black, red, caramel and peppermint; I ran past Mater

Misericordia Home run by the sisters for sick old people and headed towards the big city market.

Everyone called my father Old Glyn. It suited him. It was a loving name and now I'd have to call him that too, not my father. He didn't seem old; it must have been his snow-white hair. *But now he isn't my father, I don't feel different about him. What does he feel? He doesn't even know that I know so I hope he'll still be the same and not chase me away.* I'd see Old Glyn first and decide what to do after that. There were crowds of Friday night shoppers. I left my trunk behind the iron gate. It seemed like a safe place.

My father, I mean Old Glyn, didn't notice me at first, but very soon the trusty half-dollar was in my hand. I tucked it into my shoe with some other coins and was gone while he called after me, "Aren't you out late?" I looked back once. He waved. *It's sad we don't know each other better, and now it's sadder that he isn't my father any more and we'll never know each other better.*

I got my trunk and walked back towards Wasson's drug store. I bought an ice cream soda for five cents and tried to come to terms with what to do. Peter's mother would send me back. She lived at the bishop's palace; I couldn't go there. Tomorrow I'd get a job and a room. Right now I must find a place to sleep, one thing at a time. The druggist peered over the rim of his glasses. He looked cross. I felt conspicuous in my too-large blue serge dress, black stockings and a blue cardigan with holes in the elbows. I looked at the headlines on a pile of newspapers, trying to avoid his scrutiny. **Peace with Honour. Peace for our Time. This Man Saved Civilization.** *Just now I have to save myself.* **War Postponed is a War Won—Chamberlain**. *That has nothing to do with me.* **Eddie Shore Quits Holdout Ranks—All-Star Defenseman Signs for $7000**. *Nor does that. I'll buy a paper tomorrow and look for a job and a room.*

Out on Waterloo Street the Chinese laundry man, with his bag slung over his shoulder, went by. I shivered. The orphans knew he didn't carry little girls in his bag, but we always said he did and his bag looked heavy and lumpy when his bent silhouette shuffled past the gate. At a safe distance we'd chant, *Chinky, chinky Chinaman, sitting on a fence . . .* He frightened me so I walked quickly the other way and crossed the street to the Golden Ball Garage and waited beside the big sign for gutta percha heels and soles. I had a terrible notion that maybe I should spend the night in the basement at St. Vincent's or in my own bed. Maybe they hadn't missed me yet. Panic-stricken at such thoughts, I turned and ran the other way. I couldn't give up now.

Sitting on a bench in King's Square in the centre of Saint John, I wondered what was apt to happen to me, knowing it was up to me to make something happen. The market gate was in plain view—my link to any hope at all, yet I felt conspicuous and crossed the street away from the market and huddled on a bench in a dark corner of the Old Loyalist Burying Ground. I fed the bread from my bloomer leg to the pigeons.

Harry McGlyn's home was two blocks away, down Elliot Row. In my fantasies it was my home. Once when I had gone there, just hanging around, I blew my breath on the brass nameplate and shone *McGlyn* with the sleeve of my sweater. I had lived there for a short time, but I didn't remember much about it except his big brass cuspidor, my little feet braced on either side of the rim to reach him in his chair. Old Glyn's sister lived there with him now. Her name was Molly too. *Maybe that's why they chose me over the other babies, or maybe my name was changed and it isn't Molly at all.* On the other side of King Square, Harry McGlyn would be finishing his work soon. Perhaps I would see him walk home—but I wouldn't let him know I was running away.

Maybe I could sleep in the theater next to the Admiral Beatty Hotel. Hypnotic marquee lights climbed up one side of the word IMPERIAL and down the other. The huge letters lit up, went out and lit up again. Burned-out bulbs marred the pattern. The warped reflection in the soggy street showed the gaps too and I watched, fascinated. *If I Were King* was playing, with Ronald Coleman, Basil Rathbone and Frances Dee. My dress and black stockings implied orphan and we knew that people nudged one another when we were seen on the street. I couldn't risk going into the theater, especially carrying a doll's trunk.

It was bedtime at St. Vincent's and they'd know I was missing, if it hadn't happened already. When everybody sat up in bed and folded their hands and said, "Take my body Jesus, eyes and ears and tongue, Never let them, Jesus, help to do Thee wrong," and Sister Juda sprinkled holy water all over them and my empty bed. Would she be shocked or would she care? She'd walk up and down the long middle aisle between the rows of iron cots praying to her God. Up and down, back and forth, her shadow looming long and narrow from the bare bulb in the hall outside the bathroom. As she paced, saying her beads, her gigantic shadow grew along the ceiling, then down the wall, getting smaller and smaller, disappearing on the floor; when she turned again, her shadow would grow up the wall, along the ceiling—my bedtime story. The steady humdrum steps of the veiled shadow were enough to make you drowsy, or if your little mind was overactive it looked beastly, as if it might eat you, filling your dreams with big things that grew and receded, big faces that grew and withdrew. Thoughts became phantasmal—oversized and frightening. The big girls said there were rats. I thought it was mice who knocked the soap off the sink and chased it around the dormitory floor, pushing it down the wide steps near the toilets. I was afraid to think it was rats. I wondered if Sister Juda would be angry when she saw my empty cot or perhaps say a prayer that I was safe. I shivered and pulled a black cardigan from the trunk, putting it over my shoulders. I looked around to make sure no one would touch me in the dark. I was scared at the thought of ghosts and evil men and most of all the big market gates closing for the night. *The nuns said we all have a guardian angel. Did mine come with me to protect me or is my angel mad because I ran away?* Just then a man sat beside me on the bench. My heart flipped and tried to get out my throat.

"I won't do nuthin' to ya," he said and his big hand was warm on my cold little fist. Scared to death, I grabbed the strap of my trunk and ran as fast as I could back to the market, knowing the nighttime fear of an unloved child. Breathless and tear-smudged, I knew I must go to Old Glyn for protection.

He looked at my baggage.

"What's that?" he asked. "Is there a problem?"

"I ran away," I told him, all out of breath.

"Oh!" He weighed a bunch of soda crackers on the gleaming Toledo scale. He was busy but he spoke to me calmly like he really was my dad. He wiped a smudge off my cheek. "Here, dry your eyes." The folded handkerchief felt soft and silky; holding it was personal. I imagined he'd let me keep it and I'd always have it. He wiped his hands thoughtfully with his big white apron. "So you ran away."

He wasn't angry. He didn't say he must call the police or tell me to go back. I took a big breath and watched his eyes to see what would happen. He asked a woman who was buying crackers, "I suppose you know who this is?"

"Doris's girl?" asked a tall, nice-looking woman. I was relieved. *That's my Aunt Elsa. Doris's sister-in-law, and I know Doris doesn't like her one bit.*

At Old Glyn's urging Elsa took me home to her flat on Britain Street and I experienced a degree of security for the first time in my life. While my stomach violently threw out its last supper of hash there was an early menstrual outpouring. Elsa wrapped me in a blue chenille robe and pulled my chair to the front of the wood stove with the oven door open making lovely warmth all around me. She brought soda crackers, jam and tea and hugged me earnestly. Never in my life had I tasted anything as good as crispy crackers, butter and jam. I told Elsa, "I'll never forget this and when I'm rich I'll buy lots of crackers."

"Don't worry tonight, darling. Tomorrow we'll have to find a telephone and let the nuns know where you are—they'll have to let your mother know."

"She's not my mother."

"Who said that?"

"She did. She wrote a letter and said I was found on the doorstep at the Infants' Home. She must have made that up because Sister Juda said I had skin like my mother. So they didn't find me on the doorstep if they knew my mother, right?"

"Right, but she'll send you back, Molly. I believe she has the right, especially if she took papers out on you. Edmund wouldn't let me interfere with Doris for anything. He works on the Boston Boat tonight, but he'll be home tomorrow."

"Then I'll run away again. I won't stay there. I'd rather go to jail." In a move of defiance I turned my other side to the warmth of the oven.

"Did you tell anyone you were running away?" asked Elsa.

"Maggie Murphy dared me—she won't say nothing though. I told Olive O'Leary but she always whines. 'I'm tellin',' was all she said and all the time she's too scared to speak to Sister Juda."

"What will they do when they find you're missing?"

"They'll just send some big girls out to look for me, to Aunt Bertha's and the market. They won't think of Peter."

"Did he have anything to do with it?"

"Nothing, he just told me it was a good idea, that's all."

"He should know. Poor Bertha put three of them in the orphanage at Silver Falls when their father died. I've heard that the troublemakers at Silver Falls wear sweaters with a red circle on the back, a good target if they run away."

I wanted Elsa to keep talking to me. No one had ever listened to my aversions to orphan life or helped me understand my feelings since that birthday letter. "I don't know what else they'll do. Please don't telephone them. I wish you wouldn't, please."

"I wish I didn't have to . . ."

"I won't be any trouble. You don't even have to say I was here. I'll go away tomorrow when it's light out and find a job and I'll get a room. Please, please!"

Elsa hugged me. I snuggled close to her, wanting nothing to change.

"Darling, the nuns have to tell the police if they don't find you. You're too young to be on your own. Edmund will be home tomorrow and there's no way he'll get involved with Doris. For tonight try not to worry, just go to sleep now." And she put me to bed.

"You're kind to me," I told her and I meant it, but before I fell asleep in the safe, homey setting I thought about leaving in the morning before she was awake.

In the morning Elsa said it wasn't necessary that we go to St. Vincent's together. I was so happy. It would certainly be embarrassing to go in that gate being held by the hand while all the others in the lane stared, thinking, "They're bringing her back! Ha-ha, Molly McGlyn is back!" If Elsa or Old Glyn knew what to do and I knew there was an alternative, I would have been right there with Elsa, triumphant, showing off my derring-do, the one characteristic Sister Juda especially hated.

"Do something you'll enjoy today, Molly. Don't see your father or Aunt Bertha. Be back here long before suppertime." She gave me some change from her pocket and, indescribable joy, I thought, she trusts me! Trust, reliance on my ability to do as I was asked, was a brand-new sensation. I felt rich. Or maybe she was giving me the chance to get away? But I couldn't leave while she was going to bat for me.

Skipping along in my joy and freedom I went to visit my old friends at the County Hospital. I longed to see them again and each day that seemed less possible. I'd been sent to the children's wing, the Nesbitt Memorial sanatorium in East Saint John, regularly after an early bout with pneumonia. It was hard not to look pleased when the doctor at the health centre would say, "You must go back to the hospital for treatment and nutrition." Though I wouldn't admit it to anyone, I once dampened my chemise and wore it wet hoping I would get sick. I loved it at the hospital. I felt like a guest and wanted to stay long enough to read every book in the library. The small room was quieter than any place there and the dark wood paneling made it warm and private, like a home. I had read all the Bobbsey Twins books, *At Home, In the Country, At the Seashore, On Blueberry Island,* all thirty-seven titles and read some of them again. Flossie and Freddie lived adventures I knew nothing about. Books opened the door to a life of fantasy and excitement that I could never live at the orphanage. There were stories of mean parents, of children who didn't know their mothers, left to be raised by cruel relatives who embezzled their inheritances; about restored fortune and eventually justice; about the resourcefulness of orphans who didn't know who they belonged to, like *Oliver Twist* and Kipling's *Kim*. During my last time at the hospital, after the birthday letter from Boston, I looked for orphan stories because orphan life was not unusual in books. I loved the sad and simple story of *Heidi* and how she made her own life happier, but my favourite was the orphan girl Mary Lennox, who had hours to spend by herself in *The Secret Garden*. Mary was not strong but sickly like me, and she was contrary too, so I liked her secretly for that. She changed her world and I knew I could change mine some day. I could put myself in Emily Dickinson's lyrics too: *I'm nobody, who are you? Are you nobody too?* or *How dreary to be somebody! How public, like a frog.* Orphan kids often had mysterious pasts but some stories revealed more ordinary things. Being an orphan seemed to be natural after all. Maybe I'd be able to enjoy my life if I tried.

Hospital life was the way I wished life would be. Miss Bessborough taught school each morning, the inspector came and I was given a book once by the I.O.D.E. for being a good student. "Outstanding pupil . . ." someone wrote on the inside cover. It was royal blue with gold letters, called *The Royal Family.* When I was discharged to go back to St. Vincent's and school days were suspended, I missed the stimulation of learning and oh, how I missed my friends. My energy, curiosity and affection were stymied and each time I had to return to the orphanage I became a little more arrogant. Especially since the letter from Doris had been so humiliating and no one would help me understand it.

At the hospital ten or twelve of us were up-patients instead of bed-patients and we enjoyed our meals in a small dining room. We'd stand behind the bentwood chairs and they'd wait for me to intone the grace we sang before meals. I'd start with a loud "Be . . ." in a low key. They'd chime in ". . . present at our table, Lord. Be here and everywhere adored. Thy children bless and grant that we, may feast in paradise with Thee." Once in a while, when things didn't go my way or I was moody, I'd stand behind my chair and refuse to start the grace. Greta or Hilda, nurse's aides waiting to serve our meal, would say my name, meaning "it's time to start . . ." but I, pouting, would not give in. So grace was spoken. That was the first sort of power I remember having. I was in control of the situation and those in charge ignored me. They didn't draw attention to a silly situation and make it worse. And they didn't punish me. I learned something good from them.

I was in trouble only once at the hospital, when I was twelve. Punishment meant your bed was "moved out" and put in the infants' ward with the cribs. Wide windows separated the wards, and the infants' ward was next to the girls'. Lionel, the biggest boy, had been moved to the infants' ward and during rest hour he was standing on his bed showing his bare thing at the window. When we laughed, he dived into bed. A few seconds later he was back at the window, showing himself again. From her vantage point in the office, Miss Fraser saw him and came storming into the girls' ward. She caught me laughing under the covers and pulled my bed in a wide arc out the door, noisily down the hall into the classroom, in isolation for the night.

At first I was upset, but then I began to enjoy the shadows from the lights of the Saint John dry dock across the road. Cars approaching from the west made fascinating light patterns; the windowpanes danced around the walls, curving round the corners and merging with the dry dock lights and shadows. Cars coming from the east made the same shadows in reverse. When cars appeared from both directions at the same time, the shadows grew and telescoped and receded. Then I'd wait for the next car to round the bend in the road from the city or from Redhead and I'd fantasize about the people in the cars. The lighthouse winked and gleamed. It mesmerized like a blinking yellow eye, as did the sound of the droning foghorn penetrating the night at regular intervals. Warn and rest, warn and rest. The lighthouse beacon would beam and turn, beam and turn. Beam-warn-turn-rest. Lonely, distant lifesavers.

While Elsa was doing what she said she had to do, I approached the hospital and surprised my friends when I appeared at the long windows at the back. Children were not allowed inside the ward. They were happy to see me, I thought, *but I won't tell them I'm out of the orphanage*. Kathleen spied me first and unfastened the straps that pinned her to the laced canvas frame designed to cure her tubercular spine. She rolled off expertly as I had seen her do hundreds of times, pivoting on her tummy; lifeless legs curled up, she propelled herself to the foot of the bed with her hands.

"Hey, how'd you get here, Moll?" And then they were all at the window.

"That's a pretty dress." It was a Shirley Temple dress, soft like cashmere with a big collar and white angora trim.

"It's from my mother in Boston." I hesitated, ashamed. Could I adjust to belonging to no one and continue to say "my mother"?

"They didn't cut your hair yet."

"I don't think they're going to."

"Gee, I'm glad you came."

"Rena's going home today." Only Kathleen had been there longer than Rena, never seeming to get better; she walked with crutches once in a while, but was mostly left to pivot on her stomach or strapped to a canvas frame, flat on her back. I'd had a frame when I was a patient there. The worst-looking frame built around my bed with four big wooden posts and pulleys. Lying on my stomach, I was fastened into it with wide canvas straps that came over my shoulders and long canvas straps from a band around my waist, while the end of the frame rested on the top of the iron bedstead. Then the front end was lowered to rest on the mattress. My face fit into a small square hole in the canvas and I was expected to cough and spit into a small waxed box on the bed, my heels high in the air. They called it postural drainage and I cried of embarrassment the first time, but got used to it and soon felt I had some kind of status, being the only one.

"I'm glad you're going home, Rena," I said. Rena began to cry. She had been three years in the hospital with a tubercular hip; a long time. No one knew what it would be like for her at home in Kouchibouguac on the Northumberland Strait. When I first knew Rena, she spoke only French. Would she remember enough to get along with her family?

"Dr. Dayton married Miss McCain, ya know."

"Oh, I knew he would," We all laughed, remembering my childish crush on the handsome doctor who looked like Clark Gable.

I was happy visiting and shouting through the windows. I loved these friends, they were part of families and I felt better with them than with the orphans. Even in their illnesses they seemed more normal and now I had become an orphan and couldn't tell them about my disappointment.

In the midst of our joy that October afternoon, old Dempster appeared around the corner of the classroom in his overalls, carrying his carpenter's box. "Hello, little one!"

I froze on the spot and didn't reply. The mere sight of him was ominous, for now and then he used to stand at the ward door during rest hour, opening it just a bit, and just stand there grinning and holding himself in front, showing his part that looked like a big, old carrot. I wondered what Miss Fraser would have done about that if she had seen him. Would she punish me or old Dempster? Worse than that, though, was the time I left my autograph book in the kitchen. When I went to pick it up, Dempster teased me, holding the book just out of reach, saying, "Get it. Will you come and see me on Garden street? Get it." Each time I reached for it he backed away a little more until he had me in a corner where he grabbed my wrist and forced his finger in between my legs. I didn't cry out, afraid of making trouble, but his dirty finger was pushing and his dirty nail was scratching and his evil eyes nearly crossed and his ugly mouth puckered. I broke from his grasp before I had to cry out with pain. After that I never went any place where Dempster might be working around the hospital. The sight of him today made me sick. I had the feeling that this vile man would not be blamed if I had told anyone that he hurt me. Old man Riley was the same. He kept the furnaces going for the nuns and was always around the hospital laundry and the orphanage, rubbing against the girls when no one saw. But you couldn't tell the nuns his name or say anything because you'd be punished, you'd be the dirty one, you'd be the one in trouble. No one would believe you just for saying it.

After a while, I left my friends and crossed the road to see what was happening at the dry dock. Miss Bessborough told us it was the largest dry dock in the world and she let her students use spyglasses to watch the big hydraulic gates opening when the tide was low. Sometimes a big boat would arrive high on the tide. By morning the gates were closed and the ship low in the dry berth. Day by day we watched and heard the hammers and machinery, getting used to the sounds from across the road. Finally there was an awesome sense of adventure when the big gates opened again and the ship rose slowly with the tide until she was ready to sail. Then we talked about travels to strange lands. Often I peered wistfully at the harbour and imagined what it was like for my own mother on her long journey from Ireland.

When Elsa returned to Britain Street, I was waiting on the doorstep, feeling close to her and wondering why Doris didn't like her. Suddenly I was apprehensive that I should have gone to face Sister Juda with her. I really should have been there. We talked first about my day and I avoided looking for any message from Sister Juda, whatever it might be. I just wanted to stay with Elsa. Supper was finished before she said that the sisters would not accept me back; they would make an example of me.

"But that's not the point!" I blurted out, hoping so much Elsa would see it my way. "I won't go back. Whatever anyone else decides must be done I won't, won't, won't go back to that place." *Good news, they won't take me back!*

"The nun said you were a show-off, a troublemaker, and that you were always looking for attention?" At least Elsa was questioning me.

"Some of them were quiet, some were scared, some were stupid and a lot were sneaky. I just wanted to have fun and make them laugh, what harm is that? I have a hard time when it's quiet."

"In a place like that you have to obey the rules," she said seriously and I thought, *I'm still in trouble.*

"I did obey the rules. I took my place in the ranks, I never talked then. I said all my prayers. I had fun playing but as soon as the bell rang, Sister Juda always started picking on me, always. I couldn't stop smiling the minute the bell rang."

"The nun said you didn't go to school. Why?"

"She wouldn't let me go! I need to go! Grade seven and eight go out to St. Joseph's school for class. When I got back from the hospital she said I wouldn't be going to school yet. I knew I had to continue bedrest but Maureen Driscoll told me I didn't go to school because I couldn't be trusted to go out. That's a lie! I didn't understand and nobody explained that to me."

Elsa drained the teapot. "What's your education?"

"I finished grade six but most of it was at the hospital. Everything's better there. At the orphanage we learn a lot about British history in a small red book with small print. It's stories so I like it. Ethelred the Unready, Henry the Eighth and kings and princes and children in a tower, worse than us, and ladies with heads cut off, but it's not true, things like that. We're made to do good writing, like the Palmer method, but that's only circles and lines. I can't hold my pen that way so I get cracked over the knuckles."

"They hit you for that?"

"Sure. But I wet my bed and we get it worse."

"Is that true?"

"Of course. She lines the bed-wetters up every morning and we kneel down. 'Hold out your hand,' she always says. It's terrible. I beg my guardian angel to wake me up at night but I'm always disappointed in the morning."

"That's awful.'

"Well, she's awful, but she's not the only one. After I had pneumonia I'd get tired in school and Sister Norbert would crack me on the knuckles if I slouched in my seat." Tears were streaming off my chin and I hoped Elsa would understand. "If I leaned against the wall she'd switch my legs and my knees hurt all the time when I had to kneel down. When I showed my feelings sister would send me to the cloakroom so I'd drag my feet and pout. I'd show off, making it worse. Someone would tell Sister Juda and she kept back my letters from my mother for punishment. Now she doesn't let me go to school, but I want to go."

"What do you do all day then?" Elsa handed me a handkerchief. I think my tears were relief that I couldn't go back to St. Vincent's; but not knowing what was coming next, I was nervous, so I kept talking.

"All kinds of things," I said eagerly. I went on about putting new names on the assigned coat hooks, initials on the shelves for clean clothes and on the cubicles for rubbers, and tiny initials on the rosary rack; about scrubbing the forty-two stairs from the dormitory to the refectory. "I do a lot of things I don't like because I'm usually getting punished. Worst of all, even worse than the strap is being sent to the dark hall during recreation. I was afraid someone would touch me in the dark so I'd hide behind the coats. One night she even forgot I was sent out when they all went to bed." Elsa didn't say anything. Nervous energy kept me talking.

"But we scrub the dirty toilets for punishment too. I hate doing that."

"Who wouldn't?"

"When we scrub the recreation room, the inside room and the refectory floors, a whole row of us do patches together; two use the same pail. That's fun. Some floors get waxed and we push a heavy polisher wrapped in soft rags back and forth to make the floor shine. We even put rags over our shoes and run and slide and have a good time shining the floor."

"You make fun out of it?"

"Yeh, I guess so. Sometimes another nun picks a girl to scrub her cell. Then at suppertime that nun brings her dessert for that girl." I didn't bother to say how eighty pair of longing eyes would follow the recipient to the refectory door and back to her seat and eighty mouths would water on the first bite. I did elaborate on the bad-mark card Sister Juda asked me to make.

"A good-mark card would be more positive," Elsa mused. "Did you get enough to eat, Molly? At the home, I mean."

"Sure, there was always enough molasses bread. They never said there wasn't any more. Funny, I was never very hungry."

"Do you steal, Molly?"

I shrugged. Did that mean that Sister Juda called me a thief? "I wouldn't steal anything that belonged to somebody. We all steal bread from the bread box when we can get it and sometimes toast from a big trayful for the sisters, on our way from chapel. We're not taking it from someone hungry. We don't get toast and they have lots. I don't want to steal, I hope I won't have to."

"She told me to see that you went to confession tonight." Elsa waited.

"She must be crazy, I don't need to go."

"She also said God would punish you. I told her He already had and I could only wonder why."

"Oh don't you know why I can't know my mother, or even have a foster home? It's not fair . . ."

"No, it isn't fair. Often life isn't fair. We all have to do hard things, even when we're grown up, and it's often harder then."

"But I'm not grown up and I should know my mother. She wouldn't be mad at me all the time."

"Shh now."

"If she died, I'd understand. I think I'd understand if she didn't want me. But I can't understand why they won't let me know about her."

"You should know about her all right. You'd know yourself better then. Even if you knew what she looked like." She took my face between her hands. "Look darling," she said softly, "it's only natural that you need your mother to make you feel worthwhile. I don't know what to do about this terrible mess you're in. Just don't give up, Molly. You have time to find out who you are. Be sure you do it."

"Are you sure you don't know anything about her?"

"No child, and I'd bet Doris doesn't know a thing either."

"Is she my mother and just wants to say she isn't?"

"No, no she definitely isn't. That's one thing I do know; Doris didn't have a baby. Giving up babies is so secret. I keep wondering if she took papers and adopted you."

"How would you start to find out if you were me?"

"With your records at the orphanage. But finding out anything seems hopeless. I wish I could help."

Next morning I went to Mass by myself at the cathedral just around the corner from the orphanage. The girls from St. Vincent's were assembled in the Virgin's Chapel and I wasn't one of them! The bishop spoke about Europe's "tragic and tangled facts" and condemned the militant godless who had held an anti-God congress in London. I could see the others going to Holy Communion in the chapel. I recalled how we used to think that going to the main body of the cathedral, where I was now, was like getting out. I went to the communion rail with folded hands, kneeling in the spot where they could all see me. *They'll nudge each other,* I thought. *They'll think, " She can't go to Holy Communion, she ran away, she committed a mortal sin."* Then I caught Maggie Murphy looking out of the corner of her eye, but we didn't dare smile. She'd get in trouble if someone saw, but I could tell she was proud of me.

My prayers were fervent, not for the pope or the bishop or for Franco, or those in their last agony or for the souls in purgatory. I prayed to heaven for myself, asking with all the fervor in my soul for the privilege of knowing my mother. *And when I grow up God, let me empty all orphanages. Give me a farm and lots of children and help me to look after them all. Amen.*

After breakfast Elsa told me the nuns had spoken to Doris the day before and she had decided that I would be sent to the Good Shepherd Convent. Completely out of control, I screamed, "That's the wrong decision! What's she got to do with it? What does she care about me anyway? I won't go! I'll run away again. Please help me. Please."

Elsa put her arms around me and let me cry until I couldn't cry any more. Then we had to go.

I must have fallen asleep in St. Peter's Room after I told myself that my mind was private property and they couldn't lock me up without my thoughts. Now an oblique streak of daylight hit the tiny latticed window of St. Peter's Room. I was thankful the night was over. I imagined the sounds of rising in the dorm, washing, cleaning teeth, gargling, some crude moans but not too daring, women shuffling to the sink to empty their basins and dressing under their huge cotton nightgowns. In the early morning chill and darkness I heard the ranks move past the sewing room, the sound reverberating down the stairs with great force. Any hopes of getting out of this mess of trouble were airy dreams. I wondered if hysterics would establish my innocence or if being mute would impress more.

After Mass, Myriam brought tea and toast and I began my silent act.

"I'll wait while you eat this," she whispered. I would have welcomed her counsel. She was good at doing her duty. She looked like a farm girl, well-built and strong, fair streaked hair and rosy skin suggesting time spent in the fields, large features and big glasses forever down on her nose. I didn't answer.

"You may use the toilet if you wish."

I brushed past Myriam who turned away modestly, for the toilet was not enclosed. She removed the blanket and pillow with downcast eyes. I returned to the cell and faced the wall.

"Your tea is better if you drink it hot, Magdalen."

I'm not answering and I'm not eating. Maybe they'll understand silence; they live with it.

"If you don't want it I have to take the tray away. I'll tell Reverend Mother you didn't take it." Click.

It was the hour when I should have been on my way to the laundry; instead there was a feeling of being off work, in a way on holiday. Had some of the workers ever thought of acting up and being sent to St. Peter's room for a rest from the laundry? I had to find a pastime, something to occupy my mind. There was a pencil stub in my petticoat pocket, but nothing to write on but the walls. Next time out I'd take some toilet paper and compose something. Sounds of the day picked up in the sewing room and someone used the sink outside St. Peter's room. I didn't look out. I couldn't abide the image of my face peering from inside a locked cell and for someone to see. Cupboard doors closed, hushed voices spoke, the treadle sewing machine hummed and presently I heard the haughty rustle of Mother Monica's habit and the rattle of the large brown rosary beads that hung from her cincture. I imagined the tilt of her head and my heart raced, for her movements sounded angry. The nun would set the tone for this encounter. God, let her be kind.

"You must be ashamed of yourself. We're not surprised at your stubbornness. Sister Juda warned us you'd be hard to deal with."

"I hope she's satisfied. I'm locked in here and that proves she's right. I wouldn't expect her to give me a chance to be myself anyway." *If that's what they think of me I won't give in, never.*

The nun tightened her arms around her torso as though to emphasize the truth of Sister Juda's condemnation. "We know how to deal with stubbornness."

Helpless, I dropped my head to my lap, defying the rule of standing in her presence. I tried frantically to shut out the meaningless words that went on and on.

"It is no small matter to lose or gain the Kingdom of God. Be glad to suffer tribulation for God's sake, esteem it an honour to be chosen to suffer for Him."

Mother Monica turned the key deliberately and was gone.

Shit! I wanted to shout after her that God would be infinitely more praised if I was allowed to go to school and learn something. I wanted to scream, *Go to hell and leave me alone.* That language brought some satisfaction, but it would only prove Sister Juda's "hard to deal with" label. Frustrated, I cried at the walls and soothed my bruised face on the cool boards, tasting the salt sting of tears. What had I done to cause this uproar? The nuns were always suspicious, even a look could convince them we were sneaks. Could this madness be a test of my moral strength? The nuns were like that. They were forever telling us that their religious life was the perfect state; being a spinster was next and marriage least pleasing to God. I never wanted to believe them, I couldn't.

At noon Myriam brought a plate of hash, bread and tea. I turned my back again, sorry that Myriam was witness to my mulish game. Sorry, too, that I was failing my group leader. *She could probably listen and help me if she wanted to, but she's bound to the system, mustn't talk to each other. Servitude, subjection, she plays the part well. For all her aloofness, she's probably capable of wrestling the toughest of us into submission. If not, would she be sent alone?*

Afternoon dragged into evening. The sharp, familiar sound of the five o'clock factory whistle heard everywhere meant fathers would be going home to their children. An impossibility for me, but I indulged in the fantasy. Down in the harbour a big ship hooted hoarsely and I knew that at St. Vincent's they'd all hear it and someone would yell, "Hey, the banana boat!"

Myriam appeared again, this time with a blanket. She put a mug of water on the floor and left. Click! *Clickclickclickclickclick* I screamed in my head. Her padded steps retreated from the outer room. Another door, another click! Another night in isolation. My day of fasting and silence would only convince Mother Monica that I was the incorrigible person Sister Juda had described. Somehow I couldn't see that shouting, kicking or screaming would accomplish anything.

What else could I do? Bang the tin mug against the wall? No one would hear it. It would only hurt my own ears. *Thank you God for the blanket!* It warmed my shoulders and I wondered why they took it away during the less terrifying daylight hours. If they thought I might make a noose of it, the time would be now, in this awful black desolation facing the despair of needing my mother, or father. Yes, even a father would do. What could be more urgent? I have to know who I am before I can be anything. I can't let them see my pain but this craving absorbs all my understanding.

My thoughts turned to my own mother but I had no memories. I bet she would hold me, she might read to me or even hum and sing. She'd smell nice. I'd like it if my dad could pick me up. Old Glyn did sometimes. In a swoon of shame and longing I moved around the room. *Where is my mother? What is her name? Did my father love her? Does she know him now? Did he go to jail? Is she dead? Am I adopted? Does she think I have a home with McGlyns? Who are McGlyns anyway? Would she want me if she knew I was alone?*

Screaming silence. No answers. A comic thought occurred because I'd always wished for a room to sleep in, not a dormitory or a hospital, but a little bedroom. Well, this was a little room all right but the wishgranters were mixed up. Desperate to pass the time, I listed in my head all the people I'd known in my life: orphans, nuns, patients, nurses, doctors, priests, the bishop; or known of: Mayor McLaren, King George V, Pope Pius 11th, General Franco, Bing Crosby, Lindbergh. I started humming an old hymn, *Holy Mary Mother Mild, hear, oh hear thy little child . . .* and then a more seemly prisoner's song, *Oh I wish I had someone to live with, someone to call me their own . . . for I'm tired of living alone.*

That song was too sad. I wanted to cry again. *Where are you? Who are you?* I chanted in my head to a familiar tune, like Alice and the caterpillar: *I-I hardly know s-sir, just at present at least. I know who I was . . . but I think I must have changed several times since I came here.* Who on earth would I ever call "sir"? *I can't explain myself, I'm afraid, sir, because I'm not myself, you see, said Alice. I shall sit here, on and off for days, the caterpillar said.* That game was fun with someone, but wearisome alone with no one to laugh at or to be smarter than. *Curtsy while you're thinking, the Red Queen said to Alice.* I got up and made a deep bow. At least I felt my smile in the darkness and envisioned hundreds of nuns, black-clad from St. Vincent's and white-habited from the Good Shepherd, and wished they would do things differently, for there was no help here; no way to give or get affection, no encouragement to be better, no chance to be anything. I remembered a reading at Mass lately: *Religion that is pure and undefiled before God the Father is this: to care for orphans and widows in their distress.* James 1:27. Humph! Just widows? Did God, too, have no tolerance for unmarried mothers?

Imagination could fill the longest hours. Like, did the nuns wash their bodies? We had to pretend our bodies weren't there, obliged to wear our chemise and bathe in the dark to avoid seeing our bodies. Narrow-minded nonsense. What did they know about babies? Wherever we came from they came from too.

Myriam didn't spend time coaxing next time.

"Are you going to eat this morning?"

I shook my head and the tray was removed. *Sure, take the knife and fork away. Whatever you think I'd do with them, I haven't any idea.*

Mother Monica got right to the point that morning. "Particular friendships undermine our dedication to God. I'll have you know how much we object to your particular friendship with Germaine. She came to us a bad woman and we'll put an end to your involvement one way or another."

"I don't know what you're talking about!" I exclaimed, wondering now if the nun meant we were doing dirty things together. "I hardly know her. She scares me. Anyway I don't like her."

The nun was scornful.

"I don't know what you mean," I insisted.

"We feel differently. Somebody saw you speaking to her. Stella said she saw you exchange notes. Is that right? Do you have a note from Germaine?"

"Dear God, no I don't!" I cried boldly. "All this is not my fault. I'm always treated worse than anyone. It's not fair."

"Furthermore, Magdalen, you are restless in your work. You are not settled in your group. You are capable of contributing, you know, and you don't. I saw you and Germaine looking at each other across the classroom."

"I don't know what you mean. Everyone looks at her; how can I avoid looking?"

"Why are you not eating? You certainly make the whole situation worse by your actions."

"I can't eat in here and besides, what's the point? I don't care now." I sat down abruptly in her presence and turned my head away. *I'm not allowed to argue with a nun? Who cares? I don't!*

"I'll send Myriam to take you to the infirmary for breakfast." She touched me on the shoulder, a reassuring squeeze, then whisked haughtily away, locking the door once more. For a second I let myself find comfort in her touch but only a second. They were cruel hands that held me powerless.

After breakfast in the infirmary I was more reluctant to return to isolation from the world of semi-freedom. I resented the door clicking again on my life. Mother Monica returned and was adamant that I'd been up to some mischief with Germaine. *Maybe she means something like we touched each other, but how could that be?*

"You may return to your place in the group if you are disposed to discontinue your scandalous behaviour. When you go in twos the devil makes a third. You think about that."

How could I change behaviour that was routine, strict and scrutinized? Or change something that never happened? They were always suspicious and preoccupied with sex, forever warning us, "You be careful miss." It seemed unnecessary to me.

To while away the hours while some afternoon light filtered through the latticework, I started to write the names of the girls at St. Vincent's and people I'd known on the wall behind the door using the pencil stub from my petticoat pocket. Tiny little letters and neat categories might occupy the mind of a future visitor to St. Peter's room. Eventually Myriam appeared with a supper tray and said she would be back before night prayers, ". . . to see if you're ready." I was ready. Ready to be let out, to wash, to sleep in my own cot and to see the light of day. Summoning a measure of dignity, I was led to the classroom, bold as a lion. I would not be cowed by these hidebound women. When prayers ended, I walked with some decorum to the centre of the room and knelt, my heart pounding. "I'm sorry if I did anything to upset you. I didn't break the rules on purpose." Then, as required, I bent forward and kissed the floor. Mother Monica said something, but I didn't hear her words. Faint and faltering, somebody helped me up and I followed the rest of them into the dormitory.

It was my fourteenth birthday.

*B*ecoming more and more introspective, I ironed hour after hour certain that somehow there was another way of life for me. In the bathroom I refused to wear a chemise in the tub; I dipped it in the water to satisfy those in charge that I was moral by their standards. But I was alone and bare with a heap of heavy clothes on the floor and this was the only place I could laugh at the non-person I had become and think of myself as a person fighting for space. I moved my hands around my breasts and down my hips to know my body and I knew that the only thing wrong with it was that it was forbidden. Determination lent hope and I thought of Emily Dickinson's words that I'd read in the hospital: *Hope is the thing with feathers that perches in the soul.* There was time. I'd keep the feathers tickling my determination.

The intimacy of the confessional provided a closeness to a caring human being, a place where I could speak and get a response. This was fortunate. The priest might have been in a hurry or stuffy and disdainful; some were.

I used the mandatory confession time on Saturdays to the limit and Father Kinsella listened in the dark without imperiling privacy. It seemed I was touching him and he was touching me more directly than any physical touching. I could open the door to my personal self as far as I wanted, all the way, or even keep it closed. He understood my trying to evolve into somebody. For years I had performed the forced confessions by rote; I was taught the words almost as soon as I could speak. *Bless me Father for I have sinned, I confess to Almighty God and to you Father. It is a week since my last confession. I accuse myself of* . . . The orphans knew the list of sins by heart. *I was distracted during prayers. I was uncharitable, talked against my friend. I stole a piece of bread. I had impure thoughts. I touch myself sometimes.* All trifling errors probably never actually committed, and if they were, never with bad intentions. But we, little children, had to go into the confessional and come up with something we were sorry for, make a "firm purpose of amendment," be absolved, get a penance and have that obligation over for another week, trying not to forget a sin for which we'd burn in Hell for all eternity!

After the lock-up I examined my thoughts and feelings, realizing the one advantage we had was spiritual freedom. Meditation was urged on us. Stillness after a prayerful, bustling, tense day in the laundry was allowed and I tried to teach myself to contemplate, to focus on myself and the possibility of a world of my own. The others could fantasize forever about God, His beauty and goodness, and get downright emotional about Him. They could grow to love Him more each moment and devise little schemes to please Him all day long. They could talk to God, that was okay. Don't dare talk to anyone else though. A few got carried away with sanctimonious faces and downcast eyes like something from the Middle Ages.

Kneeling in the confessional box I heard Father Kinsella counseling the penitent on the other side, closing my ears to the whispered words. I thought I was ready but when he slid the window open and rested his ear close to the latticed space I started to say, "I accuse myself of. . ." but I could not say that I had committed a sin that caused the fuss with the women.

"I need someone to talk to Father."

"Yes, my child." He listened as I unburdened my story.

"I regret what happened, Father. It wasn't my fault. I suppose I must ask forgiveness for being stubborn."

"Don't point a finger at yourself," he said. Hushed and private, he looked right into the grillwork, making his involvement personal. "There'll be enough people doing that during your lifetime. Whatever you have done till now, place on my shoulders, never think of it again, never confess it again, never worry about it. Go in peace."

Each week it became easier. He knew my voice and listened. I could just start off by saying whatever I felt. "Father, my life is empty. I'm so discouraged. I want to do more with my life than just iron."

"St. Augustine said that yearning makes the heart deep, my child. Can you not think of that and be peaceful?"

"No, no it's not peaceful . . . I'm lost." There were no recriminations, no risks. He never hurried me. I always felt better for having talked to him.

"Pray my child, be patient, God loves you."

Patience! A cardinal virtue! I took time to think about it. He waited like an angel.

"Father, I'll try to do what I'm obliged to do and not be angry. I'll try. But I am hostile and agitated and impatient. With your help I'll try harder and I know someday my life will be changed."

I overlooked the reality that for years, at St. Vincent's, and here, if anyone was in the confessional longer than the fifty seconds it took to rhyme off your sins and an act of contrition, get your penance and absolution, the others thought that you must have committed some big mortal sin, something awful, and they snickered about it. I was indifferent to their opinions while I used the confessional to relieve my impatience and foster some hope. Being able to affirm my feelings of hopelessness, knowing there was one person I could talk to privately, who listened and reacted, gave me a new lease on life as it had to be lived for the present. For as long as I live I'll remember Father Kinsella's benevolence.

Within six months, I was moved to the packing room in the laundry, the prestigious place to work. Monday and Tuesday we counted clothes, sorted and marked them, and "visited" the pockets. The temptation to keep found money was outweighed by the approval one might gain by disclosing it and, in any case, it was no use to us in custody. The fumes of the chlorobenzene deodorant were a stimulant and I inhaled them deeply. This peek into the hampers of the well-to-do let me fantasize about the mothers and daughters who owned these soiled garments, who knew each other and lived together. Now and then the girls in the packing room caught a glimpse of the driver who brought in the dirty laundry, leaving the baskets on the delivery platform and picking them up again on Friday. When the delivery ramp was open and a current of clean air blew in, I imagined walking out, down the street. *Out into the world*, the nuns would say. But some nun would scream, the driver would probably chase after me and wrestle me back to captivity. No use thinking about it. Still, that open door was tempting.

Other days in the packing room we put the laundered clothes on designated shelf space, then packed them in bundles or baskets owned by the customers. The neat and methodical system was a challenge. No heat, no steam or noise, a polished atmosphere. No praying out loud either. We few workers had to use our heads to check laundry marks and count pieces, often going to the machine room or ironing room to locate items to complete a bundle, well aware of our senior standing.

The psychology of the confessional worked for me. The understanding and compassion of the priest made all the difference. Having ability, I was given more to do in that unreal world. Cutting hair, for example, and hearing gospels on the weekend. Each woman was obliged to memorize verbatim the gospel for that Sunday and recite it to a few designated persons. *Haircutting and gospels*, I mused. Some cuts were funny. I made amends for the bad haircuts by being lenient with the gospel recitations and it was natural to go easy on some women who couldn't memorize easily. For me it was a great memory exercise that I enjoyed and took advantage of.

Doris McGlyn came from Boston to visit that fall. We sat in a parlour divided by a wooden grille, a floor-to-ceiling barrier. Mother Monica unlocked a small window in the grillwork so we could be more at ease, but she stayed with us throughout the visit. Frantic inside, but timid in the nun's presence, I told Doris I'd rather not be there. "I'd like it better if I could live with you. I can work and look after myself, you know." But it wasn't easy to say anything about the laundry in front of the mistress. I wanted to like Doris again. She was a link with the world I longed for. While I was distracted with a hunger to ask her who would or could release me, she spoke eagerly of her various operations, quality of pain, quantity of stitches, doctors, hospitals and scars; how often she had been near death and how proud she was to be a Yankee. When I mentioned Elsa, Doris mocked, "Don't worry, that one won't be around to see you." We didn't even touch each other except when she kissed me good-bye. Then I reached through the open grille for this sweet-smelling person and my hug was longer because I was showing with physical contact what I wasn't permitted to tell her. Waves of panic smothered me and I nearly fainted knowing I'd be left again and I cried. Doris missed the point and said not to be upset because she was leaving when all the while I was crying because I was staying.

I asked Doris for money for Gregg shorthand books, typing and a bookkeeping manual. Mother Monica was allowing those who could get the books to use the recreation hour for self-teaching. To do so required infinite patience and discipline and so far only two of us were trying. She had found an old Underwood typewriter in the attic and had made a bib that hung around my neck with the other end tied to the sides of the machine, to avoid looking at the keys in this self-taught exercise. Seldom did I join my group and the class became used to seeing me busy and apart; in their petty innocuous way they seemed proud that two of us were achieving something.

The opportunity to learn became an obsession with me. More and more, the nun singled me out to do little favours for her, beckoning me from the ranks saying, "Father Howard will be visiting on Sunday. You remember how much the girls enjoyed the retreat he preached. Write an address for Father." Or, "Father Kinsella's seventeenth anniversary is Holy Thursday this year. Prepare a talk to go along with the Mass vestments Myriam is making." So I wrote a long piece, *Seventeen paschal moons have risen since our beloved Father, Christ's brother, Mary's other son, knelt before God's altar and received from the hands of the bishop the Power of the Keys; the Power to Loose and the Power to Bind* . . . Or she would say, "The bishop has been ill. He is honouring us with a visit on St. Patrick's day, can you do an appropriate poem or address?" *Nature discards her sombre cloak for a beautiful mantle of spring,* it started. Psychologically, the motivation was a godsend for my impatience and eagerness to learn.

Every so often Mother Monica wrote *petit sacré* messages to the women, lauding some virtue, reproving a shortcoming, offering encouragement. They were personal, like telling your fortune. We looked for hidden meaning, wanting her to know we tried to be better, wanting her attention. Once she asked me to help write some of these messages. I was flattered. Not that I would direct them to individuals. They were merely new words, ideas, a little gleaning from the ranks. The nun's message to me was, "You have redeemed yourself, Magdalen. God expects more of you, pray for perseverance."

She showed quite plainly that I had at least somewhat fulfilled her demands on me for righteousness and, while she was condescending, life was simpler that way. I still didn't aspire to any status in this group; my all-consuming ambition was to get out.

I believed that the nuns tenaciously set up individuals for critical scrutiny. We never knew, when accusations were levelled, if the nuns were manipulating character to strengthen it. Breaking the spirit was more to the point but conformity was the rule and the nuns didn't consider it cruel at all. There was a little clique in the class who were faultless—obedient, silent, humble, pious—a little coterie with downcast eyes, exuding self-satisfaction. They never really laughed but they prayed like saints, sang like angels, tittered appropriately and were selected to take charge in the refectory, yard and halls. Paragons of virtue, on the right track and never off. Beings with a superficial sphere of authority who had ceased to think about life. There was a larger faction of more normal women. We worked hard and took pride in our efforts to satisfy the powers that be. We sometimes fell short. There was still some hope for us in the game of life if we didn't lose all self-determination. There was also the "always in trouble, hard to deal with" bunch. "She's off the track," everyone would say; St. Peter's regulars who compounded their problems by hating the rules. "That One," the nun would say, "be careful of That One." Quietly I thought, *There but for God go I!*

With permission and help I organized a mission group and was named president. A meeting each month during recreation period was a diversion with skits, question periods, a mission field to study and a publication, *Pro Deo Et Patria.* This was a godsend for the two of us teaching ourselves to type. Collecting nickels and dimes received in the mail or in the parlour and sending them to the Foreign Missions for the Rescue of Pagan Babies became an objective. Sometimes we were allowed to sing during recreation. There were many spectacular voices, the roundelays and harmony so beautifully natural. Love songs were forbidden, but *Whispering Hope, Home on the Range* and that type were acceptable. I observed the incongruous fervour of the assembly singing words of *Home Sweet Home* with cynicism.

During Sunday spiritual reading period, I searched through the few books available, seeking information on this community of nuns and learned that the order had its roots in seventeenth-century France and this particular order of sisters was founded in 1835 to specialize in social work with delinquent girls. ". . . women in personal, social and family difficulties who were unable to function adequately in their lives and who were brought back into the fold." Hence the name Good Shepherd. There was an interesting note about the sisters and how they trained the women so their lives were not wasted. They were taught to do exquisite needlework and weaving, the demand for which could never be met. The women earned an ample wage. Some supported their families on the outside, some saved for their departure. The mission was ever and always to value and reveal the beauty of God's image in each person. This was contained in a very old volume and the locale was France, but that bit of research gave impetus to my time in the laundry. Maybe, just maybe, there would be some recompense when these days came to an end and my life started. There was no hint of such a scheme, but the possibility seemed equitable.

One day Mother Monica suggested that I might be the reader at mealtime. I was nervous for the spiritual readings were strained.

"Of course you can do it, Magdalen," the nun insisted.

As if I had a choice!

The spiritual readings were difficult to read and hard to understand; or they were lives of the saints, improbable, hard to believe. Very suddenly the nun changed that. One day the entire mealtime mood was altered when I opened the book given to me and read the words "Rachel caught her breath in amazement and sat down before the fire, the letter in her trembling hand . . ." The women couldn't believe it; they were taken off guard. I thought I'd made a terrible mistake and, looking up, saw the sparkle in the nun's eyes. She nodded and smiled in that way of hers and my voice picked up the excitement. From that day on every other mealtime book was a story, a happy alternative to all that holy reading. The women listened eagerly and it seemed they were more willing to listen to the spiritual stuff in between. Also, this uplifting turn in the routine let me read the supernatural things with more fervour and understanding than before. There was power in my position, not over anyone else, just an affirmation to myself that I was somebody giving something to others. I was thankful when the mistress arranged favourable situations for me that eased the restrictive life.

When I was nearly seventeen, Mother Monica slipped a small book with a brown paper wrapper from under her habit and said I should read it carefully, then return it, making sure I showed it to no one. Her prudent smile left me terribly curious. I hurried to the corridor. To my amazement it was sex instruction: *Letters to Mary*. I studied the human male chapter but, in truth, I lacked a healthy interest because all thoughts of our body had been banned. It had not occurred to me, ever, that anyone, least of all a nun, would think anything of my physical growth and undertake to tell me what it was about. My mind and time were filled with work and religion. Once, though, I had a dream about the altar boy Francis. He seemed to virtually float on the sanctuary steps, beckoning me. I became a bystander watching myself, naked, fearless and eager, drift towards him, his hands skimming but not reaching my purity. I was the beholder and receiver, wanting the exhilaration of the dream to go on and on.

I kept *Letters to Mary* in my petticoat pocket for a while. Some parts were interesting, but I failed to understand why the nun thought I needed this information. How could I understand white slave traffic or syphilis? I was in no hurry to return the book, fearing what Mother Monica might ask me. My interest centered on male physiology and the only man to enter my world was the priest. While I would recite the Latin mass from memory, my mind focused on the body of the man before the altar. We all loved this handsome, gentle but firm person, and now I was mindful of his shoulders, his mouth, his hair. I imagined his consecrated hands could soothe and please just as much as his words in the confessional. Conscientious scruples took hold of me for there was no denying the list of new words. Finally, one morning on the way to the laundry, the opportunity arose for a discreet handing over. The nun tossed her veil behind her right shoulder in that characteristic way and said, "Come to my office, Magdalen."

I followed and knelt down. She closed the door and swiveled quietly on her soft shoes, arms folded, hands hidden up her big sleeves, a half smile on her lips, brown eyes gleaming. *I guess I'm not in trouble.* I lowered my gaze to the floor.

"Stand up Magdalen, or have a seat," she said pleasantly. I stood up and immediately wished I had chosen the seat. We were eye to eye and I wasn't able to assess the book or to say that I had learned anything of value from it, or understand why she had given it to me.

"Well," she sighed and hesitated. I looked at the floor again. "The time has come for you to leave us." I considered sitting down before I fainted, but this was a shock I could abide.

"How come?" I asked, disbelieving.

"Mrs. McGlyn is of the opinion you are old enough. I'm afraid I don't agree with her. A few more years with us would make you stronger, better able to face the temptations of the outside world. I hope the book helped?"

"Not really," I blurted out. "But I know right from wrong, Reverend Mother, I'll not disgrace you. What is Doris's plan? Where am I to go?"

"You will be on your own," she said ruefully. "I have a letter to give you and some money she sent, and a parcel of clothes in the sewing room. Right now you may take time to collect any personal articles you want and bring them to the sewing room. Remember to keep holy silence."

I walked from the office, my thoughts in a whirl, my feet all out of control, bumping into chairs in the rec room, wanting to run and skip and shout *whoopee!* The thought occurred that I might have been gone days earlier had I returned the book sooner. How long had the "parcel of clothes" been on the premises? In my small space in the dorm I emptied the wooden washstand, patted the metal cup that someone else would use, *ha-ha, no more ice on my wash basin on cold winter mornings.* Stella went about her work and I wondered, *Does she know I'm going or does she think I'm taking my stuff to the infirmary?* I collected shorthand books from the cupboard in the recreation room and walked through that space for the last time, jubilant, shedding the loathed melancholy, head spinning, spirits soaring; I still could not believe it! I stood at my place and looked around at the empty chairs, wanting to wave—*See you all!* I didn't understand the discipline that forbade saying good-bye. Now and then one of the women had disappeared and no one had known the circumstances of her departure. I hurried towards the sewing room still disbelieving; I had to get there before the dream ended.

I felt the nun's eyes on me as I handled the new clothes with awe. Silk stockings and a garter belt—no more round elastic garters that cut off circulation! A bra that fit, *little* underwear with lace and a navy blue princess-style dress with an adorable bolero that felt gorgeous. Doris was stylish; you could say that about her. My trusty little doll's trunk was on the bench in the inside room adjacent to St. Peter's room. I opened it quickly and fingered Molly's childish things with supreme tenderness even if they were just an orphan's dress and black stockings. Little girl's things. I added Magdalen's then stole into St. Peter's room and looked behind the door. They were still there, the names of all the girls at St. Vincent's I had written with a pencil stub three years earlier, tiny, methodical and neat, earmarking the black girl, the Indian girl, the cripple, the girl with a glass eye, the simple girl called Maddy, the oldest, the baby, my likes and dislikes. When confronted, I had denied putting them there. How strange they were not erased.

The letter from Doris began, *My darling daughter Molly, During my last visit I got the impression you would like to leave the convent. I've been thinking about it and can see no reason why you shouldn't have the chance off* [again that made me smile] *looking after yourself if that's what you want* . . . She had enclosed twelve American dollars.

The real clothes felt light and so smooth. There was no describing the feeling of silk stockings on my feet and legs! *This can't be happening to me!*

Brushing my hair loose, I rang the three short bells to summon the nun who told me to follow her past the infirmary into the sisters' elevator; past the particular shining cleanliness of their halls and rooms to the parlour.

At the chapel door, I willingly made a final visit. I was glad to kneel in the place that would no longer be mine and my thoughts were distracted from prayer. No more obligatory litanies, novenas, retreats, First Fridays! No heavy clothes or chapel veils. No more trying to please to get attention. Confession only if I wanted it. In the wavering candlelight my earnest prayer, my only prayer was to the Mother of God: "More than anything in this world, let me know my real mother, amen." I vowed before God's altar, "I'll never come back to this spot, never voluntarily and I'll not break the law. I am walking away from here forever. Thank you God, thank you."

In the front parlour Mother Monica stood smiling. "Be careful, Magdalen. You have a pure expression, a face people will turn to look at. Be careful . . . maybe you should braid your hair, don't cut it though. You must buy a pocketbook. Be careful."

"I will."

"We've ordered a taxi for you. Your mother said your Aunt Bertha would help you get settled. Go there first, she is expecting you. Oh, I do hope you will make out all right, but you be careful."

"Don't worry, Reverend Mother, I will. I'll make you proud of me." I looked into her eyes and meant it. I felt no sadness at parting. *Just let me go and I'll prove it!*

On Monday, April 13, 1942, the same portress who had admitted me to the Good Shepherd Convent opened the huge oak cloistered door to liberation. "*Deo Gratias,*" she whispered and was otherwise reverently silent, eyes lowered, but at the last moment the wrinkled old face with faded peaceful eyes gave me a lovely smile that I would keep in my memory for years.

The closing of the door was consummate. Here I was, newly born, standing on the steps of the Good Shepherd Convent with a tender sense of independence and I wanted to cry to the world, *Here I am!* Would that I could proclaim my name, my mother's name, on this first day of being myself. *Not to worry Molly, now we have the freedom to face that challenge with hope and optimism and we'll make it our first independent act. I'll go to Aunt Bertha's later. Here we go.* The taxi was waiting.

"Take me to the Infants' Home please, Cobourg Street."

He drove up Cliff Street past St. Vincent's. Freedom from that woebegone existence had ironically cost me more than three years' confinement. But would those years have been any better at St. Vincent's? I dismissed the taxi and in the vestibule of the Infants' Home, I, a young woman nearly seventeen, wondered if my mother had really left me here, on this step. It was an elegant place to be left with its bright brass fittings and spotless ornamental tile floor, leaded stained glass in the impressive door. *Did my mother place me here, ring the bell and hide, maybe behind that chestnut tree? Did they ever find the other bootie? Naw, Doris must have made that up. I belonged to no one, just to her. It was her fairy story. She even called me Princess. My life, an accident, began here . . .*

Sister Rosa's arrival interrupted my daydream. The nun was childlike, barely four feet tall; her small face and thin body seemed so petite now. I remembered how she often came across the lane to see "her babies" who had turned four and had left her care. They showed a special affinity for her. She welcomed me lovingly.

"Sister, do you know where my mother is? What is my name? Tell me who I am?"

"Calm down, Molly," she smiled. "First of all I have no information. If I did you'd have no right to it. McGlyns took you and that's that." She reached up and tweaked my pale cheek. "I'll say this though, you have skin just like your mother's."

So they did know her personally. The imprecise particulars become more equivocal. Am I to walk the streets looking for skin like mine? Must I peer through a microscope and ask skin-a-likes, Are you my mother?

"Sister Juda said that, too. Do you really think it's fair that I don't know my mother? It's only natural I want to know. You are obliged to tell me."

She shrugged her little shoulders and threw her hands forward in a gesture of helplessness. "On the contrary, it's the law. I think she was one that died; yes, she died."

"Whose law? It's all wrong. And I don't believe she died. You just thought to say that now. Besides, it must be against the law to keep that information from me. I have the right to it. I wasn't adopted." I felt a weird and wonderful emancipation in arguing with a nun who wasn't in complete control of my every utterance. "Look Sister Rosa, I'll probably leave the city. I should have a birth certificate, everyone needs a birth certificate don't they?"

"That's not the point Molly. You were taken and that's that."

"It *is* the point. I insist and I'm going to stay here and wait until someone tells me my mother's name."

Sister Rosa threw her hands out exasperated and said nothing.

Controlling myself, I tried once more with the vital question. "Can't you tell me anything about her?"

"No, nothing, but I'm sure she was one that died. Some did, you know."

"Well then, tell me where she's buried. I'll go to her grave. At least that would be some consolation. I'd find comfort going there."

"No, no, I know nothing about her. There were so many babies." This stubborn Lilliputian nun meant it. Confidentiality was the issue and she was unyielding.

It's not the end. I'll never give up. I'll find other ways.

I walked down Cliff Street and the doll trunk seemed heavier now. Passing Wasson's drugstore I was reminded of my defiance a few years earlier and went in and ordered an ice cream soda, quite unabashed this time. The same druggist peered over his glasses at me, only now I was not frightened or guilty. Looking at the newspaper headlines again, I read that the "war postponed" the night I ran away was in high gear and India was begging independence from Britain, insisting it was less likely the Japanese would invade India if they were not part of the British Empire. I didn't understand war, I was satisfied it was far away in England. I bought a bright yellow scribbler and a pencil and reached Aunt Bertha's weary and hungry. Bertha was restless and worried that I was on my own, "After all, you're not yet seventeen."

"I will be in a month. I won't be a care to you, please don't worry."

"A friend of Peter's, her name is Terry, has a room on Elliot Row. She wants to know if you'll share it. Three dollars a week. She teaches, she's easygoing. I have a key, we can walk over and see it after we have a cup of tea."

The house was a block past Old Glyn's, just forty numbers on. We went up long stairs in the cool, dim house and the room was a lovely surprise. Large windows, two beds, lamps and large dressers. The bathroom was at the end of the hall and the telephone in an alcove under the stairs on the main floor. I had never used a telephone. I'd learn to. Bertha wrote down the number of her employer and left me there to wait for Terry.

"Peter is married," she said. "He lives in Toronto now. I wrote and told him Doris was letting you out."

You're right, I thought. *She let me out. I'm independent! Independence Day April 13, 1942. I'll never be subservient again.* My brief tenderness for Peter was unimportant. My only quest now was to find my mother. Doris would not approve, that was certain. And Bertha would be on her side, she'd tell me nothing, even if she knew. Doris seemed to have had the right to send me to the Good Shepherd and she had told them to release me. She'd sent me clothes and twelve dollars. Just the same I'd prefer to be free of her influence now.

Dismissing Doris from my thoughts, I opened the new yellow book and wrote the word SEARCH and added the date. The page looked mysterious. Where will this venture take me? I sensed fanfare and a drum roll. I found Terry's radio and swayed happily to the music and couldn't believe that this person, who had been on her way to the laundry at eight o'clock this morning, was here, free! Singing, dancing, soon to be laughing and talking with a new friend.

Terry was older than I was, and that was an advantage for I had so much to learn. Her smile, large dark eyes, high colour and short-cropped dark hair were attractive. It was simple and natural to accept her friendship, so easy to respond. But it would take some time to render mute the pangs of conscience I felt about particular friendships.

"What was that place like?" Terry asked the next day.

"It was awful. I suppose there were some good nuns who had their favourites but not me. We got up at the sound of a bell, knelt to pray the morning offering immediately, paraded from the dorm at the sound of a bell, knelt in the rec room behind our chairs to say morning prayers, blessed ourselves all together at the sound of a bell, paraded to the chapel, not a word was spoken. Then we worked all day. I was unhappy, it was awful."

"There's a teacher at school who wants to take you to a movie."

"Honest," she said at the look on my face. "You have to start sometime. Listen, if we double-date would you go?"

"Oh, I'd like that. Sure, tell him I'll go."

"His name is Leigh. He's blond, he's funny, kind of thin."

Our first date was planned. But more than that, I found my first job that morning, in a restaurant, typing menus, seating people and taking cash. I told them I'd wait on table as well or do dishes or anything for experience. I would be paid eight dollars a week and some meals.

"Terry, can you believe I have a home, a job and a date within two days of getting out?"

"This old city will never be the same again! And guess what, when you've worked for a while, it'll be easy to find a better job. Here, put on some lipstick, a little. You don't need any other makeup. Try a dab of perfume though."

Lipstick felt waxy and I looked different with it on. It was okay. And a dark theatre was a fine place to hear my first insinuations about romance. It was a funny movie and I laughed with the audience and learned something about the sexes. Leigh held my hand.

I wanted desperately to see Old Glyn but was afraid of what Doris might have said to him, maybe blamed him. And if he gave me a half-dollar would it imply an obligation? If not, would that indicate the end of our involvement? I didn't go. Instead, I walked through the old market, down the far side, away from his shop.

He looked the same. I was sad watching him while he did ordinary things like greeting people, weighing food and wiping his hands on his apron. I didn't see Elsa, quite certain that her kindness had caused bad feelings with Doris. In time I hoped I would see both these good friends to thank them for helping me on a grim night.

Sunday I went to see Aunt Bertha, eager to boast about my first six days in the world, impatient to let her know that I was capable, hoping also that Bertha's account to Doris would be supportive. I watched her bouncing corpulence as she prepared tea and I felt the wooden floor creak and yield when she walked. Her jolly full-blown face was bereft of wrinkles under a frame of gray curls and terribly thick glasses. I remembered the prestige of her position in the mayor's kitchen, the brick hearth, copper pots, her grand authority over the maids in uniform, the treats she saved for me.

It had been easier to sneak out from St. Vincent's to see Aunt Bertha than it was to see Old Glyn. When Sister Angeline's back was turned I could slip through the side gate, always with a ball in my hand in case she saw me coming back. Sister might think I'd gone behind the fence to retrieve the ball; at least I'd insist that was the case. Then, Bertha was head cook at Hazen's Castle, a large property adjacent to the orphanage with three hills, one small and gradual, one steep and one with three bumps at the bottom, fenced from Hazen's main property for the orphan's sledding in winter; a mass of daisies and buttercups in the summer. A diplomat or parliamentarian or someone lived there, I wasn't sure about it, but it was a treat to be able to walk into that kitchen and be fussed over.

Aunt Bertha's next job had been in the bishop's kitchen. That was important to the nuns. One day I was surprised when they prayed for the bishop's cook during Mass because she'd had another heart attack. Now, there was no glory in her position as housekeeper for a Jewish merchant and his son. Her room was as small as a nun's cell with a narrow bed hardly comfortable for her girth. Today she was distracted by a phone call from Peter. "He says this is not the place for you to start your working life, Toronto is. He called Doris and told her there are good jobs and you'd be better off there. Do you want to go?"

Things kept happening too fast. "How far is Toronto?"

"Oh, you'd be all night and most of the day on the train. Peter would meet you. He said you'd earn good money in Toronto, you could get into an office or a wartime job. He knows."

I had been insensible to the reality of Canada at war and its effect on family life. The nuns seldom mentioned war news, just now and then when we prayed for General Franco. "He's a good Catholic. He is a good man . . ." Sister Juda said. Otherwise the war seemed remote and far away. Now, in the real world, the talk all around me, the practice blackouts, poster slogans and food ration books brought it clearly to mind at the mention of a wartime job. On the twenty-third of April, ten days after my rebirth, I was on a train to Toronto. A uniformed airman left his seat and sat beside me. Terry and Leigh had walked me to the station and we all laughed at his self-consciousness for he carried the silly little trunk, he even boarded the train and saw me settled in a seat. Everything was easy with Leigh. I'd wanted to know him longer but here I was saying good-bye to someone who liked me, a new part of me willingly ripped away. And Terry! It was hard to say goodbye to her, but we made promises. That first week I had experienced touching and handshakes, Leigh's arm around me, even a kiss. Now the warmth of an airman's thigh aroused a fondness. *He likes being close to me.* He slipped his foot under mine, our knees touched. He held my hand and my arm grew weary.

The conductor brought a pillow and a blanket for the long night. Now the airman's hand was freer to stray under the blanket, from my knee to the top of my stocking. Deftly he unfastened the garter. *Who does he think he is? No one is going to run me from now on,* and I looked pleadingly to the conductor. He cleverly assigned another seat and I hobbled towards it, holding the top of my stocking behind the blanket, away from my beguiler and the sensation of wanting to sit by him and not wanting to. I was confused and I was amused.

Through man's love and woman's love
Moons and tides move
Which fuse those islands, lying face to face.
Mixing in naked passion
Those who naked new life fashion
Are themselves reborn in naked grace.

Stephen Spender

TORONTO ➤ 1942

I DIDN'T FEEL like an orphan on the train. I was dressed in real clothes and going to a definite place and doing things like other travellers. I was on my own! Aunt Bertha had given me a gift of her opal ring encircled with tiny diamonds. I studied it with delight, holding my hand up to admire it until I saw someone watching me so I folded my hands on my lap and looked at my ring covertly. My only fear now was that of going farther away from any trace of my mother. Well, they said she was gone from there too. *I'll risk anything to find her. I'll get a job, go to Boston, maybe get a job on the Boston boat. One way or another I'll find her.* Sister Juda said my mother was nursing Mrs. O'Connor. Maybe Doris knew her. The thought persisted: find Mrs. O'Connor first and then find the nurse. Simple? Maybe.

Or maybe we'd been apart too long. Maybe my mother had a family life of her own and kept her secret to herself. Maybe she didn't need a daughter. Well, I needed her, and I wanted to know what she looked like and find out something about my father too. I wondered if she'd talk about her love for him? Were they sad when she left Ireland? Did they plan to meet again? Were they married? Do I have sisters and brothers? The maze of questions was maddening!

Changing trains in Montreal at daybreak was daunting. I stood alone as the walls of Windsor Station went up and down like a teeter-totter, enduring a vertigo-inducing nausea. Pangs of sorrow and remorse added to my suffering when, in the washroom, I found I'd left my new ring on the sink in the train when I washed my hands. It was gone, just as if I had given it away. A Traveller's Aid woman gave me some juice, saying, "You're so ghostly white," then led me to the Toronto connection.

Aunt Bertha's son, Peter, lived on Charles Street with his wife Anne, a short block from Yonge and Bloor in the heart of Toronto. I was surprised to learn that their home was one large room in an old house. That night they pulled out their Murphy bed and made my bed on the couch. The first Sunday four priests came from a nearby college and Peter poured beer for them from tall green bottles. It was natural for me to be respectful of them, but I was ever so careful not to mention the Good Shepherd for one priest was from the Maritimes. "Yes, Father, I am from St. Vincent's." "An orphan? You poor child." They laughed aloud at some undercurrent of humour and I overheard Peter say, "She's so green . . ."

I felt out of place and went for a walk. Would I always be a real person with a pretend name? Saying off-hand, *Oh yes, I went to Convent School. Whereabouts?* they might say. *Oh, in the Maritimes.* Or worse, Do you have sisters or a brother? *No, I'm an only child.* I'd rather be truthful and say *I belong to nobody.* Everybody belongs to someone, they'd say, or maybe they'd just think I was crazy and leave me alone. I stood still on Yonge Street; the feeling of freedom on a spring day so joyous I laughed and threw away the prejudices and concerns of my life.

Being careful to establish my route I turned west on St. Mary Street and walked through a beautiful archway to the university grounds. Confident young people walked together or alone, all with purpose, belonging to someone or something. I swore to myself, *I can't be satisfied with a grade six mentality. I won't accept that I can't learn more and I won't feel guilty for wanting more from life.* Apart from Mother Monica's gesture of permitting self-study for the few who grabbed the chance, the nuns placed little importance on intelligence and potential. At St. Vincent's, with basic primary education, if one showed initiative or spoke up, she was labelled "bold" and punished. At the Good Shepherd, *you* weren't *you.* But if you learned to conform to the rule of prayer, silence and the laundry, the days could be endured so long as you had hope that they would end. For me they had ended and with this new beginning I resolved: I will make something of my life. I will control my own attitude and nourish my self-esteem and I will be singular.

At 74 St. Mary Street a room-for-rent sign dared me to knock on the door with some assurance. The room was large with a private entrance, a pullout couch, a hot plate and few other amenities. Cold, clean, cheap. The landlord, Mr. Wrattan, a wiry little man with thick glasses, showed me the bathroom upstairs and the telephone in an alcove under the front hall stairs. Was I naive to think that having a telephone for the tenants was a kindhearted gesture? He said he should have a deposit. Walking back to Peter's, I thought about the independence of a room of my own. I'd get a job first and then talk to Peter about taking the room.

Peter and Anne made tea and toast in the morning and left for work. Anne told me to get into their bed and enjoy a morning's rest while I still could. "You'll be working soon enough." I did that, enjoying the luxury at an hour when the girls in Saint John had been to Mass and were now at work in the laundry. One morning I slept soundly until I was conscious of Peter lying beside me, straining towards my black body hair, dripping on my thigh, his sex huge and unfamiliar. Peter touched me and I struggled from the bed as a delirious spasm started. In the bathroom there seemed to be another person in the mirror, not me. I felt anger at his betrayal and curiosity too, but we never spoke about it. Peter merely accused me: "You have a come-on look. You should be more careful."

I moved to 74 St. Mary Street the day after starting work at Simpson's rotogravure department, typing and proofreading for the catalogue department. The other women called me "the little convent girl" and I quietly acted the part while I learned everything possible about the office. Watching the ads for a better job, I saw many advertisements for laundry work but, for all my experience, I vowed to shun laundry work for as long as I lived.

Restricted cooking was allowed in my room and I bought food for the first time. I couldn't learn to cook on a two-plate burner, but it was a big advantage to have it. Mr. Wrattan found an old console radio and installed it. "It doesn't go with the room," he said twice. Whether he wanted me to pay extra or just be aware of the favour, I didn't ask. I had cake and ginger ale and swayed to the music of Don Messer and the Islanders to celebrate my formal beginning, my first home, my ten-fifty-a-week job and three-fifty-a-week room. I heard mice in the fireplace at night but the chimney was stuffed with newspaper and maybe they couldn't get out. There was no criticism from Peter or Anne about my move; they had expected I would live on my own. They made an agreeable report to Doris.

Across the street from my room, a short walk on St. Mike's campus led me to St. Basil's church on Bay Street. At daily Mass Father O'Connell recognized me from that first Sunday at Peter's and told me about Young People's Club on Tuesdays.

"How old are you my dear?"

"Seventeen in a few weeks, Father."

"Oh, one must be eighteen to belong to Young People's. However, because you are alone we won't mention your age and you won't either."

The days flew by at work. I took pride in being helpful but I would have seized any opportunity to be a nurse or a teacher or a secretary. The evenings dragged while I waited for Tuesday to come, that unparalleled day when I could belong to a Young Peoples' Club. Piling my hair high to belie my age, I chose a two-tone mauve crepe dress, the colour of lilacs and violets, criss-crossed in a soft Grecian drape, and high-heeled sandals, both from Doris. I hobbled stiff-kneed through the college grounds to the Church hall.

Young People's Club met in the church basement. The girls sported pageboys, soft sweaters with pearls, skirts and penny loafers; the boys wore corduroys or flannels and sweaters. I was overdressed. Father O'Connell said, "Hello, it's nice that you've come," and I felt better. A boy played the piano. I moved in that direction to watch him and at the end of the song he smiled at me. Soon they played fabulous dance records and I watched the rhythm of the dancers, knees swinging, feet in unison, so much to think about all at once! I thought about being held by a boy as I noticed arms around waists, around necks, cheek against cheek, a hand pressing low for closeness. I felt like an intruder. Then when they jitterbugged I wanted to laugh and clap. The piano player startled me when he asked me to dance.

"I don't know how," I said shyly.

"I'll show you. It's easy. Just move to the music, like this." He began to sway to *Elmer's Tune*.

"I don't know how," I repeated. "Everyone will look."

"No, they won't. They're too busy having a good time. Let's try a little right here." He lifted his arm and I backed away.

"No, maybe next week. I'll come back and you can show me then. I'd rather watch now."

"O.K. Can I walk you home later? I'm Julian McBeath."

"Sure." I told him my name. After that many boys asked me to dance. Each time my refusal became more refined.

It was a short walk home through St. Mike's campus. We sat on the porch steps at 74. I was comfortable there, watching others come and go, talking if I felt like it with no pressure to talk at all. Julian was tall and slight with a sharp face, sad blue eyes and wonderful brown hair. Like Joseph Cotton, I thought. He told me that even if he weren't a student, he wouldn't be in the services because he was a conscientious objector.

"War is a waste of life. I hate to believe military service is necessary. I'd rather do farm work for the war effort."

I couldn't talk about the war but I knew it was fearsome and harmful, maybe beneficial to some. I didn't think about it very much.

"I'm not too young to sign up, you know. I'm exempt as a student. I don't want to take advantage that way but it's useful while I figure out what I can do."

He tapped a cigarette on the Winchester package and put it between his lips. "Sorry. Want one?" I shook my head, not bothering to say *I don't know how*, amused at the thought of me smoking, mindful of his pale hands and flawed skin, of something pathetic in the serious squint when he blew a smoke ring.

"How can anyone shoot people they don't know anything about, or drop bombs on families?" He paused to flick something from his arm. Maybe a feeling he was brushing off. "I'd say a lot of guys are in the service because they had to go or the money's OK. Before conscription some went to get away from home, some to learn trades, like flying for instance. Some were even riding the rails when the war broke out. There's DVA land grants and university tuition involved too. There's a lot of reasons to join up."

I liked his hands, delicate with long pale fingers and intriguing fuzz curling around his white cuffs. I'd never seen that before. His thick, curly hair was irresistible and I could watch him while he spoke and inhaled, charmed by this university student who wanted to talk to me. His shirt had a tab collar with a silver bar. He wore a gray suit and carried a gabardine coat. He seemed a lot older.

"I'll get my thinking straight someday. Right now I find myself thinking about high school friends who joined up and got it. I had a buddy; he's lost in action. He used to talk about flying a Spitfire over Britain. He was only twenty-one. His parents don't know what happened to him. I know two other guys who got it. An awful thought."

"It must be awful."

"Right now I prefer to admit I'm an objector, even if I am a student."

He said it was a struggle to stay at university. He hoped to go to Osgoode Hall Law School in the fall. His father couldn't help.

"I've won public speaking contests and debates. I have a pile of trophies.

Then I won a year at university from the Lions Club. That was for public speaking too, I wrote a speech about Wilfrid Laurier and here I am, muddling through the final year on my own."

His eyes were sad.

"I love playing the piano, I've never had lessons but it comes easily." He smiled; the resentment left his eyes.

"You know, sometimes I worry because I want to drink every day. My roommates are at the King Cole Room or the Embassy every night. I don't have much money but I go along, someone always buys. I hope to God when I can afford to drink I'll find I can handle it."

I had nothing to say about these things. I just wished I could protect him from having to go to war and convince him he could drink without worrying and study without hardship.

"I've been drunk at parties. It's so easy. My dad drinks every night, he's Irish. But he works hard and who'd deny him a few beers? God, there's got to be more to life than work and beer. I don't know though. He seems content with his plebeian life."

"McBeath doesn't sound like an Irish name."

"No, it sounds Scottish but it's not spelled that way, there's an a in it like breath. It irritates me when people say McBeeth. It is Irish and pronounced McBeth. My grandparents came from around Connemara. Both my parents came from the Ottawa Valley. My mother died five years ago when I was seventeen."

He's able to talk about both parents and his grandparents. He doesn't know I couldn't do that. He kissed me good night and promised we'd meet at Young Peoples next week. I soothed the first whisker sting on my face and smiled at the reality of having been kissed, ever so briefly, by a man five years older than me.

Next club night I wanted to see Julian again but stayed in my room because I couldn't go back and keep saying *I don't know how.* Instead I wrote to Mother Monica, telling her about my job, elaborating on the joys of self-regulation, hinting that I had enjoyed a night at Young Peoples, emphasizing it was at the church hall and thinking, *I could be at the dance right now and here I am writing to a nun.* When Julian knocked it was just as well he identified himself before I opened the door. His head was shaved bald! I stared at him. "Whatever happened to you?"

He ran his hand over the top of his head and grinned. "Oh, that. I keep forgetting. The guys did it."

"Why?"

"They had a few beers. They were looking for excitement, exams were over. They said I was proud. You can't do much when four guys are holding you down with a razor on your skull. Look, it's easy to get used to. It'll grow. It's only annoying because I'm going home and I've got a summer job, but it'll grow. Come on, let's go to the dance."

He had come after me and he had more reason to hide than I did. And he said he was going home soon! Julian made dancing seem easy.

"Just put your arm on my shoulder, give me your hand, now move your feet to the music. Just follow me, Molly. See, nobody's looking."

It was easy to go where he propelled me and when I tripped over his feet because I was thinking about being in his arms, he just laughed. *He's wonderful. I never want to stop dancing.*

I missed him when he went home to Niagara for the summer. Mostly girls came to Young Peoples then. The college boys had all gone home. The young guys were in the services and the few who did come were boys with jobs who could take you to a movie, to the Island or dancing at the Palace Pier or Casa Loma. When a serviceman was home, he had a buddy with him and there was fun double dating with girls from the office. Or someone would get word that a ship was in and there'd be sailors at Club Top Hat. It was easy to go with a bunch from work. Thinking now about boys—and men—I remembered a profound question I'd had when first menstruating. Instruction from the nuns was scanty; they were determined to restrict our interest in our bodies and our sexuality. My early reaction had been, what do boys have? If I'm going to have this until I'm fifty what do boys have? There must be something; we can't be singled out for this. They're human too; don't they have some waste to get rid of every month? Now it dawned on me that boys were worse off. They were afflicted all the time with hardness, but it was difficult to understand why it had to be my problem. "Poor me, help me, please, you've gotta . . ." At least girls adjusted to once a month. Nevertheless I thought, *I'm young, I'm free! I'll get used to boys. Will I ever get used to freedom?*

It was a good time to ease into a social life and a fine time at work, but I persevered until I found a better job at Trans Canada Airlines at Bay and Temperance Streets. The stimulation of airline codes, wartime travel reservations, the bumping of non-essential business *(nebus)* or non-essential pleasure *(nepla)* seats for must rides *(mx)* and *furlo*, and transmitting weather conditions to other cities where Trans Canada Airlines flew, was exciting in this new, strategic business of air travel. My salary was now eighteen dollars a week and shift work an escape from the tedium of eight to five. I celebrated my new job by sending a big treat of ice cream for everyone in the Penitent's class and a sterling silver dinner bell, hoping it might replace the big brass bell with the black wooden handle that awakened the women at five-thirty each morning.

One afternoon in August Julian was waiting for me when I left work. He was lonesome, he said; he had hitchhiked to Toronto because he had to see me. We had dinner at Diana Sweets and went across Bloor Street to the Promenade music store. "I want you to hear something I love. I miss it when I'm home. Not as much as I miss you though." In the shop he asked for a record at the counter and we went to one of the soundproof booths for listening. "This tenor's name is Beniamino Gigli. Just listen to him sing."

The song was Bizet's *Agnus Dei*. Beautiful music but made more beautiful because Julian sang along in a remarkably sweet tenor—*miserere nobis, dona nobis pacem*. He played the flip side, Gounod's *Ave Maria*, both songs sublimely familiar from convent days. We played it over and he sang again. Julian grinned. "It's obvious you mean a lot to me. You make me happy."

We took the long way home past the museum to Philosopher's Walk, around Queen's Park and through the campus towards Burwash Hall and St. Mary Street. We were steps from my door and lingered in the privacy of Victoria College arch, sheltered from a summer shower. We shared long, ardent kisses—it was strange to be so vulnerable with Julian and find other guys so tedious. I had never felt this much happiness in my whole life, all my senses in tune with his. The sight of him, the sound of his quick breath and the feel of his hammering heart, the taste of his mouth and the wonderful smell about him. I didn't want him to go but he said he had to hitchhike back to Niagara while there was still some daylight. Inside the room when we said good-bye, I felt again the heat of his arms and the inner agitation of my whole body. Julian drew away finally.

"I've got to go, darling. It's getting late. I'm in love with you, Molly. Can you believe it?"

"Yes. I don't want you to go. Is that love ?"

"Maybe, I hope so. I'll call tomorrow and see what you think then. G'bye." He ducked back in quickly out of the teeming summer rain. "I'll wait a while. It should let up."

"I can't believe this rain." The words filled a gap while the storm streaked and teemed. We sat apart, talking about anything, shy in the unplanned privacy that had literally dropped on us from the sky. Eventually I opened out the daybed and suggested he get some rest while he waited. He said he'd rest in the chair. Amazingly, I slept. The luminous dial said two-twenty when I saw from the street light that the chair was empty. He was gone. Then I rolled over and found him asleep beside me. I covered him and he stirred.

"You're awake," he whispered.

"Yes."

"I should go but there'll be no cars till about six."

"I'll call you early," I promised and tucked the cover around his shoulders. His touchable presence made my heart pound. Only once in the convent did I get to the heart thumping stage meditating on God's infinite love. A disembodied Being was fine to pray to or ask for blessings—untouchable. But Julian was real, clearly touchable, lying a little apart from me, very exciting. I rolled over from the sagging side of the cot and stretched the length of him. He turned and drew me close as naturally as if he always slept this way. I snuggled in the crook of his arm, loving the smell of his clothes, hearing him snore softly, his face against mine, I stretched to be closer and he kissed me again and again. I responded mindlessly until nothing else mattered and his hot bare flesh was heavy on me.

"I've imagined your breasts under your clothes. They are as perfect as I thought they would be, my little convent maid." Tumbling waves of rapture rolled over all of me. Our hearts raced against each other, his voice was hoarse. "Open up my love, let me in."

"I don't know how Julian, show me how, show me everything."

"Follow me darling, just like dancing, follow me."

We were loath to make any kiss final, but at five-thirty he had to leave.

"You're mine now, Molly. I'll never let you go. Does that make you happy?"

"Happier than I've ever been."

I walked to work in a celebration of love. I didn't look different. Nothing around me had changed, but I was different. The humanness of love had awakened the invisible parts of me that wondered about passion and my self-awareness was sky high. Summer sun dappled through the trees, it was a grand morning, no *mea maxima culpa*. Just surrender and belonging and I loved it.

Julian came back to Toronto in October and entered the law course at
Osgoode Hall. He had turned twenty-two and together we were so full of
expectation, so hopeful he would gain independence through education.
Often during the work day, I glanced from the second floor window of the
office on Bay Street for the chance to see him on his way to City Hall or the
Registry Office from the Richmond Street law firm where he articled in the
afternoons, handsome in his gabardine topcoat and forever carrying a file
folder. My whole being wanted to proclaim my love out that window. When
he learned that I watched for him he would linger on the corner and look
up at the window. Others in the office would call, "Your boy friend's out
there, M.I." M.I. was my code name at TCA.

One weekend we hitchhiked to Niagara to meet his family. His dad sang
and recited poetry with an expressive lilt. Julian's aunt was fragile and shy, a
magnificent cook. The oven door was held in place with part of a
broomstick, but the crispy roast, fresh vegetables and homemade pie were a
marvelous first-time home-cooked treat for me. After dinner his Aunt Kate
asked him to sing. His sister played the beautiful old piano and, without
coaxing or excuses, Julian sang Gounod's *Ave Maria* as sweetly as Gigli
might have. Then he sang *Because* as though we were alone in the room. His
dad said he missed the days when his children were home and they all sang
together; now they were gone and scattered. Julian winced when his aunt
called him her *great man*.

"She used to call me that when I was little. Now because I'm in law she
thinks I'll be prime minister someday. She has her heart set on it."

Masquerading as a convent-bred girl with Julian and his family was all I
could manage. Someday, when the right time came, I'd tell him about
myself. Besides, he had the wrong idea that girls grouped together in a
dormitory fondled and cuddled one another. His roommates got this absurd
idea while spying on female students in a residence across from Newman
Club, hoping they'd see something not meant to be seen. I pouted when he
went on like that. It made me wonder about Germaine and the dark
mysterious streak. "C'mon now, it's true," he'd tease and I might have told
him about Germaine and other things, not mentioning the laundry, but that
wouldn't prove to Julian that nothing immoral took place in the dormitory.
It didn't as far as I knew. But because I kept this secret I couldn't tell Julian
that Mr. Powers called me into the manager's office when I'd been working
at TCA for a month. He was a quiet man who reminded me of King George
VI.

"Do you have a record?" he asked kindly.

"I beg your pardon?"

"Have you been in trouble with the law?"

"I—I don't know what you mean."

"We requested a routine reference from your school and . . ."

And the Good Shepherd sisters had written back even though they hadn't been named on the job application. I had put *grade nine and a commercial course*, no school name, just the correct address. The Good Shepherd sisters had been specific about their type of operation. Tears filled my eyes before I could stop them. Would these unfair marks of disgrace be a stigma throughout my life?

"No sir, I've not been in trouble with the law but I was homeless."

I could tell he didn't like the sight of tears and I hoped I didn't sound guilty. It was hard not to be embarrassed.

"Don't worry, you're doing a good job, the reference was just fine. That's all. You may go back to work now." There was no way to share that pain with Julian.

Ironically it was Doris McGlyn who presented the chance to be honest. She came to visit before Christmas and showed such contempt for Julian that I was embarrassed and hastened to tell him that she was not related to me. "She never took care of me and I've never lived with her."

"Why bother with her then. What right has she?"

"I'll explain it all when she's gone. I'll work it out."

Doris fussed with my hair, putting make-up on my face while I dressed for an end-of-term Christmas party. Treating me as a little girl, but it was too late for that.

"This boy has such a small face and he has pimples." My head was aching from her fussing and antagonistic prattle. Besides, everyone had pimples.

"I don't suppose his folks are much?" spitting on her thumb and shaping my eyebrows.

"They're nice." My words sounded cautious. "They're ordinary people. I was welcome in their home."

"I take it they're not rich?"

"No, they're not. Julian's putting himself through school."

"Doesn't he have any rich friends? It's important to marry someone with money. It makes a big difference how you'll live."

I ignored her.

Julian was reluctant to come in but he did, looking good in his double-breasted suit and vest, pale blue shirt and tab collar with the chic silver bar. He strode toward Doris in the small room. Smiling, he offered his hand, which she ignored. She scuffed across the room, dropping into a chair. The floor shook. We left hurriedly, muffling our nervous giggles.

"It's a good thing she put you in that boarding school. She must be crazy. You're lucky you didn't live with her."

"It wasn't boarding school, Julian. I was in an orphanage and I hated it more than I can ever tell you."

He held me close in the middle of the street while we waited for the Bay streetcar. "Just forget her," he whispered. "I'll take care of you."

The ballroom of the Royal York Hotel roof garden was breathtaking with sparkling pink lights on a revolving Christmas tree and poinsettias everywhere. There was pink punch that put me at ease with the college girls in their white kid gloves. Their dresses were elegant, mostly short for the war effort; mine was tailored white wool with red saddle stitching on the collar and cuffs. When the lights dimmed for dancing, I was a princess in Julian's arms.

"I love you Molly," he whispered right into my ear.

My feet were like feathers just brushing the floor. It was so simple to be happy. Julian tightened his arms and said wistfully, maybe cynically, "It's as if there were no disease, no maladjustment, no war; everything is hunky-dory in the best of all possible ballrooms."

He crooned with the orchestra, *Sierra Sue, Minka, Day and Night-Night and Day.* I thought, *This is really true, the streetcar isn't going to turn into a pumpkin at midnight and leave me here in my laundry clothes!*

"Hey Cagey," a dancer called. "We're in 747, come up for a drink."

As they whirled away I asked, "He called you Cagey?"

"Yeah, when I play cards or shoot craps with them I'm careful. I have to be."

In the room a big guy thrust drinks at us.

"Norm van Hattan, meet Molly," Julian called over the noise.

One whiff of the rum and coke and I passed it to Julian.

"Make her a weaker one."

I saw Norm give Julian a smart-aleck wink. "Sure, sure."

The smell of rum was awful yet I sipped it for a while. Just as I poured it into the bathroom sink, a debutante ran through the door and lunged for the bowl. It wasn't over quickly, so I held her head and rinsed a cold cloth until she felt better. I searched for Julian in the crowded, smoky room and saw the cynical curl of his lip and the arched eyebrow just as he told a blonde, "You have defeated the mirth, you asshole."

"Whas'he talking about?" she slurred.

"*I* think *he* thinks you're a party-pooper," someone shouted and everyone roared.

I beckoned to get Julian back to the dance. He raised his hand as though he had the power to still the mirth. "Methinks the lady doth protest too much."

His friends laughed uproariously, but Julian came and put his arm around me so I didn't feel the fool. Near the elevator he said, "I told you I shouldn't drink. I'm glad you got me out of there because I'd get worse. Some of those parvenu babes piss me off."

He crooned again to the music while we danced, *You'll never know, if you don't know now*. I wondered if he would ever direct vulgar words at me and if I could shield him from things that "pissed him off." Some of the rapture had gone from the night.

We lingered under the Vic Arch, for Doris would surely be awake.

Julian took a tiny box from his pocket. "I don't have anything of value, Molly. I won this medal debating. It's important to me, it's engraved, and I'd like you to have it for Christmas and because I hope you'll marry me when I finish law school."

My head reeled with the things Julian didn't know about me.

"What's the matter?" He tilted my chin as I turned away to hide the swell of tears. "Darling, what's the trouble? Tell me. Please." He offered his handkerchief then dried my tears himself.

"I don't know who I am. I thought I'd tell you when she left but I'll find my own mother someday." I turned away from him in panic.

"Shh, it doesn't matter." He held me up, he was strong for me. "We'll talk about it when you're ready. In the meantime I'll be your father and mother, your sister and brother too if you want, I'll make it all right for you, my Molly."

I was relieved he knew.

The rooming house on St. Mary street had three stories and a tenant in the attic too. There was one bathroom on the second floor to serve everyone. Someone was always waiting to get in, even knocking. Not much better than the orphanage. *I'll make my life better, just give me time.* I was at work next day when Doris moved my belongings from the back room with the private door to the front room. A bay window facing St. Mary Street and St. Michael's College playing field made it better. It was a homier room with a mantelpiece, closer to the phone and the bathroom, farther away from the back kitchen where the landlord slept on the other side of the wall where our love began. It cost five dollars a week. I resented her assumption of authority and the suggestion that I forward a portion of my earnings to her fell on indifferent ears. *She can't think I owe her anything. She once laid claim to me but she didn't mother me. She has another husband, his child lives with them. There must have been room for me years earlier.*

During the move Doris found a book hidden in my hatbox. Julian had borrowed it from the library, a subtle message for me. He had also written a Christmas card referring to the Christmas dance. "We'll have one more rendezvous darling before I go home for the Christmas break." The book was *Sex, Marriage and Birth Control.* His card was my bookmark. Doris sounded worse than the proverbial fishwife when she started her tirade.

"So that's what he calls it, eh. A rendezvous. Fancy, isn't he. Mark my words, miss, he's out to get what he wants. You behave yourself." How disagreeable her parsimonious taut mouth. I ignored her rancour.

After that rainy first night Julian and I tried to avoid the things that society and the church said we mustn't do, though sometimes we needed to love. Julian quit smoking and I did part-time waiting on tables at Diana Sweets for extra money to help him at school. We lined up for hours to see *Sergeant York* at the Uptown theatre and saw *Casablanca* three times that winter. Once we made lovely love in the old Tivoli theatre, an afternoon stolen from the office where he articled.

Too soon the school year was over and Julian went home to Niagara and his summer job. I moved into a larger room on Prince Arthur Avenue and missed him every waking moment. On weekends I took the ferryboat, the *Northumberland* or the *Dalhousie City*, across Lake Ontario to be with him and discovered that separation made our reunions impetuous and physical. We talked of marriage often but after satisfying each other it was simple for him to say, *When I finish school.* Julian would travel with me on the boat back to Toronto and we couldn't separate, so I'd ride back to Port Dalhousie with him. Then he'd sail back to Toronto with me. I'd walk backwards all the way to the street car, waving to him on the ship's railing late at night, so much in love.

After a particularly rough lake crossing, when the seasickness was more distressing than usual, I suspected I was pregnant and couldn't imagine what would happen next. We knew it could happen but we were too naïve to be prudent. It could be he expected me to learn something from that library book. I told him I'd go to the Medical Arts building and look for a doctor. I scanned the index in the lobby for an obstetrician. Dr. Foulds stood by the table where I lay and said, "There's no doubt you are going to have a baby."

My first sensation was that of drowning. Drowning in tears. *What now?*

The doctor took my hand. "Go ahead, cry, it's all right. Is your friend in the service?"

"No, he's a student."

"Do you want me to tell him? Is it going to cause a problem?"

"I'll be able to tell him. I'm not afraid. It will be a problem. I'm surprised, though I shouldn't be."

The doctor put pressure on my bare shoulder and I derived tremendous courage from this man I'd never seen before. He accepted my condition, maybe others would do so. "Good girl, this prescription will help your sick stomach. Call me the day after tomorrow for confirmation from the lab, or drop by if you prefer." He told me he would be joining His Majesty's service soon and could not be my doctor. He recommended another.

I walked to Queen's Park and sat under a big tree trying to grasp the seriousness of having a baby. *Just like my mother; another little lovechild never meant to be. Does this happen to a lot of people?* I had been too naïve to even think it could happen to me. *Imagine, creating a baby; I'm still trying to sort out my own childhood. If Julian will share it with me I'll be okay. But if he wants to break off with me? I'll go. The one truth I am sure of today—you will know your mother, little one. Nothing on earth will take you away from me, no one will make me give you up.*

I wanted my mother to know. How I regretted neglecting my search during the months I'd known Julian. That procrastination hurt now. There was so little to go on, where could I start? *Oh God, I wish Julian was here beside me, I'm ready to tell him, I'm strong, he'll feel my courage and we'll be strong together. His fondness for drinking? His emotional lows? They don't matter, we'll manage.*

When Julian phoned I thought I was casual when he asked how I felt. "I hate being separated from you," I told him as loneliness overwhelmed me.

"When I finish school Molly, we'll never be separated again, I promise. You haven't asked me how hard I've been studying. I haven't closed my books since you left. Now that my job is finished I'll study all weekend and after I write my torts supplemental we'll celebrate. How does that sound?"

"Sounds wonderful. See you Tuesday."

Two-and-a-half hours later he tapped at my window, books under his arm. "I can study here better than there, now tell me what the doctor said."

I clung to him and he knew at once.

"I've thought it out, my darling. You can count on me, you must know that. We'll get married just as soon as we can make arrangements. I'll ask the chaplain at Newman Club."

"I love you, Julian."

"I love you more." His arms hurt but it felt right. "I'm going to show you just how much I care. If I don't register at school by the middle of October I'll get my army call. So I'll enlist in the RCAF before then and with luck I'll get into air crew."

"Will you have to go away?"

"I'll have to go for basic training, but that should be in Toronto. And then some specialized instruction, I have no idea where. With luck the war could be over before I'm sent overseas."

He *had* thought it all out. I hadn't thought beyond telling him, least of all had I thought of him enlisting. "Your scruples about war?"

"Listen darling, banish from your pretty head that I'm enlisting in the air force because we have to get married. You just start thinking we're getting married because I'm going into the air force, OK?"

At Newman Club, Father Whelan's reaction to our marriage plan was not gracious. "You didn't have a winter coat last year, Julian. How do you propose to look after a wife this year? And what will happen when the children start to come? Stay in school. Marriage can wait."

At my church Father O'Connell's response was different. He probably guessed our plight. "Would two weeks today be convenient? Nine o'clock? Bring two witnesses. You'll both have to go to confession."

Doris lamented on the phone; "If you wait you can have a big wedding." Who on earth would I invite? My own family? If I knew who they were! It was a mere formality that I called her at all.

Julian wrote his torts paper and we celebrated putting away the books for an indefinite period. There was comfort, he said, in knowing that the Department of Veterans Affairs would help him through school when the war was over. People thought kindly about servicemen and the brides they married in a hurry. That guise suited our circumstances.

The night before my wedding day we shared drinks with our attendants at a corner table in the Embassy Hotel. Julian's attendant was to be big Norm, mine a friend from the TCA office, Irma Robertson. I asked Julian to show me the ring he had chosen that day, and there in front of Norm and Irma, he snapped at me, "Do you have to make a spectacle of everything?" I understood he was tense, but I wished he wouldn't put me down like a child who had done wrong. I longed for some semblance of a family, some real friends with whom to celebrate, rather than sitting in a corner of the beer parlour in the Embassy Hotel switching beer glasses while Julian drank half of his then half of mine, switching again before the next round. "I'm sorry Molly. Drinking makes me act that way. Let me see my girl smile again." And I smiled because I really wanted to.

It was a glorious morning for my wedding. I walked down Avenue Road on my way to church, my pale blue suit set off by a navy hat with a broad soft brim and navy shoes. I carried no bag and wore no flower. The Park Plaza doorman, resplendent in navy with gold braid, brass and white gloves, had always reminded me of Old Glyn with his white mustache, gentle face and elegant stance. We often exchanged good mornings as I walked to work. This day I told him, "I'm being married today!" "Here," he said and kissed me on the cheek. I wanted to borrow him to escort me to the altar. I wanted to tell everyone who passed by that I was getting married, to collect a coterie of happy people from the street and take them along as my witnesses. So conscious of my baby going to my wedding, I reinforced my promise, *You'll know your father too!* Such a magnificent morning! What a wonderful world! At the entrance to Young Peoples where first we met I got frightened. *Maybe Julian won't show up! He should stay in school, he doesn't want to go to war. He doesn't have to marry me.* But Julian was already kneeling at the altar when I entered the church alone. He came to me with open arms and took me to kneel beside him at the altar rail. The candles shimmered on our solemn promises to each other.

The four of us celebrated at a wedding breakfast at Murray's in the Park Plaza Hotel. Later, in the twin-bedded room at the Royal York hotel, which cost Julian five dollars, with beer cooling in the sink there was sadness in our passion. The maid rattled some keys and walked in on our nakedness. Julian shouted, "The room is occupied." After, Julian sat at the window, savoring his beer, deep in pained thought and shaking his head disbelievingly.

"The city I came to conquer. I thought I could make it. At home the lawyers I caddied for, the car dealers, the big shots all said, 'You're going places son, stay in there and study.' And the millionaire industrialist and a senior lawyer each signed a note for a hundred and fifty dollars for me. Then I sweat wondering how I'm going to pay it back while I'm studying. Now it's over, perhaps for the better, who knows?" When he reached for the bottle on the window ledge it tipped, disappearing. Horrified, I looked over, but it had landed on a marquee. He got another.

"What's it all about, the years spent striving and searching, competing to be somebody? Why does it come so easily to some?"

I couldn't answer his questions.

"You know, in 1936 I had a teacher who spent a month in Germany during the summer. She stood up and told the class that fall, 'There's going to be a war and you young boys are going to be in it.' She had tears in her eyes when she said that and I felt sorry for her. But I've never forgotten. Her prophecy has come true and it's terrible. She knew more than our government did."

He reached for my hand and put it to his lips. "Pray for me darling, I'll do my best to like what I may be doing for your sake."

His family said they were happy about our marriage, but there was a certain melancholy about his quitting school and going to war. It was happening to everyone and everyone expected it. They knew his finances were touchy and they acquiesced, agreeing that DVA benefits would help him eventually. His aunt hurried to invite the family home for a weekend dinner, to bake a cake and hear Julian sing *Because*.

There was a tense moment on our brief honeymoon to Niagara when Julian and his dad returned from the home of the bootlegger on the street— a weekend ritual. Julian looked so dejected, so humiliated, I couldn't bear his misery.

"Darling, what's happened?"

"Shh," he pulled me to him. "You'll hate me for this but you have to know. I lost all the money we had in a crap game. I was trying to win for you. Can you forgive me?"

"Yes."

"I'll make it up somehow."

"The money I brought too?"

"Yes, yes. I'm sorry . . . Dad doesn't know."

My love soared to new heights. *He did it because he had to. Necessity knows no law. Caring for—being cared for matters most.*

Julian went off to Manning Depot at Exhibition Park for induction into the Royal Canadian Air Force. There were days of formal admission ceremonies, vaccinations and quarantine and finally, when I was allowed to visit him, he did not have a pass to leave the barracks.

"I'm going home with you just the same, Molly. I have to love you, I can't wait a day longer. Come on, we can get out."

No strong arm reached out to pull us back, no service police barred the way, we just walked out onto Strachan Avenue. Then the fear of being off base gripped me. AWOL! In uniform, needing proof to return.

All along the street servicemen cuddled girls. "I have an idea," he said. "Let's go." On Garrison Road by Old Fort York he found a big bush. He spread my coat on the ground and we moaned our urgent pleasure to the stars. Then we walked right back through the Prince's Gates at Exhibition Park with others coming and going. There was no problem.

*J*ulian was posted to Guelph on a wireless air gunner's course. I continued working and lived for his letters and his furloughs, often changing shifts to have more time with him. Doris's reaction to news of the baby was that I should go to Boston. "The city will be hot in the summer and it is so pleasant in Beachmont by the sea." I did not want to be beholden to her; nevertheless I was curious about living in a house with a family—especially that particular house.

After Christmas we considered Doris's offer and I arrived in Boston early in March. She lived in a small, two-story frame cottage just a block from the sea in Beachmont. Set back from the street in the shadow of a much larger old home, it had a quaint front porch and old-fashioned charm. It was a small house and I was to share the front bedroom with Doris. Her Husband, George, was relegated to the back bedroom which, it appeared, belonged to his daughter, Anne. I felt dismay at putting him out, but when Doris arranged things you didn't question her.

Julian should have his posting when the baby was a month old; I could follow him then. For now I wrote to him each evening and waited for the mailman each morning. My letters were repetitive, walks by the sea, seeing the doctor, what little knitting and reading I did, love words, waiting for the mail. . .but he wanted letters daily and I had told him if he wrote often I'd write oftener.

> Darling Airman, It's a beautiful spring day. I was out walking
> along the boulevard, how I wish we could walk together, arm
> in arm. I watch others doing that. If you were overseas I

wouldn't walk by the ocean. I look at the sea and thank God
you're on this side. Just seeing that incessant water separating
some lovers is awesome. Glad you're doing well preparing for
exams, also waxing and polishing on clean-up day. Learn all
you can about waxing and polishing! I miss you so much and at
times feel unworthy for coming away. Wouldn't it be dreadful
if the baby WAS due in July instead of May? That's what I told
Doris, though. It'll work itself out. Till tomorrow.
My love forever.

Julian wrote about the weekly tests in Morse procedure and radio theory.

I'm not interested in all this stuff but it won't hurt me to know
it. We had quite a ceremony here yesterday as we got ourselves
a new Commanding Officer. I spent the day standing at
attention, getting inspected, and listening to powerful speeches
by our inspiring hierarchy of Group Captains and Wing
Commanders. Last night one of my bunkmates produced a
bottle of whiskey and insisted I share it with him and before we
knew it the whole quart was gone. But don't worry about me
drinking too much, I don't have the money. Of course poker is
far beyond my reach. There are a few things I'm interested in—
you, our child and making a success of my life in our own little
world and acquiring a position of independence in professional
life. I don't mention your mother very often but I do appreciate
her giving you a home at this time. I know she has never
approved of me but it's of no importance to me what anyone in
this world thinks of me except you. If you ever changed towards
me now I would rather never see you again than find out . . . .
Good night, darling.

Your Mother! Julian's reference to Doris brought a terrible gloom for my
neglect. It was up to me to find ways of searching but where could I begin?
Not at St. Vincent's and not with Doris McGlyn. *There once was a young girl
walking, as I do each day, with me kicking against her womb. A young girl maybe
with my thoughts. Don't be impatient baby, don't rush into this world, make it
respectable for me. If you can, be late.*
Catholic Welfare in Saint John had answered my letter, saying they had
no information. That was that. Now I had time to think about new angles.
One day during my walk I stopped at the library to examine the Boston
phone list of O'Connors. It was the only clue I had. The lists were long. I

should find a way to take the pages home to Toronto to study. I had to find Mrs. O'Connor. Even if I had my mother's name, she would have married long ago, making it impossible to find her in phone books or directories. Still I braved half a dozen phone calls one afternoon when Doris was out, my heart pounding with the daring of beginning something that could have such far-reaching results.

"I'd like to reach a woman named Mrs. O'Connor. She employed an Irish nurse about six years ago, I thought you might . . ."

"I don't know anyone by that name."

"You must have the wrong number, no one here . . ."

"Is this some kinda joke?"

"I have no relatives here, sorry."

"If you're one of them looking for a woman who gave you up, leave her alone."

"Meet me someplace honey. Maybe I can help you."

And the final call: "Yes my name is O'Connor. I'm a nurse."

"Is it convenient for me to ask a few questions?"

"It's not good right now, but you can give me a number or call back."

"I can't give you a number, I don't live at home." I was tense waiting for the chance to phone again, not knowing how I'd handle questions. When I did call the number was not in service.

So much for that effort. I dared to write to the registrar general, expecting my real birth certificate to be a sealed document. Nevertheless there was a chance that the name McGlyn might be cross-referenced with my real name and they might give it to me. When we had gone for a marriage license Julian told the clerk I was an orphan. He studied the Selective Service registration I carried for my identity and merely asked, "What name do you go by?" I secretly hoped he would be obliged to do some research for I had no adoption papers. But he was casual and issued the license politely. Maybe he was an orphan too and was being kind to me.

I wrote to St. Vincent's and the Infants' Home and, feeling venturesome, even tried St. Joseph's Infirmary where I was born. As the saying goes, nothing ventured, nothing gained. If Doris should see any mail that made her curious, then I'd deal with that if it happened. Then I decided to pack the letters away, to be mailed from Canada as soon as I was back and had my own address.

Most days I slipped away from the cottage to sit on the steps and read Julian's letters alone by the sea. A peaceful atmosphere of gulls and sky, waves and wind, sometimes a lone person ambling along the rocky shore. There I could daydream and hope and long for my love. Sometimes, after weeping over Joseph Cotton in a movie, I'd slip into a coffee shop and put nickels in the jukebox to play "You'll Never Know." No great classic, just a simple little song of love that made me cry. On May sixth Julian wrote:

> It's Saturday night and I'm lonesome. How I long to be with you but it's not possible so I'll not dwell on it. I'm reading Bertrand Russell's Conquest of Happiness. He writes that a certain amount of boredom must be endured by every individual if he has a purpose. Be that as it may, I am still very lonesome. The radio in the lounge is playing My Blue Heaven, ". . . just Molly and me . . ." It makes me remember that the months before you went away were the happiest of my life I was supposed to do an hour's drill tonight for being ten seconds late coming out of the mess hall to parade. It's hard to keep out of trouble of one sort or another. Once they get a married man into this outfit they've really got him. We have a sergeant here who calls us cock-a-roaches. Can you believe that in a democracy? I loathe the system that places men in involuntary servitude to other men. I don't like flying. I worry too much about the sound of the engine in our little training aircraft, what I'm supposed to be doing, about the pilot, about dying, about you. Sometimes I feel like walking out of the camp and not stopping until I see you. You are my reason for everything I do. The thought of you keeps me here.

Julian finished his course and exams and was leaving for Boston on furlough when our baby daughter was born at Chelsea Memorial Hospital. Labour lasted throughout the day on May twenty-first. The baby arrived at one in the morning, a priceless birthday gift for me. Julian hitchhiked nearly six hundred miles over two days. He was tired and thin, his uniform rumpled but never in my life would I expect to behold a more handsome sight. My arms were open and I laughed as he hurried to my bed in the big ward, hugging and rocking while other new mothers looked on. Maybe it was sad for some of them, service wives, service widows; I didn't know. My man was here, we had our baby, we were a family.

"She's perfect, Julian."

"I know, I've seen her. It's hard to believe we made her. She has dark hair like you."

"And beautiful blue eyes like you. Oh, hold me tighter, something terrible happened here yesterday," a spontaneous outcry I couldn't help. "A poor woman died having her baby. She was older, it was her first baby. . .so excited when she came in, then she kept saying she was dying. There was a horrible rattling sound, she kept calling 'help me.' Her poor mother was crying. She was here in the ward and we were all frightened."

Julian's arms around me helped me forget the shock.

* * *

*I*n Chelsea, near East Boston, nurse Kathleen Shannon O'Connor tucked her fourth son into bed. "Good-night wee Tim, God Bless." To the urgent call of "Mama," from the boys in another room, she merely answered "Cummin'," in her quick, soft Galway brogue.

Downstairs she dropped into a big chair. With terrible cold symptoms and aching feet her sighs were pure relief that this was her night off from the delivery room at Chelsea Memorial Hospital. "We've been so busy wi' all the babies, they all seem to be born at night lately. But they're begun at night, aren't they though."

Michael O'Connor dropped the newspaper to his lap, as softly and thoughtfully as he did most things and looked at his wife. She was tall, though not too tall and had the look of a woman who worked hard, a permanently tired face. Around her sons, though, she was fun-loving with a gentle nature and a stunning smile. Her hair was typically Irish, a thick waving thatch of glossy auburn that set off the whiteness of her smooth skin and gray-green eyes.

"Have you heeded Sean's newest caper, Michael?"

"To be sure, that mischief-maker has taken to callin' the boys by number. Aye, 'struth, I've noticed."

"He's number one, he'll only answer if they call him number one. He calls the little ones two, three, four, five and six. Another way to annoy Thomas. Wee Tim and Patrick don't care. He's a good boy all the same though." She took a deep breath and let out a long shuddering sigh.

"Kathleen don't cry. I know it's your daughter's birthday."

"No, no it's not that. She's nineteen today, you know." Her voice broke. "A mother died today, Michael. By the time we got her in delivery it was too late. A section might've saved her. Her poor old mother was frantic." God is so good, she thought, but why couldn't that poor soul be blessed with the gift of a wee baby when I think I'm starting number seven. Silly me, thinking number seven, like Sean.

"I remember old Mrs. Duggan in Ireland," she said to divert from the sadness. "She came to deliver the babies. Everyone had Mrs. Duggan. She was so capable, puffing away on her clay pipe, in her bare feet." Kathleen laughed out loud at the memory. "She helped everyone and herself with barely a fistful. Mrs. Duggan didn't go to your family did she? So many babies . . ."

"No, no. You've asked me that before. It would be too far. Remember there were no steamrolled paths then, no tarmacadam, just dirt roads with deep cart tracks. If you needed Mrs. Duggan you needed her in a hurry. There may have been another midwife in Spiddal but I didn't know anything about it."

"I knew being the eldest. We had a baby every two years. Old Mrs. Duggan would lay the dead babies out too if necessary, in the parlour. We never had any, thank God. Ma never went to the workhouse either. At the top of the street, they took women in for difficult births. It was free, but if you were poor, and who wasn't, you were made to feel you were cared for on sufferance."

The big chair surrounded her. Michael lifted her feet and placed a footstool under them. "All the same, Michael, somewhere out there is a daughter of mine. I must believe that she had a good home with parents who love her."

"I'll fetch you tea," he said.

She was inclined to think of home tonight, her mother and her father, God rest them. What kept coming back was the contentment she knew as a child. They were hard times then but now they were so dear. She realized that memory plays tricks, making that which was arduous seem easy and sentimental She remembered the cow they got for milk. They led her from the back yard each day to a grazing field, through the kitchen and the narrow front hall to the front door and back at night so she wouldn't be stolen. It was the only way out in that row house. And when she was large with calf it was nigh impossible to squeeze her through the narrow hall, her wide belly all green where she scraped the paint from the wall, the marks still on the wall no doubt and the scratching sound still familiar. She could see her sister and brothers singing round the kitchen hearth, barefoot, happy. The fire at floor level, portions of it separated under the big pot, a small one baking a bastable of bread, a smaller fire under the teapot and like as not a fire under the flatiron. There was always scrumptious food on the peat fire for endless people, her Mam was best at that. She'd get pig's bones from the butcher and simmer them all night, ever so slowly; she'd slice the lard off the top and oh she made delicious pastry with it. She'd scrape the bits of bacon off and make a grand soup. After that she'd mash the soft bones and add the mush to the soup. And could she make a suet pudding! She never wasted a scrap, my Mam. When she made elderflower champagne she'd gather the blossoms from the elderberry tree and put them in a large crock with the berries, cover it all with slices of thick toast and unseeded raisins. You could almost hear it ferment. And the chickens all over the place, pecking and clucking, in and out the back door, the laying hens under the counter near the bucket of water from the village pump. Her brothers, when they reached five or six, had to fetch the water half a mile from home, that was their job—bringing the water home. They were taught to balance a bucket on each side. It was better in the wet weather because then the barrel under the rain spout was full. It was often full in Ireland. Upstairs there were no beds for any of us, just straw ticks. Except John, the envy of all. Over a long time he'd made himself a feather bed from feathers everyone plucked year after year until he had enough. It was soft and warm and swelled high on either side of him when he dropped into it. She still wondered who took John's mattress when he left and followed her to Canada. The straw ticks were changed every year. You found your corner and there was plenty of covers for all. Hard times? But what is harder than now? I want to go where I belong, it's utterly hopeless.

She wanted to see Mam and the little row house again more than anything in the world and that was most impossible now. She'd never forget that time, her only fourteen, working in Paddy Burke's pub and the horror of the ambush at Ballyturrin. A lorry load of Black and Tans crazed with looted drink, rounded up the republicans, taking pot shots at anything that moved. Her brothers, only ten and twelve, and other boys would round up bodies in the morning. She saved Sean Fahey's life, everyone said. He was on the run and she pushed him through Burke's skylight and he jumped to the lane, just in the nick of time; then she calmly served the soldiers chasing Fahey. "What is it ye want?" It seemed now that that was an exciting time in Ireland but it was a very uneven society, brother against brother, civil war, Ireland looking for her freedom from Britain, Ireland involved, courageous, unafraid. But the society created was far narrower than intended. When she left home at seventeen to become a maidservant her life changed.

With the passing of time her personal sadness did not wane—the girl in service whose life was changed by serving her employer beyond her job.

Fear, shame, deceit, hoodwinking her mother; telling her, as the eldest, it was time to go to America. Mam did everything to help her go and Kathleen didn't tell her about the baby, all the while afraid she knew. Mam stitched her a new suit, pleats on pleats, so full and voluminous and gave Kathleen her own plum-coloured hooded cloak and bought her low-cut black shoes and collected all the fare, some from the boys, to be sent back for John to go when Kathleen was working on the other side. She'd returned the fare at once and John did follow her to Canada and sent the fare home for Francis. He came and sent the fare for Matthew. Matt never came. He joined the army in England and went to war. Kathleen lost trace of John and Frank. She suspected they weren't doing well otherwise they'd keep in touch. They'd all been at the train when she left home to go to Cobh, alone, to get the steamer for Canada. John wondering when his turn to take the journey would come; Francis, only thirteen, balancing on the parallel crossties between the rails, Matt and Fergus imitating him, Mam holding Norah's hand, all rejoicing in a way at the prospect of this journey and a new life for Kathleen, but at the back of it all was the melancholy of departure. For Mam and Da it was a long and last adieu. Up and down the street she said good-bye to the neighbors and not a soul suspected she was going to have a baby. She celebrated with her family and the neighbours, all the while terrified that she must get out of Ireland now, escape public condemnation from the pulpit; never let other children throw rocks at her child and call "bastard"; protect her child's father from disgrace with his family, ruin in his business, censure from the pulpit. It was desperate. His brother arranged money for Kathleen and she had to sign a paper, something about keeping her condition private. At least she was free of the anxiety of immediate survival. She tried not to think about giving her baby away, at this point it was safe and no one could take it but she dreaded the time when she'd have to face that decision.

Wearing Mam's cloak she stood alone in a large crowd on the quay at Cobh. The hood was down and the coloured ribbon on her plaited auburn hair blew free in the salt air. Absurd thoughts invaded the strange moment when she first realized she was on her own. "Who'll be braidin' my hair now that I'm gone? I'll not be goin' barefoot any more." Alone at Cobh, the harbour of tears, the saddest spot in all of Ireland. A million young people had gone away from this port. The Atlantic liner waited once more in the sun-crested, rolling pewter water, waited for the tenders to take the emigrants out, away from home. Going should be happy, a real adventure it should be, with the expectation of coming back proud. Being pregnant made it altogether wretched and fearful. Thank God her goodbyes had been said at the train. It was easier to cry alone, wet salty tears in the wet salty air. Still, she sensed adventure. Keening filled her ears in a long, sad cry until a band struck up to make the leaving seem festive. Kathleen approached the curragh and watched a young man calling, "I'll send for ye darlin', and ye'll be me own." Cutting words. She'd die of grief before she got to Canada; she was nobody's own!

She had to go. A religion of fear and hypocrisy would make her an outcast if she stayed; leaving was critical. This trend in the Church in Ireland was so widespread, so pervasive, it had to come from the most superior body, from the top. The irony in one sense was having to leave her homeland, going to a situation where nuns of the church came to her rescue on the other side.

Oh, don't think of it now, she thought. Don't think of it at all! She pulled Mam's own shawl with the lovely fringe tighter around her body and Michael knew, in her mind, she was settling her on-again-off-again languishing bouts. He had his moments too, though his trauma was on this side of the ocean. Finding work was hard. "Irish and Catholic need not apply," a sign so common in Boston it preyed on his mind like a song you couldn't forget, repeating itself in your head all day, even in your dreams. That wasn't so common now, but he still had no work, hard for a father of six. But he did his best with the children and took comfort from that, for Kathleen so loved her nursing. The Democratic politician James Michael Curley used to look out for the Irish sometimes. Even he was in trouble now, in jail. Michael needed work and there was none. Kathleen came out of her reverie and interrupted his melancholy.

"It was hard times with eight of us and I doing a man's work. My mam still tells me when she writes, 'Kathleen, my most happy times were when you all were small.'"

"Och, memory's like that," said Michael.

* * *

*J*ulian had taken a room at the "Y" avoiding a one-on-one with Doris. He said he couldn't imagine having a discussion with her about anything. My heart was not insensitive nor my mind naïve about the tension this would cause. "I have to sleep the clock around, darling. I'm not complaining, but I've been two nights on the road. When you leave the hospital, I'll go home to Beachmont with you. She'll understand."

Finally, in the cottage by the sea, we realized once again the rapture of being together, hugging and caressing, knees and toes touching, hearts pounding that this time had finally come. Mary slept in her bassinet near us and we were astonished at the miracle of birth. Proud, so full of wonder. We walked by the sea and enjoyed hours of sunshine, but all too soon we were at the bus depot for Julian's return to camp.

"There's talk of an invasion, darling. I hope with all my heart it will hasten the end of the war," he said with optimism.

"Whether the war ends or not Julian, I'll join you at flying school in a few weeks. If the doctor says no, I'll follow you later to your posting wherever it is."

The acrid smell of short-order food and cigarette smoke made the bus terminal a mournful place to say goodbye. We avoided the words.

"Darling, there's no way to tell you what this week has meant to me. Now I'm all the more impatient for you to come back." His lips frantic on mine, he grabbed me closer with a coveting cry. Our tears ran together.

The Greyhound bus moved slowly out of the terminal. Julian waved from the window until we could no longer see each other. A morbid fear that I would never see him again clutched at my heart in the murky subway as I traveled home to Beachmont, shivering with a terrifying emptiness.

On Tuesday, June sixth, Julian phoned excitedly. "Well, darling, today is the day! The invasion of Europe has begun. I for one never expected it so soon. It's really under way!"

"I heard the news this morning. It's exciting that something's finally happening."

"And only two days ago the Allies got to Rome. It is exciting. There's more good news, really so good I can't believe it. My flying school will be in Niagara, eight whole weeks. I can have living out privileges, so ask the doctor how soon you can leave. Did you hear, honey? I'll look for a place to live and we can be together. Unless you want to stay at Dad's until you find a place you like."

"That sounds best. I'll write tomorrow."

"Listen to the war news tonight, Molly."

The familiar voice of H.V. Kaltenborn added hope. "There's gooooood news tonight. The Allies have landed in France . . . Five infantry Divisions and three Airborne Divisions landed at dawn . . . The Germans were surprised, the coastal defenses were soon overwhelmed. Over two hundred thousand Allies are ashore this evening in the area between Le Havre and

Cherbourg, the main attack taking place at Caen." The advance was slow but steady and the news regular. *The Americans have taken Carenton on their way to St. Lô. Canadians have a rough time in the Caen canal. . .and the Germans launched the first V-1 flying bombs on London from bases in northwest France on June thirteenth.* The V-1 was a pilotless plane that carried a ton of explosives. They were directed at the heart of London. German propaganda claimed that this secret weapon would destroy London. Goebbels had already declared that London was paralyzed. This progress in German missile warfare was terrifying. I dreamed of the V-1s whistling through the air. Cowering, I waited for the hit as they glided silently before they fell. A strange dream, for I didn't really know if the bombs whistled or glided. Then I boarded the train to Buffalo and a bus to Niagara, convinced that with a little more flying time Julian would be on his way to the front. I had to hurry to him before he would leave me forever. Yet, when I saw his physical presence at the bus depot in his RCAF summer khaki, tenderly reaching for Mary, I felt the future would be our own Elysium.

"Such a wonderful surprise, Julian," I whispered. "Supposing we weren't on that bus, you'd have been upset?"

"No, I'd meet the next one. Get your stuff and let's get out of here."

His aunt knew of a two-room flat on the same street, Pelham Road. I rented it next day, though it was tiny and the bathroom had to be shared with nine others. Julian returned to camp before leaving his post at Guelph for flying school. I was dismayed when he wrote:

> As you can guess, darling I'm rushed off my feet these days at outstations, cubicles built like the inside of a plane to get us ready for flying. Do these operators ever send fast! I've taken an hour of Morse this evening to brush up a bit. I got a ride as far as Hamilton this morning and another to Guelph before my pass expired. I want you to forget my silly behaviour last night. I was up tight and stopped for a beer. I met Dad and you know the rest. The night wasn't a total loss. Believe it or not I was up quite a while with Mary while you slept. When I had to lie down for a while I set her against you and she just lay there and smiled. Next thing, the alarm went off. I had a phone call from Boston tonight. I won't refer to it again but I cannot understand her aversion to us spending this month together when I could very well be posted overseas after it. I'm sorry she got angry with you for leaving. You didn't tell me. She said

some unpleasant things, trying to come between us. I was as civil as I could be. You took the only sensible course and I'm proud of you. Go on feeling dependent on me, I'll try harder to get rid of all the bad habits that make you worry. I'll never fail you honey and I'll be with you as soon as I can get home on Saturday.

All my love.

So, I'd been alone with my baby in the Leonard Hotel. I could overlook his "silly behaviour" last night. My childlike attitude that Julian should be happy surmounted anger. So, he had stopped to drink with his dad! Once I knew the situation I was never angry, but it was the waiting and wondering that frightened me. In time I guessed that Julian expected me to be angry and strangely, he got angry with me when he drank.

Flying school posting at the Niagara airport with overnights and weekends was a gift to be cherished in our first home. Julian, Baby Mary and me. Merely two years ago I'd been confined, a laundress, no hope of a normal life. Being a wife and a mother was the purest joy I could envision. Long hours in bed, we read aloud and heard good music on the bedside radio. We couldn't be far apart in two rooms, but he'd lure me back with Milton's poetic love. *"Haste thee, nymph, and bring with thee . . . Quips and Cranks and wanton wiles, Nods and Becks and wreathed Smiles."* Consenting, I always hurried to be close to him. Our overdue love was ravenous. I drew strength from his need. I felt him watching me as I ironed one evening, book on his lap, beer in his hand.

"I'll try and give you some help the next time I'm home instead of making so much work for you."

"I won't hold my breath, I'll believe that when it happens." He couldn't know how much I detested holding an iron.

"Molly, my mind's a lot more at ease now that we have a little place. I could watch you puttering around here forever with the baby or a meal or any of the things you take pride in doing, like bringing me another beer right this instant." He ducked as I motioned to hurl the iron in his direction.

My strength dwindled during the weekend episodes of "drinking at the corner" and the resultant tardiness and defensive sarcasm and the everlasting "I'm sorry darling, I'm so ashamed, I don't know what to do."

"I'll tell you what to do if you don't know. I want you with me; you want to be with me. I wheel the baby carriage over the high-level bridge to get you beer when I'm not old enough to have a ration book. Drink here for

God's sake, you won't drink as much. At that beer parlour everyone guzzles like it's going to be cut off." That little show of scorn made me cry. "Look," I said, making it worse, "I've got some things to work on too, my frightful past, the fear of not pleasing. I'm too damn submissive but I'm trying to grow up. I don't know how to handle all your apologies but I am trying."

He rubbed his cigarette butt out. "Maybe you make too much of your past. It was no picnic growing up during the depression you know. Not that I'm changing the subject but there'll be another depression after the war, wait and see."

It seemed the subject had been changed. Julian drained his glass and quoted to himself, mysterious and melancholy, *Tomorrow, and tomorrow, and tomorrow, creeps in this petty pace from day to day . . . Out, out, brief candle! Life's but a walking shadow, a poor player that struts and frets his hour upon the stage and then is heard no more.* Dramatically he spat the words as though he spurned being part of what was now part of him. "That's the beer talking," I told myself.

"Have you ever really tried to get a birth certificate?" he said abruptly. That surprised me.

"What's the use?" I cried. "I can't get the truth anyway. I'm not interested in one for McGlyn; if there is one it would be fake and I'd be furious. But if you really want to know, yes, I've tried and there is no birth certificate for me, Molly McGlyn which confirms that *she* didn't adopt me, thank God. I want the real thing and I don't know how to get it without a name."

"You have to go back to the nuns. Try again, see what happens. Are you afraid to?"

"I'm not afraid of them, no way. It's just so useless. It was hopeless trying to get my name from that nun. She wasn't going to budge."

"Didn't you tell her you wanted a baptismal certificate?"

"No."

"Well you should have. That's damn important to them. It's worth a try."

"I should have thought of that. I'll write. Sometimes I take a line of least resistance because it's overwhelming not having any lead and never getting any satisfaction if I try. I keep thinking something's going to happen. But it won't if I don't make it happen. I'll write them tomorrow."

My letter was not pleading, nor even questioning. I merely told Sister Rosa, "I don't have a baptismal certificate. There isn't one for Molly McGlyn. What do you think of that?"

Whether or not this was true, fortuitously it worked. My baptismal paper arrived in the mail sometime later and I couldn't believe my eyes. My own real name was Shannon! My mother's name was Kathleen Shannon! My God, how wonderful to know! The only other new information was the date of baptism and sponsor's name, Anna Tebbo. Father's name was blank. I recited my name over and over, *Shannon, Shannon,* enjoying the sound, getting the feel of it. I couldn't wait to tell Julian and follow up somehow.

Flying school ended and Julian returned to Guelph for the conferring of wireless sparks and his WAG—wireless air gunner's wing. The parents of his pal and crewmate, Gerry Morris, insisted I take the baby and travel with them. The ceremony was a solemn display of military force and precision with air force bands on the quadrangle of the Agricultural College, now an air force barracks. I was proud when Julian's name was called and he marched forward and saluted. With tears in my eyes I hugged Mary and told her how important her daddy was. Later, in the ladies' room at McDonald Hall, I was at ease nursing Mary. Gerry's teen-aged sister lingered to admire the baby while other women gawked in disbelief and turned away embarrassed, clucking with annoyance at the sight of a mother nursing her baby.

Then began the wait for orders. Expectant, frightened yet hopeful. When they came, along with a short leave, it was an assignment to a navigation course in Chatham, New Brunswick. Blessed relief! This was infinitely better than going overseas as a wireless air gunner. The day Julian left for his new posting, Paris was liberated, supposedly by the Parisians themselves. There was an undercurrent of social revolution and fear of General de Gaulle becoming a dictator. There was common talk of the war being over before Christmas, but it was feared the French condition would prolong it.

My query letters written in Boston, mailed in Canada, had not been answered. I wrote again to the Catholic Welfare Bureau, citing in support of my rights the name Shannon. "I was not legally adopted, therefore please forward all the information you have." Their reply was prompt, a satisfying, positive factor in my story. It put an end to the question of adoption.

> You were born Molly Shannon on May 22, 1925 in Saint John.
> There is no record of your parents' names just that they were
> from Ireland. You were left at St. Vincent's Infants' Home and
> placed for adoption with Mrs. H.G. McGlyn on March 12,

1926. No doubt when you went with the McGlyn's you went
with the intention that they would adopt you legally. However,
in many of the old adoptions, the adoptive parents did not take
out legal adoption papers. We do not know why except they
did not realize the importance of it. The children belonged to
them as much as if they had adopted them. We come across
many adoptive parents who are shocked when they realize that
their adopted sons and daughters are not legally theirs. We are
of the opinion that the placement did not go through the court,
otherwise there should be a birth certificate available under the
new name.

My God, my name really was Shannon! Now this was significant. I
believed they had more information about my parents. I'd get it somehow.
More venturesome now, I wrote to St. Joseph's infirmary again, asking for
medical records of my birth, my hospitalization for pneumonia and any
information about my mother, determined to try any avenue or alley to
know my beginning. I rewrote the letters to the Registrar General and St.
Vincent's. An overpowering sense of satisfaction gripped me when my birth
certificate arrived for it was in my own name, Shannon. There would be no
legalized fraud to grapple with, no phony registration for Molly McGlyn;
no sealed document to fight for, I was not Doris McGlyn's legally adopted
daughter! I was Kathleen Shannon's daughter! Father's name was blank.

Other new information; my mother was born in Cork. This narrowed the
territory. I now knew my mother's name, approximate age and county of
birth. I wrote to County Cork for records of Kathleen Shannons born
within a certain period; if information was forthcoming no need to identify
myself, not until I knew my mother's feelings. I refused to believe my
mother wouldn't want to know me. My lost self must be found and my
fantasies replaced with a real face. Surely my mother would be caring;
maybe my father thought about me too.

The entry in my yellow search book in August 1944 read:

> Wrote to the Registrar-General, Custom House, Dublin. Encl.
> five-pound bank draft, requested birth certificates for all
> K.A.Ss. born in County Cork in 1907-08-09. The local
> chancery office has an Irish directory of parishes I can use.

When I least expected it the mailman brought a curious looking thin
brown envelope with a harp on the flap. "From overseas," he called. I was

relieved that an overseas letter wasn't the norm. The Registrar of births in Dublin had written:

> I am directed by the Registrar-General to refer to your letter and to say that one female infant named Kathleen Shannon was born in County Cork in 1907. Her birth certificate is enclosed. There was also one female infant with that name born in 1908. Her birth certificate is also enclosed. No female infant of the name was born in 1909. We have enclosed a birth certificate for one female infant born in 1910.
> Yours faithfully.

They bore interesting details and this small connection was stimulating. These papers were from the spot where my mother's record lay. I examined them carefully. Kathleen, born first of May 1907, registered in district of Killbrittain, Bandon, Co. Cork. Father: Francis, a farmer, Mother: Margaret, formerly Forde. Dwelling place: Rathdrought, (eighteen when I was born, thirty-seven now).

Kathleen, born third of January 1908, registered in district of Templeudigan, New Ross, Co. Wexford. Father: blank; Mother: Mary Shannon, formerly: blank. (Another love child.) Dwelling place: Ballinspittal. The mother lived in County Cork, she was likely sent to Wexford to conceal the birth (seventeen then, thirty-six now).

Kathleen, born twenty-eighth of June 1910, registered in district of Fermoy, Co. Cork. Father: Diarmuid, printer, Mother: Norah, formerly Mahoney. Dwelling place: Ballinabanque (fifteen then, thirty-four now).

This letter was a link in the process, but oh how I wanted a letter saying where my mother was and how I could get to her. I wrote to parish presbyteries in Bandon, Fermoy and New Ross and several others in the Diocese of Cork asking for baptismal papers for these and other Kathleen Shannons, if any. The replies were much like the birth certificates—factual. None said *This one is YOUR mother.* Kathleen, born in 1907 had married Denis O'Neill at Christ the King Church in 1928. Not likely my mother. Kathleen, born in 1910 had also married in Ireland, but the priest specified, "There is no such place as Ballinabanque." Replies from County Wexford were impatient and touchy.

> ... send your fee for the work ... no one by that name emigrated ... in recent times I have had several queries from Canada and the U.S.A. In every case my quest was in vain

because of the lack of accurate information from the petitioner. Really, I have spent hours endeavouring to trace people in the parish registers. For me the whole business has been a time-wasting exercise, a hopelessly boring assignment.

Well said! I sympathized. Generally, all the answers were, "Having made a diligent search of the records, I fail to find . . ."

St. Joseph's Infirmary in Saint John merely wrote, "I'm sorry to tell you that our records do not go back that far." St. Vincent's and the Infants' Home did not answer.

To sustain the momentum I wrote to the Boston library for copies of pages from the city directories of 1925-40 for Shannons and O'Connors and the Saint John library for Shannons recorded during 1924-30. That cross-section should give me something to work on. The response was overlong to both requests, but inexpensive. Not knowing my mother's married name was the crux of the whole thing, but having her name at all was stupendous. I diligently researched clues from every quarter, anything to keep at it. Surely when I least expected it, something more would happen.

Writing to Julian became a focal point in my day and I made time to clutch at any straw, no matter how slight, rummaging in the shadowy corners of my past. Four pages were filled in the yellow search book. The pages were numbered to ten in bold print, and I solemnly wondered what stage of my search would bring me to the bottom of page ten. Did my mother wonder about me? Was she alive? Did she think about my feelings for her? That had to be the most natural instinct, more hurtful even than my mortification. The law stood squarely in the way. Perhaps my mother was even more anxious than I was and had as little to go on. Or maybe she had left well enough alone. Perhaps she was deeply grieved that I hadn't found and acknowledged her. But how could I? She was *there*, I am *here*, but where is *there*? My mother had left Saint John believing I had a family and a home. I can't give up.

Each morning I met the postman outside for my *billet-doux* and he became a party to my anticipation. Probably he had the same reaction all over his route from languishing service wives and sweethearts. Julian wrote faithfully.

> My Molly, It was a clear, cool day, very good for flying. We
> went within twenty miles of Saint John on our way to St.
> Stephen and I thought of my girl in relation to that city. While

reading in the library Sunday, it was gray and rainy and I could
look out and hear the gulls screaming over the Miramichi, my
thoughts of you then are expressed in a Yeats poem. Here's
some of it:

O, curlew cry no more in the air
. . . Because your crying brings to my mind
Passion-dimmed eyes and long heavy hair
That was shaken out over my breast . . .
I want so much to be with you again. Must go to the rec hall
and play ping-pong before I go daffy. Pray hard for me, I know
your prayers do me a lot of good.

Early one October morning, while Mary slept outside in her carriage, I
waited for the mailman on the steps, watching my landlady and other
women rush to the corner where they would be picked up by a farmer for
a day of cutting grapes in the Niagara vineyards. Why do they go? A fall
day in the fields? Companionship? Money, most likely. A liaison? The war
effort? My loneliness was more acute as I thought about going with them.
To dream of Julian in some grassy lair beyond the furrows of the vineyards
where tall grasses would fence in my privacy, to dream of lying with Julian
under this perfect October day. The early sun cut across Pelham Road and
a white vapour enveloped the bridge as the morning train to Toronto gave
a long piercing whistle and slowed beneath it to pull into the station. My
voice broke and it startled me. *Oh God, if only I could go to him today.* I
blinked to spill the tears and bring the beauty of the morning into focus. A
tiny sparrow hopped around the steps picking up weed seed, another
perched on a bush singing a wistful song. Then there were more, they
pecked and chittered and suddenly all flew off like leaves in the wind. A
large bird swooped downward then took off again unhurriedly, graceful
and high. I envied its jubilation and freedom to fly. If only I could fly to
Julian. The leaves rustled, like soft rain. They would soon be gone from
the trees; another winter alone. School children came. Quietly at first,
talking, gesturing. Then they ran and skipped and sprinted, swinging
hardened and polished chestnuts on a string, filling Edith Cavell
schoolyard and filling me with fascination. I'd never gone to a schoolyard
or gone home from a schoolyard. Part of me wanted to capture a lost
childhood and part of me looked in on an otherness wanting to be ravished
by my husband. Lulled thoughts, at once a childlike *berceuse* and a sexual
rhapsody.

*T*he allure of autumn, full of hope and desire, wore on to the days before Christmas. If only the war would end! Advances had been made. I shied away from daily war news. I didn't stick little pins into a map and move them forward feverishly, which I might have done if Julian were overseas. Churchill had met Roosevelt again in September, this time in Quebec. They were concerned with operations in the Far East; Roosevelt had accepted Churchill's offer of the British Fleet for operations against the Japanese under American command. The thought of Julian going to fight the Japanese was more than I could bear; sadistic barbarians with modern weapons was all I knew. Churchill met Stalin in Moscow, accomplishing nothing in Roosevelt's absence. So said the North American papers. Roosevelt campaigned and won an unprecedented fourth term in the White House. President de Gaulle's government strengthened its position and was at last recognized by the three major Allies. Eisenhower's tact and charm were praised while Montgomery was criticized ferociously. Athens, liberated in October, fell to civil war by December. Distrust of the immensely powerful Russians was universal; still, this serviceman's wife was glad Russia was an ally. Their ruthless measures could break up the Alliance, said the headlines. We might have told you so, said most people. Could anyone see victory in any of this? The leaders, enemies and allies, were respectful and courteous to each other in conference tents while thousands of human beings, who didn't know each other, blew each other up every day for five long years.

Julian wrote that he hoped to be home for Christmas. It was only a possibility. Some would not be getting leave until New Year's Day.

> There are plenty of rumours flying around about our posting
> being changed but don't worry. How is our little girl? I hope
> she gurgles when you tell her about me. The little angel will
> always have everything we can give her. Thank goodness I'm so
> busy down here I can't realize how far away I am from you,
> except before I go to sleep.

Always, just before I went to sleep I felt how far away he was. It was then, the darkest hour of every day, I'd worry about a training accident or an overseas posting on short notice. He was qualified for duty, I had to face that. Every night the rat below the floorboards gnawed loudly. The landlady had lifted the linoleum and put poison in the hole. That didn't stop it. I filled a suitcase with law books and put it over the loose linoleum under my bed so I'd feel safe. The rat was noisy tonight. I dozed, used to the dread sound, but was roused by short pings. Reaching out I pulled the crib closer, fearing for the sleeping baby. I heard it again at the window this time. Frantically stepping over the small floor space I saw Julian below throwing pebbles at the windowpane, the aircrew flash in his cap luminous in the December moonlight. My heart stopped. To see what I couldn't imagine happening in my dreams. It had to be a dream but I flew barefoot down the stairs anyway. Had he deserted? Had he returned to me despite the war? We clung to each other quietly in the dark hall, kissing, without a word. I lifted my nightie with one hand and we mounted the stairway hand in hand. In the seclusion of the flat I gasped, "I don't believe this, are you all right?"

"Yes, I have a two-week leave." He kissed my brow, my nose, my neck, my wet mouth. "Until after Christmas." He held me tight and ran his hands over my satin gown. "We've all been posted to Rockcliffe; it was quite sudden and none of us wasted time getting away. You wouldn't have believed that departure scene, it was madness. The CO had no explanation. I think it's the beginning of the end of the war or else they're sending us over."

"I can't believe you're here. You were like Romeo down there." My wild arms held him at length. He was rumpled, thin, his acne accentuated by barracks food. He had a terrible brush cut, but he was home.

"Well, Juliet, I will lie with thee tonight. Let's see for means: O mischief! thou art swift to enter in the thoughts of desperate men. Molly, Molly I love you. You are beautiful, soft as warm silk." We stepped into the bedroom and he gaped at Mary. "She's so big, she looks different. Will she remember me?"

"No, but she'll get used to you in a day or two. You'll love her antics, she's a smart baby."

Standing between the bed and the crib our passion flared to unbearable heights. Julian's hands flowed over me, cupping my breasts, stooping to find them with his lips. My hands felt the sensation of his lean back and moved over the tautness of his small hips and barely touched the virile hardness straining against my gown. "Let's get rid of this," He slid the tiny straps from my shoulders and it fell to my feet. "I should see you," he moaned. "All of you, your mouth, your smoky eyes, oh darling, darling, I love all of you."

We'd been apart too long. My legs curled around him, I pushed my softness to him and felt him lengthen in me. "Make it last, my Molly, make it last. You're lovely, so lovely," he sighed. "We'll make up for lost time."

Julian slept at once. I lay there thinking about the night's surprise, about my feelings, the love we shared and being together.

All too soon it was the postman whose footfall I consciously waited for each morning. Julian was given more furlough time. Our love was important; each time could very well be the last time and we acted that way. Rockcliffe was closer, the distance less fearsome, the news more hopeful again as the Allies advanced rapidly. So much was happening. Another Three Power Conference at Yalta with Roosevelt, Churchill and Stalin. The media said it was a failure. This time Roosevelt looked years older and had little to say. But there was action and I began to survey war areas on a map. British troops forced a crossing of the Rhine into Wesel; the Americans began to advance from Remagen and Mainz; Frankfurt had been captured. Americans under Eisenhower were on the Elbe at the Czechoslovakian border, Patton's troops were in Nuremberg, the Eighth Army sealed the base of the Danish promontory and captured Lübeck and Field Marshall Alexander broke through the Adriatic flank, forcing a large number of German divisions against the Po. The green line I drew around these places began to spiral in a winning game.

One sunny April morning with a wonderful feeling of spring everywhere my spirits soared. The air smelled fertile, the ground felt good underfoot, the face of every school child brought a lump of joy to my throat. I wheeled Mary's pram out Pelham Road, walked into a shop and like a thunderbolt the shopkeeper announced, "FDR is dead, the president is dead!" Any optimism that finally good might prevail over the evil of this war turned to gloom. This would have a terrible impact on the war situation. I thought so little about death and funerals. A few elderly nuns had died when I was growing up and we were drawn into the solemn time and paraded past the coffins and knelt to pray in a group but it seemed to me their deaths were timely. That was all. How could a person with such power be gone, just like that? The black cloak that set him apart, the light glancing off his gold-rimmed spectacles in the Pathé news, his flashing smile, his jaunty manner. There was an aura of strength about him, people trusted him, how could it end so suddenly? The shoppers were generalizing, "Harry Truman can't fill that job. Yeah, Churchill never even met the guy. The war will get worse now." Their talk annoyed me. The pungent air of the shop was dismal. Someone's cigarette smoke, so suddenly disagreeable, could only mean the sick feeling of early pregnancy. Joy and disquietude! Death and a new life. A son to go to war in twenty years time?

A week after Roosevelt died, the Americans crossed the Czech border and a week later met the Russians at Torgau, cutting the German army in half. Russia was behaving like an enemy, betraying the Yalta agreement. The world was shocked by the horror of Mussolini and his mistress Clara Petacci, shot by Italian partisans, strung like sides of beef upside down from the girders of a gas station, displayed on the front page of the world's newspapers. Two days later, on May first, Hitler, who had just married his mistress, Eva Braun, shot himself and his bride took poison. It was reported the two bodies were buried in the bunker outside the Chancellery in Berlin that was already under Russian shellfire. I nurtured a wistful hope that one day Julian would tell me the war was ending.

> Molly Darling, We still haven't heard a thing . . . the Air Commodore says we know just as much as he does about our future. It wouldn't surprise me if the Allies declare the war in Germany over quite soon and treat those who fight on as guerrillas as I don't think Germany will ever surrender. It's surprising how they keep up an organized resistance. . .it must be awful there now. Last night Johnny and I went down to the Château Laurier for a few beers and who should we run into but Buzz Beurling! I was reading his book 'Malta Spitfire' just before I joined up. Remember? He left last night for China to join up there to fight the Japanese. I shouldn't tell you this but now I think it's funny. I got pretty drunk and became convinced I was talking to Jap spies at the bar, especially when they invited me up to their room. I was crawling under the bar on my hands and knees thinking they couldn't see me, waiting for the chance to get my book off the bar. One of them said, "This guy must be crazy, look at the crap he reads." It was a Dos Passos novel, The 42nd Parallel. Johnny had trouble getting me out of there. I remember laughing all the way back to camp because I had outsmarted the spies.

Julian wasn't happy when I told him about the expected baby. And I was devastated by his pessimism on May eighth when an Associated Press news bulletin informed the world that the Germans had surrendered. Five years and eight months after the Sunday morning Mother Monica had roused the women to pray to save Poland and the whole world from Nazi tyranny. I waited hours for him to appear. I phoned the barracks, certain he'd be home to celebrate. The whole world was celebrating. I couldn't believe it when he said, "Yes, we have a holiday here too, I suppose everyone did. I slept all morning."

"Oh, Julian, I heard all servicemen got a ninety-six hour pass for V-E Day. You should be home."

"Whoever told you that didn't know what they were talking about. Personally, I don't get a kick out of parades and crowds. Besides it seems funny to be celebrating the end of the war when it's possible that for some it's just the beginning."

Disappointed, overwhelmed actually, I disregarded his pessimism. I wheeled Mary to the centre of town where the whole city had congregated. Cheering filled the air. It was a new chapter in the lives of Canadians; war with Germany was over. Cars honked, streetcars couldn't move, the conductors just gave up and got off to celebrate. In the sky, airplanes from the Niagara flying school buzzed, adding their happy sounds to the victory. People shouted, "The war is over! We won!" Everyone cheered and waved Churchill's V-for-Victory sign. Paper and streamers littered the streets, and soldiers, sailors, airmen and girls grabbed each other and kissed. Happy kids ran everywhere, everyone overflowing with exuberance for this time in history, this time in our lives, this end of the second war to end all wars. I felt a quiet disbelief, in a way; I tried to comprehend our life without war and I prayed that my children would never know war. A woman was killed when a flagpole broke under the weight of happy boys and someone lifted my wallet from Mary's carriage. The stab of fear in my heart was natural. Julian could be right. Everyone was forgetting the Japanese; it could get worse. This could be a false peace.

> My darling, yesterday we were asked to volunteer for the Pacific. I thought it over and didn't. Can't see where it makes any difference because if they need me they will, most assuredly, not consider my feelings in the matter. At the present time I feel sufficiently enthusiastic about completing my education. The life I'm leading now is not what you'd call demanding or unpleasant but I dislike service life and I always will. There is no purpose or reason to this existence unless one believes that this war is some sort of crusade against evil. If I thought I'd succumb to drinking and gambling in civilian life the way one does in the service, I'd stay in because it would be unfair to both of you. God knows I've done little enough for you. As I said though, the decision in the final analysis won't be

in my hands. We started a new course in oxygen today, for
flying at high altitudes but on the whole there is so little to do.
I was down to the sergeant's mess for a few beers and they ran
out.

I've been playing cards for the last two hours but I broke
even—I quit while I still had train fare. Johnny's getting out.
He's convinced them that he is not psychologically suited to
this outfit. Neither am I but I can't admit it to them. I
shouldn't complain about life here except it is very artificial and
you lose all initiative because we wait from day to day for
something to happen. Being away from you is the worst part,
but then I'm here because of you . . . it's all very hard on the
morale. Well, MacKenzie King is in again, whatever that will
mean. Now that the election's over we may get definite word
about a posting. Love to my girl.

I knew inactivity could be devastating for Julian. I prayed it wouldn't
destroy his determination altogether.

Though the war in Europe was over, it continued with bloody persistence
on Asian fronts. Canada was organizing a volunteer force, including the
veterans of Europe, to help the United States end the struggle with Japan
and there was much speculation about President Truman's ultimatum to the
Japanese: "Quit or be destroyed!" adding to conjecture about the secret
weapon being tested in the New Mexico desert.

Then, abruptly in August the United States dropped the atomic bomb on
Hiroshima and Nagasaki. In a flash the war in the Pacific ended, changing
history in one fell swoop. Push-button warfare, though a shocking *coup de
grâce*, meant the end of the war—which was what we all lived for and so
many had died for as well. Forty-two thousand Canadians were not coming
home and in the golden glow of Julian's homecoming I tried to understand
the cataclysm that had changed our lives. The brutal detonation had killed
an estimated two hundred thousand people. I tried not to think about that
and just be glad that in our small sphere war was over. I prayed that peace
would prevail.

The whole country was on the move. Julian came home late at night. It
was a loving and truly thankful reunion. But even then he was a prophet of
doom. "It may be the end of the war, it could well be the end of everything.
They'll blow the world up next."

"Is there a chance we could be happy in the meantime?"

"There's bound to be a depression now, you know that."

I won't say it but why do you want to be gloomy? I have so much to be happy about. I sighed.

"What a sigh is there! The heart is sorely charged." Verbal wit put Julian right in his element; his quips seldom needed an answer.

That fall Julian was back in Toronto at Osgoode Hall Law School, articling in his old firm and sharing a Gloucester Street room with his air force buddy, Johnny. They fancied themselves Bohemian romantics in their garret with beer and bread on the bare table, listening to *La Boheme*, Gigli of course; deciphering *Ulysses*, expounding on *Brave New World*, cynically up-to-date. I longed to be living with him but with the baby due, I had to stay in the little flat. There was barely enough money from DVA and Toronto was high-priced. It would take two school years, but we'd have weekends and holidays and best of all, all summer long.

On a Friday morning, early in December, on my way to the hospital, I left a note on the pillow "I hope it's a boy this time, for you." By noon I had given easy birth and in the evening Julian arrived to see his new son. Through an etherized stupor I saw him, handsome, impeccable, a little uneasy as he smoothed the hair from my face.

"He looks so much like Dad," he whispered. "Could we call him Thomas?"

"Sure. Did you see his red hair?"

"Yes, it's weird. Will it change?"

"Sure, he might be fair, not dark like Mary."

"I was blond when I was little." He lingered at the door, looking so vulnerable and apologizing for wanting a drink to celebrate.

"That's OK, have one for me."

Julian's sister chided me for my great love for him. "It's way beyond the usual," she scolded. "He's not that important, you know."

"He's important to me."

My love was magnanimous, perhaps with a touch of conceit because he loved me. When he was home I indulged his self-indulgent moods, tearing about in a subservient manner, loving him enough to try anything to make him happy; often wheeling the pram uptown to bring him a case of beer. Sometimes it worked and sometimes his melancholic depression was so deep I went about choked with tears. Our love was needful on his arrival and then, later, a salve for my tears, a mollifier for his dejection. It could have been ideal. His natural virtue was ambition, a craving for success above the ordinary. My aim was to help him achieve that goal.

But our babies annoyed him when he was drinking. Once while changing Tommy, his navel not healed from birth, I asked Julian to hold his little ankles so the baby wouldn't hurt himself. He foolishly looked at his hands and asked, "Do you have a pair of gloves?" Who could believe such nonsense, such utter detachment from one's own son? It was sad that he missed out on all the little joys that made up their lives. His weekends at home were just for him during this last year at law school. I tolerated his alcoholic highs followed by crashes into depression and was determined to emerge with him, successful. I pampered his moods but was at a loss when he insisted he believed himself to be manic-depressive and went into long dissertations about that condition. Then he said he was schizophrenic too. I researched the words at the library. The bizarre definitions convinced me he was talking nonsense. More melodrama. All beer talk. I knew I was important to him, he just didn't know how to show it. Everything would be perfect when he graduated.

During Julian's last year at school, Christina Dow, a good neighbour, asked me to go with her to the Children's Aid annual general meeting. "It's public, I have a feeling you'll find it interesting," Ina said.

She was commandingly tall and attractive in a plain sort of way. There was some compelling quality that drew people to her, an air of strength and fairness enhanced by her shyness and a sense of humour that did not wound. Proudly Scottish with a mop of red curls, she often called herself "the wee timorous beastie." She had worked for the government from the time she was sixteen. After serving in the women's division of the air force she returned with full seniority to her old department generating more energy for and consciousness of people's rights. We formed a special friendship that surmounted my troubles, for her ability to laugh and make me laugh was priceless.

The Children's Aid conference turned out to be one of those opportunities that seem later to have been destiny, or intervention by whatever gods there be. They were begging for volunteers for a few hours each week. Julian's Aunt Kate was living with me at this time and seemed to enjoy tending the children. I offered my services with a slightly ulterior impulse—to find out everything possible about fostering and adoption rules and to assess the possibility of working for the Children's Aid to supplement my monthly allowance from DVA. Very soon I was a part-time paid worker, realizing other benefits. It was a way to get information—anything that might facilitate my own search and the urge to satisfy an inherent hope that I might help even one child to know love and security.

The society had begun as a private organization, supported by donations and bequests, but was now racing down the road to total public administration and control, for nearly all its costs came from taxpaying sources. The society originally conceived its duties as those of a policing power to ensure proper care for children. When public money was given for maintenance of these children, the emphasis was more on a family welfare service, and the activities of the Children's Aid Society became more protective of youngsters rather than punitive of neglectful parents. My involvement was certainly satisfying. The danger lay in getting involved in others' tragedies: child abuse, alcoholism, juvenile delinquency, adolescent suicides, some adoptive parents' failures, most of all the sadness of unwed mothers being denied any choice in surrendering their babies. I had overwhelming thoughts of my mother, alone, in a strange country. I wondered if my supervisor, who took her heritage for granted, would understand my marrow-deep need to know who I was. But asking would expose my illegitimacy and perhaps jeopardize my job. Typing social workers' reports was often difficult: *It was touch-and-go as to whether the child would be released for adoption. Make the child's identity to be as close to an 'own' child as possible. The baby is lovely and should be excellent material for adoption. The new legal name will be . . .* The definition of a good adoptive home stressed material things.

Could there not be a better way than a new name, a new legal-fraudulent birth certificate? Real records and identifying information were sealed and locked away, deliberately, forever, presumably *in the best interests of the child.* Why couldn't a baby grow up knowing who it was? Why couldn't a mother *who was interested* be allowed to *know* about her child even though she had nothing to do with its life? To convince her that she was selfish if she did not relinquish her baby and renounce any future knowledge of the child's existence was, I felt, inhuman. If only the attitude towards adoptees beyond age eighteen could be changed to free today's babies from my kind of imprisonment. If only I could cry out publicly with birthmothers and other twenty-year-old "babies," "We have a right to know our origins, we can handle the responsibility; we can deal with the pain if things aren't as we hoped they'd be." Not every case would work but the majority would.

Government funding with its attendant restrictions was causing more harm than good to children as well as immeasurable damage in the family courts. Social workers were taking children out of their homes, instead of working with families to keep them together. Child-care professionals were being drawn into deceit and distortion to get the judge's approval for custody. It was plain that they had to label a child to get public money to flow. Group homes tripled in numbers and reports proved that child care took a nosedive. The Children's Aid just gave money out, so much per child per day, not fully understanding how group homes operated. Group homes competed for beds. It was a seller's market. It was deplorable. My work with the Children's Aid became frustrating.

If only I had the education to take a stand, get into some political office to work towards improving the system. But if one thought about all the "if only" permutations in life one could go mad. My lack of schooling made me fearful of speaking out. Impetuously I enrolled in a home study course, tenth grade. The assignments were demanding but fulfilling.

Julian was called to the bar *summa cum laude*. After four years of abnormal living, we were a normal family at last. A partner in his new law firm said Julian must get involved in the church and the community, be a Knight of Columbus, be an usher, join the Lion's Club, get on civic boards, join the Jaycees, join the golf club, and he tried. He despised the clandestine, infantile goings-on at the initiation ceremonies of the Knights, being slapped around in the dark, fake heart attacks to teach you to trust your brothers in the guise of unity, fraternity and patriotism. He tried for a longer period to be an usher at church but cringed at the servility of the task, so convinced in his delusion that the pastor directed all accusatory sermons at him. "I'm not dumb, that son-of-a-bitch is needling me." He wanted to enjoy the Lions Club. He had won his first-year scholarship to the University of Toronto from the Lions. Still he said he couldn't abide a group of men behaving like little boys, "even if they do the greatest amount of good in the community." He undertook his appointment to the Municipal Board of Health and grappled with its attendant responsibilities. He didn't criticize or ridicule them, but he chafed more and more under the strictures of the meetings. He called the Jaycees "shining-faced do-gooders" and it was clear he wouldn't persevere in that group, but one night he joined his peers in shooting craps after the dinner meeting and from then on he gambled regularly.

The golf club might have been a good thing. Julian had a natural talent and he could have enjoyed the game. But he played with his Jaycee friends and they gambled. The nineteenth hole ritual always brought new challenges, new wagers, tests of skill on the practice green, new stakes, another bet!

He became paranoid at the office, certain the junior partner was "out to get him" and got rigid and tense when "that god-damned secretary stands there at five o'clock with mail to be signed." He was happy in court. Quite often he said, "Molly, this work is more sensational than the movies. There's no drama quite so moving as human beings fighting for their rights; not their lives, just their rights." I was proud and partial when I saw him in court. He was eloquent and looked distinguished in his gown and wing collar.

Julian always stayed out in the evening to drink. One night he didn't come home at all. It was mid-morning before he called from Niagara Falls, New York, to say a friend had bailed him out of jail on a drunk charge. "Call the office and tell them I'm sick, that I won't be in today. I'll get a bus home." I lied for him and the call backfired when the junior partner called back to speak to Julian. He never did tell me what actually happened that night. Communication with this brooding melancholic was not easy. I was beginning to realize I hardly knew him, I had never gotten beneath the passion that had brought us together.

Monday nights we retired early and listened to Lux Theatre of the Air. Not much talking then. This was a time to be close, attended by the solemn declarations of the actresses who washed their skin and their sweaters only in Lux. A sobering-up evening. The end result was a new baby boy. Mary and Tom were five-and-a-half and four when Brien Patrick was born. Julian's cross manner did not escape Mary. "Oh, Daddy's gonna be mad!" she said at the news, with make-believe consternation on her little face. "When I grow up to be a mother and Tommy grows up to be a father we'll fight. What is the end of it, Mommy? Tell me."

Once upon a time I had a childlike belief that I could help Julian and we would build a happy family life together. Help him, not change him. But now he was missing so many of the triumphs and small disasters which made up the children's days. I remembered one rare summer evening before Brien was born, I'd gone out, leaving Julian to call the children in at bedtime. And that's precisely what he did, he called them in. I found them asleep, arm in arm, in Mary's youth bed, dirty overalls, muddy boots still on Tommy. He couldn't climb into his crib so Mary mothered him. Heartrending frustration at Julian's indifference overtook me and I sobbed while he sat in the Lazy-boy, swilling beer.

"You're overreacting," he slurred when I had stopped crying. "I got them in, it's not that serious." There were times when he pitifully minimized his parental authority. "Am I a good daddy?" he'd ask. "I'm not a bad daddy, am I?" "You know your daddy wouldn't hurt you, don't you?" In a wistful stupor I saw other couples laughing everywhere. At the supermarket I watched a man in his compact car tending his children, a beautifully fair boy and girl in the back seat, an infant on his lap. *Exactly like my family.* I pretended not to see how tenderly he brushed his lips on the baby's fuzzy head. The mother came by, just bursting with enthusiasm and smiling at me as she passed. I got calmly into a cab with my groceries but fell apart once inside, sobbing, asking no one in particular, Why? Dear God, why?

Our trust and confidence in each other had vanished. We didn't share our thoughts, feelings or actions about the children. I hid my problems from him to escape his anger and cursing and that was lamentable. Julian had been a child of the Great Depression. These were good times after the war; still he tormented himself with a phobia that had no basis in reality. "Don't you understand there's another depression coming? Mark my words, you wait and see." In spite of that he drank and gambled most nights. He had no system with money, no budget, no allowance for the house, yet when he was home he wanted good food and absurd situations evolved. *Yes,* I would assure him, *I did peel the mushrooms. It IS freshly squeezed juice. Oh yes, I watched the butcher grind the beef, they ARE brown eggs, the stewing beef IS sirloin. No, I won't get food near the rim of your plate. Yes, I'll fill your tea to the brim, no crisp edges on your eggs. Here's your sixth glass of water, not enough ice? Sorry. Toast not dark enough? Sorry.* There was always something missing, always something not right. His fine fingers instinctively felt the rim of his tea cup and that God-awful look of self-pity when he said it wasn't hot made me crazy. I grew angry preparing a meal, he was angry eating it. There was stark silence when we were alone. Then he implied I was trying to build a good reputation for myself while destroying him so that "when the end comes people will believe you're the victim." I couldn't believe that he meant the foolish things he said; thoughtless words loaded with sarcasm and disaffection. He was supposed to be clever. Everyone said it, constantly.

Discerning friends encouraged Julian to try Alcoholics Anonymous. Though I'd grasp at any straw in the wind, I knew his problems were more psychological. "No, no," they'd say. "It's drinking and you can't begin to know an alcoholic. They're locked up inside themselves with their own awful problems. They have to go to AA." A colleague of Julian's who went to AA probed doggedly in true legal fashion until I shouted at him. "Yes, our lives are unmanageable!" It happened one day when I was feeling good. Three months pregnant with Brien, an orange and white silk dress complemented my tan. My mood was gentle because I loved carrying my baby.

"Julian's lifestyle hasn't seemed to hurt you at all." He grinned lecherously, running his fat hand around my hip.

"You just ask Julian about it then," I shouted at him. "Not me. You creep!"

His wife, Lise, called often. "Come to a meeting with me. Spouses of alcoholics go. It helps them understand."

"I understand all I want to. I can't go. I don't want to go. I'm too busy, the children . . ."

Lise was utterly unyielding. "Listen to me, I know. No other method has helped the drinker as much as the help they give themselves through AA. Julian could find a group where he'd be comfortable, where he'd have some common interests and where there is a non-drinking friend available to socialize with away from the tavern. Soon he'd be helping others and that would afford him the confidence he now looks for in liquor. I'll pick you up."

The meeting was in the type of church hall where we had met. There were signs all over: *Keep an open mind. Remember when? Think!* Sickly blue smoke filled the room and Bill B's voice droned on. "I've never been to skid row and I'm not bragging. I brought skid row into my home. But I've had a bowel movement ôf the soul, I've spewed out of me the things that are wrong and I'm climbing the mountain, out of the depths, out of the morass of my life. And do you know what? The farther up I go the more I can see."

There was something in his eyes and his smile—it was clear he had found something. There were many men and women there who had beaten alcohol. There were words and more words: hopeful-helpful, despair-discord, stimulant-depressant, nightcap-sleepless nights, courage-fearful mess, the pairing went on and on. God, the other fellow and self. . . I was uneasy with public displays. Another AA wife had taken me to an Alanon meeting once. Telling intimate things to strangers worked for some, they needed the release and maybe it helped them. Not for me. The same woman had taken Mary and Tom into her home for Alateen meetings. My heart ached for them, I couldn't believe it was right. Hearing other teens' sad tales would compound their own worst fears. They were good about it, though, and it was short-lived. Now, I hated the gloomy room, creaky floors, scattered meeting chairs, sour fumes and the horrid smoke. I ran from the place.

My headache was gruesome. Julian came home early and sober, truly sympathetic and anxious, getting ice, massaging, wishing he could take the pain away. "What caused it?" he asked. I covered my eyes with the cold cloth to avoid his.

"Listen honey, I went to an AA meeting tonight with Victor. He talked me into it. I don't need this crap but I'll try, for you. Would you like that?"

I nodded in amazement. "Good old Victor the protector," I murmured. What a clever little coup Lise and her husband had pulled off. Taking Julian to one meeting location and me to another! If she knew Lise should have been honest with me. It didn't matter now. It was done. But if some good came of it, I would welcome that.

"I can't promise it will work. You know my dry drunks are always worse. What do you say we try?"

"We'll try." I reached for his hand. "Can't we be like this more often instead of antagonistic all the time?" He clasped my hand, his immaculate French cuffs and sterling cuff links close to my face. He flicked lint from the bed off his suit and vest. Julian was never mussed. He revelled in the texture of a towel, the specialty of a tab collar, the quality of his classic navy cashmere coat, his silk scarf, his Owens and Elms hand-sewn shoes and cashmere socks. Julian bought what he wanted. He didn't know yet we were having a new baby. I feared his reaction and I was waiting for the moment when it might be gentle. I lay still in a swoon of feeling as the hands I loved rubbed and used pressure on my aching head until it was time to get Tom up for the bathroom. The sleepy angel didn't wake up fully for this nocturnal routine. I guided him while Julian watched. He patted Tommy's fair brush cut and, in his usual Shakespearean manner, quoted, "When come such another?"

"November," I demurred when he hadn't been asking the question at all, just indulging in his ever-present penchant for the quip. His response was worse than I expected.

"Jesus Christ, I thought so! Let me out of this goddamn den of conformity." He stomped from the house in search of a drink or whatever he needed to wallow in this injustice to him.

I went to the children's bedroom and sat on the floor between Mary and Tommy, innocent in their little beds. Long lashes on chubby cheeks, wisps of dark curls where Mary had cut her own hair in the front. Tommy with his new brush cut; his father should have taken him. Didn't every father take his son for his first haircut? Wasn't it a rite of passage? A bonding? Anyway, he didn't cry, he was just a little wary. He wasn't bribed either. I cried for relief from the headache, from the blame. I cried because Julian was sick, I cried for the release tears brought and I summoned some strength in the serenity of the little room, telling myself: *There's no sense in saying I don't give a damn: I do. I love him; he's the reason I believe that I am somebody, a mother, his wife. I love that man and in his way he loves us. But this, this is a terrible way to live. We snap and snarl and this dark space between us is getting darker and wider. Some women have a deep psychological wish to be taken care of. There are those who'd say orphans have it more. To hell with that. I don't need Julian to complete me now. I won't hide or lean, and damn the social isolation. One fatalist in this family is one too many. If I have to face failure in this most important relationship of my life, I'll manage.* I dozed and kept waking up on the floor between the little beds and words went on in my head like drums in the middle of the night.

Get on your feet and be somebody!

The treadmill years rolled one into the next and Julian spoke more often about being schizoid, paranoid and alcoholic. He bragged that he had a persecution complex and admitted to delusions of grandeur with such bravado. Alibis, all alibis for drinking. He often wept at my knee in the morning with the tired familiar "I don't know what's wrong with me, darling. I'm sorry."

"Chameleon words," I told him scornfully. "Words of a weakling. It would be better if you said what you did was wrong, it shouldn't have happened, and it won't happen again."

"If I said that you wouldn't believe me and I can't blame you."

It's a trying experience to watch the one you love cry. You feel the pain you see on his face and crave to make it better. You turn away, but you can't bear it. You cry too, for sharing pain is a natural act of love; but there are circumstances when assertiveness is an act of love also. In a desperate bid to check the widening gap between us, I seized upon one of these times to suggest seeing Dr. Bell who had opened a rehabilitation clinic in Toronto. To my surprise, Julian agreed. The doctor questioned Julian, then explained that first we both must understand the facts, that alcoholism was a chronic illness of undetermined etiology with insidious symptoms proportionate to its severity. The small office was very quiet and I found solace in his words because we were now in a position to be helped.

"Heavy drinkers seek to escape the responsibility of facing and solving problems through the use of alcohol," he explained. "Unfortunately, this tends to increase the number and severity of the problems, so that the quantity he must drink to escape becomes greater. How old are you?"

"Thirty-two." Julian's voice was firm. Though he tried to impress the specialist with professional talk, Julian revealed so much about himself and his problems that he was most unconvincing when he declared profoundly to the doctor that he was merely a social drinker. The doctor watched my reaction to Julian's excuses; I didn't overdo it. I was desperate and it showed.

"I would urge you into action," the doctor said as though he hadn't heard Julian's extenuation. "I recommend that you enter the clinic for treatment." He described the voluntary routine and the open-door policy; he emphasized the volitional sessions for the benefit of the psychoneurotic. I had an extraordinary sense of relief as he gave a name to Julian's troubles. Psychoneurosis could be fathomed and treated. There was such comfort being there in the soft light of the mahogany room, hearing the calm words of this person who understood. But Julian made excuses. The absence from his job would be conspicuous.

"Treat it as a vacation. Many do."

Julian said he couldn't afford it. The doctor quashed that defense. "Consider the amount of money you spend on alcohol." The doctor knew every rationalization drinkers used to justify their habit. "You probably have recurrent mood disorders?"

"Doesn't everyone?"

"No. Not serious disorders. Do you?"

"Yes."

"Your drinking may rob your children of optimal parenting. Frequent episodes may result in a ruined career and marital breakdown. You should consider that serious."

But on that hopeful day the clever attorney talked himself out of the help he so desperately needed.

On the bus going home, Julian's attitude was playful, as though he had won something. He nudged me and whispered happily the final words of Stephen Dedalus, *Welcome O life! I go to encounter for the millionth time the reality of experience. Old father, old artificer, stand me now and ever in good stead.* His was a rueful humour, while Frost's words went round in my head, words

I much preferred: *Two roads diverged in a wood, and I, I took the one less traveled by.* And that *could have* made the difference but all that came from that session was Julian's smugness that he had done what I had asked him to do.

Nevertheless something beautiful and indispensable to my life happened after that. When Brien was four I gave birth to a fourth precious child. I made myself peaceful while I carried this baby against my heart; I soothed and cradled my belly certain it would be the last time I would have the phenomenal experience of nurturing and developing a baby whom I would hold, protect, love and enjoy. I re-covered the bassinet in downy pink, I made pink booties and bonnets, I bought a pink baby buggy, I wore a pink hat and a pink blouse and I prayed for a baby girl. I called her Molly Ann!

Julian seemed sheepish and uneasy at the foot of my hospital bed, decidedly drunk; his police friend had brought him and waited to take him away to celebrate.

Life continued sad and crazy between us. At a golf club party someone named Rob crooned drunkenly in my ear as we danced, "You knew it would be like this, didn't you colleen? I'll be 'round throwing pebbles at your window." I was bent backwards like a bow and Julian accused me of dancing too close. Someone named Neil, who had seen me preside at the PTA at school, asked me to dance. "Hello miss-holier-than-thou. You know, I think you're full of love." Julian danced by. "Hello, God," shouted Neil just as someone pushed us all together. "Christ, McBeath, you old bastard, it's good to see ya but ya look like hell."

Later the party moved to someone's house, someone rich, and Julian stood on the verandah, reeling back and forth watching his friends. I think he was being sarcastic when he said, "We've arrived darling, we've made it, we've arrived." His insecurity, his desire for the grand life, his envy of those who had it, his insinuation that I wanted it, was all so pitiful. We walked home in the cool, fresh morning and went to bed. While I wanted Julian's warmth against me and to hear his breathy moan, feelings of love were smothered.

Not long after that party we were expected to attend the Legal Ball in Niagara Falls. I loved parties. Secretly recalling the coarse laundry garb, I could still get giddy at the texture of fine clothes. This was a different group than the golf club party and, while I loved the sophistication, I disliked the pretense that surfaced when Julian was in this company. I didn't crave to be like the other wives, but Julian was better mannered and more courteous with them and I wished our life together could be a little more civilized, like this. At his law partner's home, middle-aged men congregated in the library, a hand in a pocket, a glass in a hand as they spoke of new homes, new offices, suits or actions at law and the misery of missing the football game. The women sat straight on the damask sofa and Italian chairs, squeezed into their garments, holding little jeweled bags.

I moved about. It was easier than becoming involved in a not-too-sincere conversation, oohing and aahing over things I didn't have. Julian was handsome in his rented formal evening clothes yet only I could see his uneasiness with these temperate men, constrained as he flicked imaginary particles from his skin each time he spoke.

The dinner was a glistening world of romance. Subdued music, candles, the low murmur of voices, laughter. The joy of being able to watch and listen to the most charming men. Then to smile and dance with other lawyers and a judge. I felt young and pretty in an emerald velvet gown. There was a romantic atmosphere, particular men saying my name pleasantly, merry little hugs at the end of a dance, a sort of thanks. I was pleasing them, experiencing some pleasure in myself, loving the comments. *You are lovely, Julian is a lucky man. It's a pleasure to know you . . . where has he been hiding you?* It was gracious flattery and I liked it. In Julian's arms I felt romantic again and certain we could sweep all the obstacles away and be happy. I whispered "I love you." He said my arm was heavy on his shoulder, "Please move it." I was left to watch his long gulps, short pauses and surly mood unfold; the sarcastic arch of his brow, cynical curl of his lip, curiously sensual.

"We'd better go darling." I said it gently, but just when my back was turned in the parking lot Julian delivered a sudden, cruel blow to the side of my head and unleashed his prolonged and insidious name-calling. "Swinehound, vixen, bitch, flaunting yourself in there, making a play for those goddamned cocksuckers. I'll show you!" He smashed one side of my face with his open hand, then the other, back and forth, again and again.

"Stop it!" I screamed hysterically. Shaking and gasping for breath, I attempted to grab his wrists. He hissed and held one of my arms behind my back and trapped the other with his body. "You're not so smart!" He continued his accusations and invective in such a pitiless way I ceased struggling, hoping to end this insanity. Julian squeezed my jaw between his thumb and finger, wild-eyed, awful. "How many of those guys have fucked you already, eh?" He flung me away from him.

God, oh God, what'll I do? I had to drive, he obviously couldn't. My taking the wheel caused a bogus attempt on Julian's part to get into the driver's seat. Eventually, my ears ringing, jaws aching, borrowed dress torn, earrings lost, I drove home in a torrent of tears, Julian out cold beside me. He revived enough to cause a great commotion, waking Mary with cursing and accusations, cruelly shouting that he wasn't her father. I would never forgive him for that.

That party was the bitter denouement that killed our marriage. I said I forgave him to get rid of him when he cried at my knee in the morning, but inside I began to plan a better way of life.

"You're ravishing when you're mad."

I ignored that.

"Look honey, I don't mean to make you unhappy . . ."

"Don't honey me, you fugitive from drink and gambling. Go to those women at the golf club who keep telling you you're so clever, soooo distinguished! Hurry though, you're burning yourself out and they won't want you." At night I'd cling to the side of our wartime mattress that sagged in a V to avoid touching him.

I had to make some move, do something, but Lise had said, "Hands-off. A man like that has to hit rock bottom before any sense is knocked into him. He has to make the move to quit himself."

"If this isn't rock bottom, Lise, I don't want to be around to know it."

My doctor shook his head. "It would take an analyst," he said, though he didn't suggest a way of getting Julian there. There was a touch of irony in his question, "Are you a perfectionist? Maybe you expect too much." He even had the effrontery to ask, "What are your drawers like?"

"What?"

"Are they all neat and tidy, just the way you want them?"

"Of course they are," I cried.

I cried at the injustice his alcoholism was inflicting on us, because I loved Julian. I searched back through some of his letters for assurance that we belonged together, for some certainty that he really loved me. What I found instead was evidence that he must be crazy, mad as a hatter, whatever that meant. The letter had come from Chatham, just before the unexpected leave and posting to Rockcliffe.

> My Molly; I spend so much time with you on my mind that it is wonderful to be able to sit down and know that my thoughts are being transmitted to you. I don't know what I'd do if ever I didn't have you now . . . I love you in such different ways . . . [he

named several] . . . and in another way which I cannot
understand - something dark and cruel, worse than physical
attraction. It's incredible to me that I can feel so differently about
one person. Sometimes when I feel like this I try to think of
anything that will make me hate you. . .[reasons for hating,
including going away to Boston]. I don't know why I torment
myself like this. Do you think there is a streak of insanity in me?
What makes me like this? I want you to understand me
completely.

I couldn't understand, I'd never understand this person who claimed to
be a conscientious objector, who beat, neglected and insulted the one
person he claimed he could not live without. "He's sick," they said. "He's
sick." Lise sounded like a broken record.

"If he's sick, Lise, that means he is not responsible."

"Right."

"Funny, he manages very well not to be sick all day at work and in other
relationships with varying degrees of interaction. He can hurt me in private
and bruise me where it doesn't show. That's not sick, that's premeditated."

Frantic but determined, I decided to take more home study courses or
find an evening course and when school was out in June, take the children
and just leave. I gave up on Julian. I began to record feelings of self-
assessment. I found strength reading the early journals of Anaïs Nin, though
some found Nin tedious and pretentious, others narcissistic. I saw her as
magical. *Why am I not happy? What do I regret? What do I want? What can I
do about it?* I came to terms with some of the panic. *What do I have? What do
I need? What will it take to bring have and need together?* Certainly the
disentanglement would have to take place between my own ears since it was
clear to me no one else could help me.

The clutter of the law reflected Britain's 1857 Matrimonial Causes Act; if
I wanted to assert my rights not to be beaten, I'd have to leave bed and
board, otherwise the police or prosecutors would not intervene. They said
women used these officers as leverage to bring a man to heel. They said a
prosecutor couldn't believe a woman is serious about her complaint when
she continued to live in the same house with a brute. There definitely was
a double standard when it came to violence inside and outside the home. If
women tried to use legal or social services for their protection, their
attempts only led to worse violence. Sadly I learned that secure people often
said that the victims of abuse asked for it—or deserved it. I felt trapped by

Julian's most cruel manner, especially when his high school chum, Stan, a Provincial Policeman, parked his cruiser in the driveway and they drunkenly ridiculed ethics, in my home. They asked each other the Alcoholics Anonymous twenty questions and roared with laughter as they answered "Yes, yes, yes . . ." They joked that wife-beating was a man's right and accepted in most societies. In a blithe mood Julian told Stan there was a British law under which a woman couldn't be beaten with anything except a whip no wider than a man's thumb. And an obsolete law of the Isle of Sark brought out their sadistic humour, for it allowed a husband to beat a wife so long as he didn't damage the eyes, break the arms or legs or draw blood. Shameful destructive talk. They thought it humorous. I observed Stan one evening when he gave Mary twenty-five cents then grabbed her wrist saying, "Give me a kiss." This twelve-year-old actually handed the quarter back to him.

I endured the trauma of Julian's two car accidents in a short space of time, the first a serious one. Saturday afternoon, while drinking, he went off to deliver a gift bottle of Canadian Club to a real estate salesman for some professional favour. I tried to drive him there; "I need the car for shopping . . ." It didn't work. When he phoned from the kitchen of a rural home late that night telling me he had an accident, he asked me to taxi there. The taxi driver saw Julian's car between two trees, all but demolished. He was in a horrible state, sitting before a warm stove, holding a towel to his bloody face and a large gash on the back of his head. The poor woman was too frightened to speak. I got him to the taxi and the driver told me, "We can't leave the scene, there's too much damage. The police have to be called. You can say you were driving. Oh, they're here already." I left the taxi to divert attention from Julian, but the officer went directly to the cab and looked in the window.

"You get Mr. McBeath to the hospital, we'll follow. You come with me," he said. Shaking, I was able to tell him that Julian spoke to me from the woman's home and I arrived by taxi. He was kind and led me to the cruiser then went to the car and lifted Julian's brief case out the rear window. "It's heavy," he said depositing it in the back seat of the police cruiser.

"Probably law books," I tried to say, hoping it wasn't booze. My teeth chattered loudly and I shook as we followed the taxi. At the hospital he placed the briefcase beside my chair. He didn't open it.

Mary was an angel at home, giving me freedom to spend time at the hospital, though Julian's attitude was anything but amiable. "For Christ's sake find me something to piss in." He spewed the words after the orderly left the room with an empty urinal. "I'm not giving that cocksucker a specimen for the police. That's what he wants." I brought him a drinking glass which he filled a few times, and over the noisy splash he argued that I was disappointed he hadn't killed himself. A neighbour policeman phoned next morning and said he was happy to tell me there'd be no charge laid for drunk driving. I suppose I was relieved but in my heart I knew it was not fair. Same procedure after he broadsided a car while driving his partner's Cadillac. They were frightening times and outwardly Julian was not self-critical after these mistakes. In the guise of anger at me he raved that I wanted the accident to be fatal and, to make me feel guilty, he ranted as though I had caused it. A reverse psychology tactic so banal and beneath his profession.

I cried after that shock. I had been on the perimeter of Julian's drinking for so long, had been sucked into the swirling vortex and now I was trying to crawl from the whirlpool and I was losing ground; trapped in a relationship where you suffer because it's the way it's supposed to be. Grim-lipped, choked up, forever and ever. No way! There was no support anywhere to help me separate from him, but I had to go and I had to be certain there'd be no crawling back. As certain as the child who ran away from St. Vincent's only, *Please God, don't make me pay as much for this running away as I paid that first time.*

Our rented house was sold that year. This became the catalyst for our separation. I didn't have to walk out on him; the separation was mutual. Still, he made it difficult. "Do whatever the hell you want. You won't take my children and you won't get any money from me."

His concern for his children was new. A ploy to keep me there, to frighten and prevent me from going away. But he was dealing with a mothering instinct with which he could not compete. *If he thinks I'm the bitch, swine or vixen he calls me, he'll soon learn I can be as protective and scheming as any mother fox, bear or sow. We'll have our Armageddon and Julian will learn that my affinity for him is nothing if he threatens my maternal responsibility.*

It was quite in keeping with Julian's manner that his vehemence was directed at me alone. I engaged a Toronto lawyer who did not delve for information; he knew. He lunched with Julian to discuss the separation and told me, "He has agreed to contribute minimally to the children's upkeep. What do you want for yourself by way of support from him?"

"That's a hopeless question if ever there was one. Julian has never supported me and it's pointless to think he'd start now."

"Okay, whatever you say. But we should go after some support when he has recovered a financial balance."

I agreed to there being no legal document, just Julian's agreement to his colleague. Sadly, by this time I wasn't devastated at breaking up. The determination to start again was all I needed and I was eager to go. Thank God we didn't have material things to haggle over. In the final untangling of bonds I wept for the intangibles—intimacy, shared hopes and parenting, all immolated.

Pity me not the waning of the moon,
Nor that the ebbing tide goes out to sea,
Nor that a man's desire is hushed so soon,
And you no longer look with love on me.
. . . Pity me that the heart is slow to learn
What the swift mind beholds at every turn.

Edna St. Vincent Millay

TORONTO/SAINT JOHN > 1962

*A*S I LOADED the old green fifty-five Monarch with clothes, toys, linens, dishes, school books and sports equipment an ambivalent mood swamped me. When the packing was done late Saturday afternoon I drove away from Niagara alone, leaving Brien and Molly Ann with a friend for the night. The small city seemed dismal. Kresge's windows filled with plastic windmills, mops and pails; Buehler's butcher shop windows with empty enameled trays and green fringed paper; Hattie's ancient dry goods store; the Royal Bank and Julian's office above it; the small jewelry store run by the Petersen brothers, the older one tall and lean, handsome and gentle with his Gary Cooper voice and winsome smile. I sometimes fancied him. Past Bissonnette & Joy, Haberdashers, who actually had bowler hats for sale. Once, early on, Julian wanted a bowler hat. It didn't suit his small features; he looked like a kid wearing his father's hat. I returned it to the shop for him. Past Diana Sweets where the waitresses knew how to plunk everything Julian preferred down in front of him. Eaton's Annex; Household Finance next door where I'd borrowed money on the strength of my fifty-three dollars a month allowance when I was nineteen, saying I was twenty-one, then going to Home Outfitting to buy beds and chairs such a long time ago when life was all expectation and desire. I had an urge to drive past our rental homes if only to prove to myself that I'd made an attempt at home-making for my family, first in the two-room flat on Pelham Road, close to the tavern where Julian had done a waiter's work to earn money for school—near his father's place where he sang *Because*, alone to me in front of his family. I could see Mary here, months old, sitting in

117

her playpen occupied with blocks or a rag doll, the Ink Spots singing on the radio, *Gonna dance with the dolly with the hole in her stocking.* Always, at the first notes she'd scramble to her feet and do a vigorous dance, rattling the play pen and beaming with the pure joy in her large, innocent eyes. Tommy's life began here. Next I drove out to the wartime house on Boulton Boulevard. A misnomer for sure, a mud road where coarse gravel had been dumped, making it impossible to wheel a baby carriage or even walk with heeled shoes, and the families, all returning veterans, had to plant their own lawns. I had planted forget-me-nots around the steps. On this last look at the bungalow tears filled my eyes as I remembered Mary's little fist full of dandelions: "Look Mommy, I picked you some lilies." Brien Patrick had started life on Boulton. I decided to finish the route, like a closing ritual, making it final. So, on to Collier Street, more wartime homes where veterans were wait-listed for the bungalows with paved roads and basements. I had been proud and happy homemaking here and life was more or less settled. Brien was three weeks old when we moved in; he was a good baby and I had a sense of well-being when I nursed him, knowing I'd have a large bowl of chocolate ice cream with sliced bananas after he was fed.

An odd memory assailed me now. Julian promised to go to the house and light the coal furnace the night before we moved in. He didn't. I remember trying to light the fire on January second with a few sticks, ignorant of the chains that controlled the air flow, frustrated as hell, my new baby next door waiting to be nursed. When Julian came he stood at the top of the basement stairs in his white silk scarf, good gloves, cashmere coat, explaining to me how it was done but indicating his clothes prevented him from doing it. He was right; he looked debonair and elegant. Molly Ann had started life on Collier Street. A former tenant had planted forget-me-nots and I could see her now, strands of golden hair across her gentian-blue eyes, a pudgy little fist filled with tiny blue flowers saying, "Here Mommy, I picked you some don't-forget-me-nots." Bad memories here but good memories too. Piles of folded diapers smelling of fresh air, lots of clean towels and sheets representing work accomplished. Satisfaction on Friday when the house had been cleaned, and the smell of wax and polish made a pleasing combination at day's end with the heat smell from the oven where the Friday macaroni and cheese bubbled. Coming in from play, Tom would invariably sniff and ask innocently, "Who's coming?" Later we rented a furnished house in a fine area of the city. South Drive. Lawyers lived there, and doctors. But it was too late by then. Here memories of high school days and my children's lives developing were important; that was all. And Molly Ann, who had been in kindergarten half-days, on her first full day of school, calling from the back door after lunch, "I'm going back to school now Mama, good-bye." With no response from me, or Brien who was escorting her, she called louder, "I have to go to school this aft. Did you know? Hey everybody, I'm going back to grade one now." Some memories were sweet.

Julian didn't bid on the South Drive house when it went up for sale. *Get out of here*, I told myself. *That's finished.* And I beat it out of town. As the dismalness of the small city receded in the glorious September evening I sang out loud to myself *O! What a beautiful morning, O! what a beautiful day . . .* I was on my own again!

*L*ife took a positive turn and everything worked out better than I had hoped when I moved to Toronto from Niagara. The children settled easily, though the move affected Tom most. At seventeen he was quiet and often stayed away after school. I feared he might be gambling but could not accuse him. *Just be there. Don't nag. Just emphasize your expectations.* He knew they were high, he'd measure up. Secretly I hoped Tom would be partial to me, depend on me and not blame me. As for the other children, Mary's life at university was a boon. St. Joseph's College Residence on Wellesley gave her a new outlook on life. She would be fine, a good student. Molly Ann entered grade two and was content to be the responsibility of her grade seven brother. School was a block away and I could watch them go off together in the morning before I went to work at my new job with Aircraft Appliances & Equipment half a mile away. I went home for their lunch hour but they were home before me after school. It worked. Love prevailed in every issue.

Brien would be happy anywhere if he could play hockey. He was a popular player on two teams, making friends at every turn. His Humber Valley team went to Quebec City for a week that first winter to compete in an International Peewee Tournament at the Winter Carnival. I took him to Union Station and noticed that some parents were going on the trip—couples! My envy surprised me. I had a potent vodka that night and unleashed the tears that were inevitable now and then. Only now and then, alone, could I open the dusty doors of regret looking for reasons, thinking of yesterdays and remembering the hunger of wartime separations. Sometimes at night the mattress took a punching as I sat on the empty bed, asking an unremitting *why?* to heaven. There was no answer, no reason why two people who loved each other should hate each other and live separately. But it was over. I would not serve time for our inadequacies.

Apartment life in our new family complex was good. Julian's small deposit in the bank each week made a difference in how I could organize our lives. I found secretarial work immediately and close to home. It was the early days of feminism and, we were told, changes were necessary; be independent, more autonomous; gender discrimination must change. *They* spoke in unison, *they* were educated. I wasn't. Someone had to bring coffee, answer the phone, take dictation and type, and cover up. I just made sure I didn't try to be smarter than I was supposed to be—for now. It was the norm to pester a secretary for a date, she worked *for* men. I grew to detest that word and was adamant that I worked *with* . . . In time, I made application to Atkinson College at York University for part-time evening courses. They asked for my reasons and for a letter from someone supporting my academic ability. I told them I had been hindered and frustrated by the lack of higher education so, happily I was admitted as a mature student starting with the humanities and adding social science. One subject at a time would keep me busy. How I enjoyed "striding the halls of academe", well aware of the privilege. Going to school at last! I put a closure on the past, liking myself better in this endeavour. Still, every now and then the mattress took a punching at night; the loneliness and privation were real.

A shocking headline in The Catholic Register took my breath away. *Saint John Diocese closes Orphanage. Bishop states.* Sure enough, St. Vincent's was closing after a hundred years. I had a great urge to celebrate, and to know more about the bishop's decision. He actually said that some orphaned children would grow into bitter, confused adults without a home environment. No kidding! He also said that leading childcare experts claimed that children are better off in the care of foster homes, not institutions. "It is the feeling of all concerned that the whole child can be better served by the rich stimulation of an active family environment. Families provide security, stable relationships, a chance to live in a community and to face adulthood with maturity." How about that! I suppose I should admire his words. How wonderful that someone had admitted and tried to correct an inequity. I dared to hope that the Good Shepherd had also shut down.

With information gleaned from my Children's Aid Society work a few years back I wrote to Ann Bell, adoption coordinator for Saint John, asking for any family history or record, sending along a copy of the Welfare Bureau missive, stressing "I have never been adopted and I am entitled to. . ." The closing of St. Vincent's might well facilitate a satisfying answer and now was the time to try and get it. For three months there was no reply. I wrote again, insisting that at least my letter deserved acknowledgment ". . . for I was direct in my request, either information is available or it isn't. Kindly review my letter." It took several calls before Ann Bell explained, "I'm alone at this job and very busy. I'm out of the office often. I am sorry."

On a spur-of-the-moment whim I decided I'd go to Saint John during the summer holidays. I hadn't been there since 1949. That year, Julian's aunt had come to stay with us and she was happiest looking after the children, so I had taken a series of office jobs: for an accountant at tax time, federal election work and latterly, permanent work for R. A. Hanright, Consulting Engineer where his private secretary, by being strict, instilled in me a work ethic that would see me through many jobs in my life. I lacked training and knowledge and Marion was a model of perfection in procedures, grooming and dress. She demanded perfection in the specifications I typed, eleven onion skin copies, all to be corrected if a comma was out of place. I welcomed her rules, learning daily, whereas when the nuns had enforced any rule on me, my resentment flourished.

I had earned a vacation but more than that, I had the most natural urge to show my children to someone, preferably my mother. As that was impossible I took Mary and Tommy on the train with me and I showed them off to Mother Monica, of all people. Mary was five and Tommy three-and-a-half that summer. I took them to the city market for dulse and we went to King Square to watch the pigeons. To my great joy we found Harry McGlyn sitting on a bench in the Old Burial Ground. Children coming from school called to him fondly, "Hi Old Glyn." He leaned forward on a white cane and I could see when he took a watch from his vest pocket and squinted at the large white face, he was nearly blind. Joyously I sat beside him and spoke for a while before I identified myself and proudly presented my two babies. He looked old; still the gentle smile was the same. It was wonderful to see him again. Mary and Tommy chased pigeons while we talked.

"Can you tell me anything about myself? Doris said she wasn't my mother, another time she said she was."

"Don't let her fool you," he answered.

That didn't tell me anything. I tried another angle.

"Why did you and Doris take me?"

"She was afraid to have a baby."

So they did "take" me. "Why didn't we stay together?"

"I couldn't please her. If I gave her the world it wouldn't be enough. There was no pleasing her."

"Do you know my family name? Can you remember it?"

"I never knew it. She didn't either, I'm sure of that."

He gave short answers to direct questions so I left him alone. He was having fun convincing Mary and Tommy they could catch a pigeon if they put salt on its tail. Then he took a new half-dollar from his vest pocket, no apron this time, and pressed it into my hand with such delight it almost seemed he had been waiting for this day. I hugged him and choked up. He was emotional too. I promised to bring the children to his home next day. His sister still lived there and he said she would cook a Restigouche salmon.

"But right now," I told them, "we're going to the Sugar Bowl where Mommy used to buy candy when Grandpa gave her fifty cents." I showed them the treats, the same great big suckers, green, black, red, caramel and peppermint, hard hats and big pieces of fresh fudge. "I saved my sucker sticks for knitting with string," I told them. "See the small hammer? That's for breaking hard candy and peanut brittle. Here's five butter balls for a cent and jelly babies and a whole box of Hundreds and Thousands for another penny." I couldn't believe the Sugar Bowl was still there. I remembered keeping my money in my shoe for safekeeping. If Sister Juda saw it or somebody told her, she'd ask, "Where did you get that?

"I had it," I always said. The orphans all said that—I had it. Sure enough it was a saucy answer from a most willful girl. Mary tugged my skirt, I laughed at the big wax buck-teeth in her tiny mouth, breaking the reverie of long ago memories of Sister Juda. I told her that the teeth used to be my favourite when I had pennies to spend because when the fun and the flavour were gone you could chew the wax for a long time.

I took them to see Sister Rosa too. She was older and smaller and still insisted with emphasis that I had no right to information about my mother. I couldn't tolerate her *ask me no questions and I'll tell you no lies* approach. It seemed to me that a simple humane attitude such as *we're sorry about your state of life, it happened to a lot of people, mothers moved on and we had no contact with them. That was encouraged.* I'd understand that instead of that god-awful condemnation, you have no rights, it's the law. Not only was it stupid, it lacked humanity and kindness. I gave up on the Saint John connection then and let my life in general get in the way of my determination.

I was happy I went to Saint John in 1949 for Harry McGlyn died that winter. Now I'd try once more. This first summer of our separation Brien was excited about going to camp on Lake Simcoe for two weeks. Tom would be a counselor there. Mary had won the job of lifeguard at our apartment complex and would care for Molly Ann. I took the train to Saint John to see Ann Bell, to try again to find any trace or vestige of my mother's existence or whereabouts. On the phone, explaining that she was doing the job on her own, she sounded young, but showed compassion and I liked her when we met.

"First of all," she advised, "if I were you I'd find out where the orphanage records were sent when it closed." Surely she must have that information in her job and like everyone else, tried to keep people like me at bay.

"I know that," I said impatiently. "I've written to the chancery office twice, that's where they are. I wrote directly to Father Walsh. He ignored me. Everyone ignores perfectly natural questions as though they were foolish and not worth answering."

"Please don't feel that way, Mrs. McBeath. They have never been receptive to orphans looking for information, they avoid confrontation as long as possible. You wouldn't believe the number of lost children from your time. Can you imagine the ramifications of that era? Leave it with me for today and call me tomorrow."

Saint John always presents an eerie presence on a foggy morning. Just as I remembered it, I awoke to a fog-blanketed city and felt right at home. When we met, Ann Bell handed me a photocopy of a one-page record from the Infant's Home. "It's the only thing I've been able to get," she said. "There wasn't much record-keeping back then. It's sad for me and I realize it's frustrating for you not to know about your natural background. I regret I can't be of more help."

"Why this is fantastic! I'm so excited." We studied the paper together, proof that my orphanage days were not illusory. Child number five hundred and eighty-three. Child's name, Molly Shannon, where and when I was born, where and when baptized. Mother's name - Kathleen Shannon. Religion - R.C. Address - Ireland Cand. (or Gord). Father's name - Francis O'Hara. Religion - R.C. Address - Bresak, Ireland. Occupation - Mental doctor. Recommended by: Father Savage. Taken by: Mrs. H.G. McGlyn, March 22, 1926.

One word couldn't be understood looking like Cand. or Gord. "Maybe it means Canada," the woman suggested. It wasn't Cork. I dared to ask the big question once again, "Is there anything anywhere to tell me where my mother went? Where I might find her or what her married name is?"

She shook her head. There was nothing to lead me to my mother. Still, these new facts were exciting. Francis O'Hara, mental doctor, Bresak. Knowing that name was a link to my father. I was not a mythical birth. The absence of a father in my life had hurt deeply though I had never admitted it to anyone. *O'Hara is a nice name, and very Irish.* I tried it on . . . *Molly O'Hara.* I liked it. This was a most exciting piece of paper. I went to find a lawyer. If there were other clues in Saint John, I was ready to pay someone to find them. Then I realized I didn't want to part with this old-yet-new connection with my beginnings.

"By all means we'll make a copy for us."

The lawyer, Lou Gagnon, decried the sadness of my formative years with the so-called penitents at the Good Shepherd Home. "The nuns should have told your own mother when you were returned and they should have kept her on record as long as you were unadopted. It was a crime of indifference that you were left homeless and a worse crime that your developing years were spent in a laundry. How horrible."

He said all that and more. I was putting the matter in good hands.

When I went to Waterloo Street that afternoon, expecting to visit Mother Monica, there was nothing there, just a parking lot and the stone steps I had taken to freedom years earlier. A giddy feeling took hold as though something good had swooped in and annihilated a tyranny, all that remained was a pleasant vista, albeit a parking lot.

I sat on the steps. Twenty years earlier I had walked out a door now gone, down these five steps detached from that door and from that strange abnormal life I once led. *I'm better off now, I've been loved, really loved and that love gave me my children who are everything in the world to me.* I went into the cathedral next door, up the long aisle in a wave of nostalgia; out through the Virgin's Chapel to the churchyard where the asters still pushed through the blacktop. The orphans used to play hide-and-seek there in the architectural corners. The gate to the sister's courtyard at St. Vincent's was unlocked so I ventured in. It might have been twenty years earlier. Everything looked exactly the same, especially the grotto and the statue of Our Lady of Lourdes, lovingly washed to a gleam by the nuns. The orphans used this yard when they went in procession to the chapel in fine weather or to the cathedral for confessions. The poor weather route to the chapel was through the large basement kitchen with its dank furnace areas and coal bins, shadowy stairs and frightful doors. As long as we live, I thought, every St. Vincent's girl will remember the night the girls screamed. Some small person in the front ranks saw a shadow and screamed, then everyone screamed and turned and stampeded the long distance back to the recreation room. A hundred meditating nuns in the chapel heard the cries. We were not sent back to the chapel that day.

Down the long outside steps, now covered with red outdoor carpet, I ventured along the basement hall to the refectory, treading the same shiny red brick floor, seeing the same worn wooden tables, only fewer, with peeling paint on the thick legs. No backless chairs now, no tin plates or mugs. The same small basement windows, still barred; I watched feet walking along Cliff Street and remembered my childhood yearning to go with anyone walking by. Up one flight of stairs, the rec room seemed smaller, the benches gone. It was now a sparsely furnished club or study room, bookshelves where the rosary rack and bad mark card used to hang. Not a soul was there. Up the long narrow flight from the rec room, the old deviltry of my youth conjured up the specter of Sister Juda puffing her way down the stairs. I waited reverently while the vision passed, then tore up the stairs two at a time as if I were ten or twelve again. I was set to charge another giddy flight to the upper dorm when two men wearing soutanes entered the hall.

"Oh, oh. Am I trespassing in a monastery or a seminary?"

"No, no," they laughed. "St. Vincent's is a residence for graduate students. There are just a few here at present for summer school."

No one could tell me why or when the Good Shepherd had disappeared, just that the nuns went to Toronto and the girls were *sent out*. Now that was an amusing phrase from the past. All my young life things had been *sent in*— clothes, furniture, treats, pails of peanut butter, barrels of apples. How bizarre that in the end the girls were *sent out*.

From St. Vincent's I took a walk through the cavernous city market in memory of Old Glyn. Still in good use after nearly a hundred years, but different from modern-day markets: business was carried on in the entrepreneurial tradition by permanent retailers, not farmers. One was apt to discover anything here, stalls laden with fine cheeses, buttermilk and headcheese, the aroma of fresh bread, Digby Bay scallops, fresh fish, fiddleheads, fruits of the sea and dulse, a tangy, purple sea vegetable gathered along the rocks of the Bay of Fundy and dried in the sun. I loved its peculiar taste and bought a small bag for more than a dollar; while savoring its particular fresh and salty flavour, I reminisced about buying a large bag of dulse for six cents. The orphans would spread a small piece with their tongues over a single tooth, or two or three teeth, then smile a toothless smile.

Feeling close to the spirit of Harry McGlyn, I roamed through the old building that resembled an inverted galley hull, built of hand-hewn timbers by shipbuilders nearly a hundred years back. This was where I'd seen my foster father. I had wanted so much from him, family, love and security. A woman appeared in front of me, lights glancing off her golden brown curls and big glasses, her excited words dismissing my memories of the only father I could claim.

"Molly," she called. "Is it you? Molly McGlyn? Can I believe my eyes?"

I smiled first, showing a big black space in my teeth, then flicked the dulse away and we laughed hard at the memory. It was Mildred, one of the many girls my age at St, Vincent's. We had always been partners in the ranks that started with the wee girls at the front, through the different heights, to the tallest at the back. We were the same height and sat together in the refectory and knelt together in the chapel. We had been sort of friends. She was easygoing, we all called her "the judge." I don't remember why.

"We went around together, remember? Recall when we used to sneak out and come here? You always got money from your father. Oh my God, remember when we'd sneak out to get cookies from your aunt Bertha at Mayor McLaren's house and after that, Hazen's Castle? I can't believe this."

"Oh, I remember! Here, have some dulse."

"Look at the barley toys I just bought. Take some. I never see these in the stores at home.

"Where's home?"

"Toronto, I'm visiting my daughter here. Would you believe I had a daughter before I got married?

"Really?" I wouldn't be so inclined to announce the fact. "And you kept her?"

"No. Yeah, I had to give her up, she's adopted but we know each other and we see each other in the summer when we can."

"That's important. Good for you."

Barley toys were hard candies, clear yellow and red animal shapes of all sorts that we got at Christmas: horses, cows, bears, kittens, birds. We'd suck them for hours giving them different shapes, making them last. I bought a bag for old times' sake.

"Gad, I even ate tooth powder when we were kids I craved sugar so much."

"Let's go some place and talk, get caught up. I live in Toronto now too. Let's have a drink."

So we had a drink to the memories.

"Remember the book you got from the I.O.D.E. for being smart, she took it away?"

"Oh, I got that at school in the hospital. God I was proud of the inscription—*To an outstanding pupil in the City Schools*. Juda gave it to my foster mother who never gave it back to me."

"I think Juda hated you."

"I thought she did. Sometimes now I give her the benefit of the doubt; in that milieu I deserved it, maybe. I was stubborn. It's funny to hear you say it though, I still believe that she punished us, me especially, for her own personal bias against the sins of our mothers."

"Wasn't she good at sewing though, teaching us embroidery and darning; she kept us at it, but how sarcastic she was. Molly, at times she seemed to cut me right in two. And banging our heads with her thimble and pinches that left our arms black and blue."

"Yes, how we'd push our sleeves up showing our bruised arms to each other, like a badge." Instinctively I rubbed my arms to assuage that memory.

"You look good, Molly; you were so sickly, did you get over that?"

"Pretty well. I have what's called bronchiectasis. Do you remember when I had pneumonia when we were small, and my times in the County Hospital? It's from then."

"It sounds bad."

"No. It has a troublesome name but it's not bad if you understand it and take care. I enjoy perfect health."

Dozens of names were recalled, some I had totally forgotten. "Remember Emma Mae?"

"Oh, Emma Mae and bath night!" She was in charge of bathing. She was the homeliest girl of all, heavy with protruding teeth and bulging eyes, a receding chin and her hair fastened with bobby pins in little dips along her cheek, black and straight, a caricature from the comics. We'd line up, five at a time, each wrapped in a used sheet as we'd waddle towards her. She'd throw us quickly into one of the two tubs. "Sit!" she'd say when we could barely ease ourselves into the scalding water, or sometimes cold and dirty water from several other bathers. She'd scrub our little limbs with a big floor brush and yellow laundry soap called OK soap and before we could close our eyes or mouth we were pummeled in the face with a soapy flannel. Some dared to bawl. Then Emma Mae would hold the sheet up and lift us out. We'd go to the toilet cubicle with a bundle of clean clothes and dry off with the sheet. We didn't have towels. When we got older she'd tell us impatiently to "warsh yourself" and when the wrapped sheet trailed behind and a bare bottom showed, she'd order, "get onder that sheet, you." I could see Sister Juda sitting in the hall outside the bathroom, stitching stocking mates together before they went to the laundry and putting names on clothes with a purple indelible pencil that left a stain on her lip when she wet it. And she'd keep saying, "Don't dawdle, you can't dawdle."

"Guess what Mildred? Now I dawdle and I love to watch my children dawdle and I make sure they have all the hot water and all the time they want in the bath. And guess what? I put a warm cloth on my face and neck at night and I coo to my heart's content still. It's lovely."

"Me too."

"'Woe betide you,'" I said, imitating Emma Mae's favourite threat. "Remember she called us trollops and 'rabscallions', imagine rapscallions, or worse, trollops. We were only little kids. I often think about the orphans' picnic. It's so good to see you again, Mildred." She signaled for another drink.

Could anyone forget the orphans' picnic? Once a year we were herded off to St. Joseph's school with the orphan boys from St. Patrick's Orphanage at Silver Falls and *marched* to Union Station for a train ride to Torryburn on picnic day. I hated being paraded, but there was a certain exhilaration as we stepped along to the charity band and we got into the mood, all greedy for a good time, for the balls and dolls, kazoos and whistles and the little tin wheels that made sparks, for the games and races, for the hot chicken meal and Washington pie and strawberry drinks. Somebody put a lot of effort into the orphans' picnic; probably the Knights of Columbus. Every morning was wet in Saint John. How we prayed it wouldn't be on that day.

"I think the best part of the orphans' picnic was the train ride home. We were so happy and tired out and we still had to walk from Union Station to Cliff Street."

"How about that boy you liked from the Silver Falls orphanage? Have you ever heard anything about him?"

"Oh never." But I remembered. I had noticed Billy McCarthy every year at the picnic. He seemed tanned, had curly hair, a nice smile and white teeth. I talked about him so the others teased me and dared me to get his autograph. I did, proof again of my willful ways.

"He wrote in my autograph book, Mildred. It's funny now. We were so anxious behind the bushes that he wrote upside down on two pages. I still have it. Someone saw us and for a long time afterward Sister Juda took me aside during recreation and asked me who I had intercourse with. I honestly didn't know what she was talking about but she poked me in the stomach and finally I had to admit to what I thought was 'discourse' with poor Billy. God knows what they said to him or did to him."

"What on earth did he write?"

"Well, it was childish and it's silly but I still have it. It goes, *The Picnic, August 9, 1938. My dearest Molly* (imagine that!), *Old Casey Jones one stormy night tried to get to heaven on the tail of a kite, the kite's tail broke and Casey fell, instead of going to heaven he had to go to hell. ha ha, Billy.* Our focus was all on heaven and hell then. I said to Billy that day, 'I always look for you at the picnic.' He said, 'That's nice, I look for you too. Maybe we'll know each other when we get out.' We were thirteen."

"Remember the time we learned to dance the minuet for Bishop LeBlanc, the time he came back from Rome?"

"Sure. Even today when I hear *Minuet in G* I hum to myself, *three and one and two and three* thinking how we tried so hard to dance the little steps for him, who was so pompous, so righteous, accepting our childlike effort, maybe condescending. Who knows? We were happy kids to be pleasing him. The music was so unlike our lives, it was light and free and happy." Could I be blamed for being so critical? Maybe then I didn't find fault so readily. It's likely the resentment has grown over the years.

Mildred looked marvelous. "It must be nearly twenty-five years since you ran away."

"Almost," I answered quietly. "Do you know what? In my dreams I'm still running down Cliff Street with my doll trunk. In my dream I'm not fretting, I'm liberated. I'm smiling. That stuff will be in my subconscious forever. And I have a recurrent dream of Sister Juda coming down the rec room stairs. She doesn't walk, she just floats from top to bottom. Today when I went into that place I stood aside at the foot of the stairs and *felt* her presence."

"Recall how she strapped us, especially you. Remember how she lined the bed-wetters up every morning to 'take your medicine'. Jesus! I can still see you walking around with the goddamn white welts on your red wrist, and you holding your arm until it stopped hurting. I always stuck up for you, we did for each other, kinda like sisters."

"Hold out your hand" Sister Juda croaked with her thick leather strap ready. We knew the familiar command but no child ever offered her hand for strapping without being told "Hold out your hand." And if we drew back, a natural reflex when someone was about to hurt you, the strapping, in the privacy of her cell, on the bare bottom, was worse. We'd howl in protest to let the others hear. In trouble that deep you could go the limit.

"Remember she'd put a pillow over your head if you screamed, then sit on it and hit so hard you could hear her beads flying and her sleeves swishing. That was hard on her, ha-ha. It wasn't funny then but it's funny now. I can't say out loud what I'd like to call her."

"Mildred, beatings were a way of life especially for the bed-wetters, we had the devil to pay. I'd take the four big safety pins out of the corners of my quilted pad, rinse it out at that deep sink and hang that red rubber sheet on the foot of my bed. I got over my shame, I had to, I had no control over wetting the bed."

"I don't think those nuns would have kicked dogs but they sure gave us no affection, it seemed so easy for them to dislike us."

"Maybe some were dedicated but what training did they have? Their power over us far exceeded their ability and they certainly weren't affectionate." I sighed, remembering.

When strapping didn't cure the bed-wetters, an even more public punishment was devised—kneeling at the front of the refectory during breakfast, without food from the night before, arms outstretched in the form of a cross, wet sheets pinned to the miscreant's shoulders. I was a fainter and often fainted from hunger.

I felt like screaming Enough! when Mildred recalled other times. I groaned and thanked God I was only passing through Saint John. *The theft of our childhood*, I thought. *Nobody's children*. Shouldn't it have been the most natural thing to love innocence? To comfort a child with a touch? They called themselves Brides of Christ. Weren't we God's children? Maybe the cold discipline had taught me the possibilities within myself. I had learned to endure.

When we parted, I walked towards Britain Street. I'd never contacted Aunt Elsa since the night I ran away but I wanted to see her. It was a slum, a shambles, and the sidewalk-hugging houses spilled urchins. When I inquired at Elsa's house, the response was, "Fuck off."

I left Saint John when the tide was turning in the wide and foaming Saint John River and I watched the landscape in this history-proud city drop away outside the train windows. Through valleys and rolling hills, fields of daisies and buttercups, pasture land and verdant potato fields, the train clattered along, the land slipping into the summer afternoon. The fields brought back memories of the times I would stretch a blade of grass between my thumbs and blow a piercing whistle, watching heads turn and the nuns become agitated. I would turn my head too, feigning innocence, laughing up my sleeve for having penetrated the gloom of childhood with a forbidden whistle. Whistling made the Blessed Virgin Mary cry, they said! Chewing gum did, too! And crossing your legs!

The long, shrill train whistle, reminiscent of my first train ride from Saint John, brought heartache for my failure at marriage. However, regret could not alter anything that Julian or I had done. The train moved slower through a little village. Wooden houses and open barns appeared and flew into the gathering darkness and the blurred lights from secluded farmhouse windows made me lonesome for Julian in my life.

Long talks with adult adoptees who have given years of their lives
to the frustrating search for their past have convinced me that
we cannot continue to let the past rule the present. Surely if a
young adult who has grown up with love has the strength to
accept the reality of her beginnings, her birth parents and
adoptive parents can do so as well.

Margaret Mead

TORONTO ＞ 1968

NOTHING COMPARES with sustenance and humour for healing; the ability to laugh at one's self is good medicine too. So what could be better for a working single parent than an invitation to dinner from a friend who could toss pun and rhyme about brilliantly? My dearest friend Christina Dow, whom we called Ina, had transferred to Toronto. A long-time civil servant, she had facilitated my job with the Children's Aid Society in Niagara when Julian was still at Osgoode Hall. Her mother, Marion, with whom Ina then lived, had spent a few of her early years in the kitchens of Stirling Castle in Scotland and was a connoisseur of good eating. The children knew Ina well; her sense of humour, original and waggish, never offended. Molly Ann called gleefully after me, "It'll be a laughing dinner for sure, Mom."

She looked wonderful in a blue tartan gown that softened her too-red hair. Homely, wholesome and candid, there was that old feeling of being safe with a friend as we shared aperitifs in her firelit den. Lively *Eine Kleine Nachtmusik* soared around me but my equanimity of the moment was broken when she asked in her pleasant brogue, "Why don't you run in the provincial election next year?"

"Is this your new brand of humour, Ina?"

"I've never been more serious. Will you listen to me?"

"I will."

"The female count in the Legislature is infinitesimal, a mere one out of a hundred and eight and that one is only the third woman to win at the polls in Ontario, ever." Her brown eyes were steady, waiting for the impact of her words. "Women in Ontario obtained the right to be candidates in 1919 and the first woman was not elected until 1943."

"So?"

"For your information, twenty-five years later, we are represented by only one woman and 263 men in Federal Parliament in Ottawa. Regretfully there is a tradition that women can run but not win. We are not part of any decision-making process because we are not *there*. Men debate all the issues which bear directly on our lives. Besides, you could use a challenge to put your life in a more satisfying perspective. You sound bitter some of the time."

"That's an old habit that goes back to not getting my own way when I was growing up. I *am* getting better."

"Sure Molly, bitter and bitter every day."

"If you say so. What about experience? You're not serious."

"Where do you think one gets experience? Get in and get it. You've done enough community stuff to think on your feet. Your Children's Aid work, that was good experience. There's major reforms due in child welfare, there's developing interest in adoption procedures, hordes expressing hostility to closed records. In the new Child Welfare Act last year the most fundamental things about adoption weren't raised. Besides, I believe you could make a difference."

I had always hoped that someone in politics would raise the issue of adoption as it was defined, especially the concept of adoption beyond the coming-of-age, but it couldn't be me. Without the least intention of being serious I said, "You are funny, just which party label do you have in mind? Independent Feminist?"

"Don't get fidgety now. You were an active Young Liberal once. Your picture was in the paper when finance minister Abbott was in Niagara. That gets noticed. But it's your Children's Aid work, volunteer and otherwise, that will help you."

"I wasn't active, as you say. I went along with Julian because he was, that's all. Children's Aid? That wasn't long, I didn't make a career of it. It's impossible; I know nothing about the procedure or the issues or party dogma. Being a woman wouldn't be the biggest hurdle, I *do not* have enough education."

"The time is right," she insisted. "There are nine new ridings with the current redistribution. The hundred and eight seats become a hundred and seventeen to be filled. Think about it."

"No way. I'm interested in child welfare and opportunity for women, but tell me, whose idea is this? How could I afford it?"

She sipped her scotch, neat as usual, and her unwavering stare was familiar. "It's my idea. I presented your running as a matter of interest to one of my clubs. To a member they vowed support. I can't help in any visible way, I have a non-political job. But I can be your sounding board and your friend. Oh yes, it's expensive but there is help. The party has a special fund, *Women in Nomination.*"

"No! There'd be other requisites, formalities, legal qualifications and education."

"Simply, anyone qualified as an elector is qualified as a candidate. "The most common source of disqualification is 'corrupt and illegal practices.' Any person holding or executing any contract with the government— members of Her Majesty's Forces and civil servants, that's me—cannot be a member of parliament, may not even be a candidate. Candidates should have talent and interest, and," she held her glass in a festive gesture, "no *exploitable* weaknesses."

"What happens to all those people who lose an election?"

"They just bind up the shattered ego and the financial wounds and decide if they'll try again. You're lucky. You'd have your studies to fall back on. How's the course?"

"It's interesting but slow. I've earned a third of my credits towards a degree at York."

"That seems fast enough to me."

"I've just finished a third level course in Celtic Studies at the University of Toronto. I liked it. I'm doing modern Canadian fiction this year and I'm obliged to read a list of books but not the books I prefer. Essays take so much of my time. There's something else I'd rather be doing. I may postpone the courses for a while."

"What for example?"

"I want to finish something I started to write."

"What?"

"A book. I've put years of notes in chronological order and I'm obsessed with the idea. I ask myself if I want to get a degree so my children will be there to applaud, or do I want to finish what I've dreamed about for many years. I haven't time for both. Getting a degree isn't going to change my opportunities for work at my age, my book is more important to me. But that's a story I'll tell you another time."

"What's it about? I'm amazed. Won't you tell me now?"

"I can't. Not yet. You know I grew up in New Brunswick. I don't have a basic education and no matter how hard I study now, the mold was cast. Deprivation of all high school subjects is a gap that can't be filled."

"The upshot of all education is being able to do what you think you must do or want to do. You're able to take on politics; education's not an issue."

"It's an issue with me. Have you ever listened to yourself on tape?"

"Yes. Nobody likes the sound of their own voice taped."

"Ina, when I moved to my new apartment in the Colonnade, my children had a housewarming party. It was fabulous, full of laughter. They each took a turn and, with excessive detail and humour, pinpointed the jobs I've had and the laughable things about them. It was astonishing. I wasn't aware that they were taping but when I listened to the tape alone I laughed out loud for two hours. Two startling facts emerged. I'd had eight jobs in six years, and hearing my own voice on tape was terrible evidence of lack of upbringing—I mean it, Maritime colloquialisms, lack of confidence and, as you say, a bitterness. My voice was flat and whiny, even while we laughed. But, it was so brilliant being with them. I felt as though I had risen to their level of competence."

"You have something wonderful in those children."

"How well I know. Hearing them roast the series of jobs I've had out of necessity, I sensed their pride. They paid attention to my life as a single working mom. They understood all along."

"How's your present job?"

"It's good working for the NHL; and expansion is definitely interesting. It's up to me to make something of it. I will."

"Do the children see their father?"

"On a social basis I think and on family occasions. I'm well aware that they are adult now and may relate to him and may be friends. Still, it's sad that at this stage of our children's lives Julian and I do not have each other."

"You wouldn't go back?" she asked skeptically.

"No. I love where I'm living; that area between St. Mary Street, my first room when I came to Toronto, and Prince Arthur Avenue, my second. The ambiance and style of the Bay-Bloor area inspires me, I'm at home there."

The whole university atmosphere had a bittersweet tinge. What I didn't have as a youngster I was realizing now as a mature student and through the children. Mary and Paul were married and living in Baltimore. He was doing his Ph.D. at Johns Hopkins University. Mary was enrolled at Notre

Dame of Maryland and teaching as well. Tom was working for IBM, his wife Sharon in the chartered accountants course. Brien was just entering the University of Massachusetts on a partial hockey scholarship. Molly Ann would go to St. Joseph's High School in the fall. Life was satisfying in the district where I had lived, loved and married. It was good to be back, like having another chance.

"Grab this opportunity at politics, Molly, it couldn't come at a better time for you. Was it Bacon who said, *Opportunity turneth a bald noodle after she hath presented her locks in front, and no hold taken?*"

"Look, maybe I can help behind the scenes." I remembered the exhaustive three-year study on child welfare, and while the new Act had made advances, so much of it did not work. For one thing the religious crux was still there and making children wards of the Protestant or Catholic Children's Aid divided them on a religious basis, limiting their chances of being adopted.

I longed to tell Ina that these matters were intimate to me, but my illegitimacy was a topic I could not discuss without chagrin. If I could find my mother then the yearning, embarrassment and frustration would take flight. I'd be so proud of being her daughter everyone would know.

"I know you'd do things your way," she pestered. "You might even lend the House a vibrancy. You can be tactless, that's not always bad. Just don't be intimidated."

"That sounds like a speech. Are you finished?"

"Yes."

"Will you give up now? I can't be a politician."

"Okay, okay." So she asked me why I shut myself away socially. *She's curious about Julian*, I thought. He did spend Christmas, Thanksgiving and birthdays with us. As much as I had loved the man I married, I resented what we had become. I did not show that pique to my children and always welcomed him to family affairs, which he enjoyed.

"There's an old expression, Ina, kick against the pricks, and literally, I've had to do that."

"Touché, Molly. But you have to be open-minded."

"You're a fine one to talk, you don't date."

"That's different," she snapped. "I've always been single, you haven't."

"I'm ashamed to tell you how much I've tried to find friendship but the price is always sex. Men don't pause between the glance and the grab, you know."

"If you say so."

She wouldn't want to know about the characters with whom I tried to be sociable, especially when I had a downtown office for the soccer league, open to all comers to stir up interest in the game. Like meeting Cliff, an actor, in the Cav-a-Bob bar for a drink. He liked my blue silk dress and said so.

"You have hardly any makeup on," he noted.

"I don't use much," I said, scanning the familiar room for a familiar face.

"Don't look away when I'm talking to you." His narcissism was too much. The pianist played a love song. Cliff held my hand and sang, *The Second Time Around.* I snickered.

"You're the first woman who laughed when I said I loved her."

"Do you say it often?"

He shifted. He had something on his mind. It was his fifteen-year-old daughter. "She needs a mother," he whined.

"Me too," I murmured. "Me too!"

"What?"

"Nothing."

There were others like that. A detective named Martin who presented me with miniature gold handcuffs. "For your charm bracelet," he said. "Seventy-five dollars," he lamented. After a date with a man called Peter, I received a muffled, anonymous phone call. The voice hissed the most unpleasant words. I sent the handcuff charm back to detective Martin's home next day.

As for my date with Peter, the conversation went like this:

"Little Peter likes you."

"That's nice."

"He couldn't go to sleep last night. Poor little bugger just sobbed 'Daddy, I want a mother.'"

Sure. Me too, me too!

"Ina, too often when I try to be sociable, or human you could say, I find myself cornered with a foolish, self-centred man, some even say, *You have that look, you promised.* If one more would-be lover tells me he wished we had met when we were younger, I'll scream. You'd give forth yourself with a few classic puns if you knew about some of the situations I've been in. Even my hairdresser slobbers into my neck as he holds my coat. 'T'se your friend, I geev you everyting, I want notting,' and feels my behind. Don't judge me on the subject of sociability with men."

"I won't, I'm sorry. Surely there's decent men out there."

"Certainly, all married to fortunate women. But saying they're fortunate doesn't mean they're all great marriages. I secretly dated a good man a few times and it was so curative. He referred to his wife and Julian as 'the madam and the madman' and we laughed a lot."

"Were you living with Julian then?"

"Sure, but Julian's neglect invited it. There was a little bar over the Niagara River on a country road in New York State; we called it Schotzies for some reason, probably a parody on the proper name. We talked for hours. At times we danced to a nickelodeon, you know, Sinatra, Mathis, Andy Williams, slow love songs, so simple and calming like *The Twelfth of Never*. I still have a dress I wore then. It's an alive memory, Ina."

"Were you discreet?"

"Did Julian care about me? He seldom came home to us and in my gut I knew I was being vengeful. So what? When a liaison is furtive, Ina, it's emotional, then it's dangerous, and it can end up heartbreaking. We knew that."

I'd said enough. Ina was sensitive.

*D*uring the next months I had a lot of enthusiasm for getting involved, through Ina, with interesting people who were serious about child welfare issues. Surprised at their intensity, I took it personally and was grateful.

"See how *you* can make a difference," she told me. "It's friends, it's numbers. Take ten people with ten friends, it's a pyramid and things get done. Keep in there."

I read everything I could find about women candidates. It fascinated me. One newspaper suspended its long-standing partiality and asked:

> Is it plain old male chauvinism keeping the number of women candidates down or do women lack the confidence to jump into the political fray? There are seventeen women running in the upcoming provincial election from a total of three hundred and forty-nine candidates. The figure is startlingly low relative to the percentage of women in the population and in the work force. Still these are the early years of contemporary feminism and there is interest in womens' achievements and changing status. Consideration must be given to the need for a better female presence and women should join forces to elect a more equitable balance of lady politicians.

Election day was gray and cheerless and the rain kept many voters at home; nevertheless it was intense. The Conservative Party won again, its eighth consecutive victory since 1943, but their majority of the last parliament was cut to sixty-nine seats. The Liberals gained six seats, giving them twenty-eight, and the New Democratic Party received a surge of support winning twenty seats, an increase of thirteen. I rejoiced with the NDP. They, above all, were determined to change the Child Welfare Act. Three women were elected to sit in Ontario's twenty-eighth parliament, two for Metropolitan Toronto and one for Hamilton. Ontario was in command of her own resources and established beyond question as the senior sharer in the nation. Like all things else technology had come to government. There were hordes of statisticians, coded libraries, computers, new social perspectives but still, for some, sealed birth records and legal/fraudulent birth certificates.

*In dealing with the state we ought to remember that its institutions
are not aboriginal, though they existed before we were born; that
they are not superior to the citizen; that every one of them was once
the act of a single man; every law and usage was a man's expedient
to meet a particular case; that they are all imitable, all alterable;
we may make as good; we may make better. The law is only a
memorandum . . . the statute stands there to say, yesterday we
agreed so and so, but how feel ye this article today?*

Emerson

TORONTO ≻ THE SEVENTIES

WITH OR WITHOUT government assistance (or government impediments), adoptees and the less fortunate were going to persist in fighting for that which is due to anyone by just claim and moral principles. However, in the new assembly of the Ontario government, a proposal to revamp the adoption process and to legislate a newer form of open adoption was vetoed by the cabinet. The New Democratic Party had drafted an amendment to statutes governing Access to Adoption Documents and Original Birth Information for Adults. The standing committee on social welfare had spent long days of persistent debate on the criteria for: a) Access for Compelling Reasons; b) Access on Demand; and c) Controlled Access to birth data. Now Bill 114, an Act to revise the Child Welfare Act, was before the House on the Order Paper for a Second Reading. Many of the Members had spoken to it, many against it. From the government seats the debate had been hostile and taunting. Some even introduced controversial facets to sidetrack the issue and wear everyone down with the negative aspects.

I was in the Visitor's Gallery in the Legislature of Ontario at Queen's Park and felt an overwhelming reverence for the grandeur and power of the old House. The rich red carpet and polished brass chandeliers, originally gas-fed, were magnificent. The royal coat of arms behind the Speaker's chair was carved from a solid piece of mahogany. Original hand-carved work on the walls, of Canadian sycamore and mahogany, was covered for the time being by soundboard to improve the acoustics of the House. A mere eighty-two years ago, a lunatic asylum had been torn down on this site and some said the ghosts of three female patients and one old soldier still walked the tower and the halls, maybe pausing in unoccupied seats today.

The NDP had brought in an amendment to Bill 114 aimed at satisfying all the progressive thinkers in the assembly. The dissenters were vociferous. The issue should be totally devoid of partisan politics with a free, non-party vote, but the outcome was certainly predetermined in a House where the count was 69-28-20. The Conservatives would vote as a bloc and simply veto the bill.

People milled about beyond the oak door to the Chamber. The burnished warmth of the imposing door closing suddenly brought to my mind the horror of the old oak door at the Good Shepherd Convent as it closed behind Aunt Elsa. But then, the unmatched freedom on the day I left the Good Shepherd Convent could be symbolic if, when the Ontario Legislature ended this day's session and that magnificent door closed again, there would be freedom for adoptees to know about their biological background.

The pomp and circumstance of the Speaker's daily procession to the Chamber began and he placed the mace on the table, symbolizing the freedom and powers of Parliament, indicating that the House was in session.

Ross McClellan, NDP for Bellwoods, had moved an amendment that "subsection 1 of section 80 of the bill be struck out and changes made, specifically, that the Registrar General shall, where an application is made in the prescribed form by an adopted child who is 18 or more years of age, supply to the adopted child on payment of the prescribed fee such information as is necessary to enable the adopted child to obtain a certified copy of the record, before the adoption, of his or her birth. . ." He said, "Let me deal with what this amendment will do—it will provide information with respect to an adult adoptee's birth record under what I believe is a very restrictive set of conditions. This is not a revolutionary change. It is, if I can use the words of the honourable minister, a very reasonable and cautious change . . ."

"You're not quoting me," The Honourable Keith Norton called out.

"Yes, I am quoting the Minister of Community and Social Services. You said it was reasonable and cautious and it is reasonable and cautious."

"I said this amendment was more cautious than the first change."

Mr. McClellan addressed the House in a long speech, quoting from the study directly, reiterating openness and honesty, rights and change saying,

"The question of coming to terms with one's own identity is a normal and natural part of the adoptive process. There is nothing abnormal about wanting to know who you are."

The Honourable Bette Stephenson, Minister of Health and Welfare, was decidedly hostile to the Bill. Her denouncement had been delivered in her well-known *sotto voce* and might have been less formidable had she shouted it. She told the House she had wrestled with the subject for some time and it was an issue in which the government must show leadership. "I speak in opposition to the amendment as it has been proposed."

"Hear, hear!" the government members shouted and thumped their desks. The minister paused for effect and looked around the room deliberately.

"Why are we so willing to interfere with the lives of thousands of families without being sure of what it is we are doing?" asked Keith Norton in a long speech citing qualitative studies and quantitative argument and destruction to adopting families. "The basic concept of adoption is essentially a legal concept." He gave support to the thousands of adoptive parents who entered adoption lawfully and were given assurances of confidentiality. These assurances, he claimed, were not to be ignored, repudiated, disclaimed, quashed or countermanded by those who would change the law *ex post facto*. He pitied natural mothers. "I'll not get into an anecdotal discussion about them but I know whereof I speak, having spent a period of time as guardian *ad litem* to minor unwed mothers throughout that difficult time when they had to face their decision." His incisive words impacted on the House.

"Life isn't always fair, and some have to make decisions for better or worse and go on from there. Sometimes we change the law too quickly because minority groups, groups with vested interests, pressure us. I would urge everyone to consider carefully the contingent fallout from this action."

"The Honorable Member so loquaciously defended the adoptive family and the natural parents," said Elie Martel, NDP Sudbury East, "but had not one word for the adopted child, or rather the adult that adopted child has become. I say the most tragic aspect of adoption as we practice it is the government's unwillingness to recognize we are *not* speaking of children in this amendment. Arguments that deny an adult direct access to original birth information become rationalizations in defense of discrimination." While he talked further, some of the long-time Members shared jokes as though they were in a club. Pages ran hither and yon delivering waggish or droll messages. Interjections ran rampant for some time when an Honourable Member, Margaret Birch Scarborough East indicated that families were being destroyed by learning the truth.

"Table that documentation, if there is any. That's a little dishonest . . ." called Mr. Martel.

"I ask the member to withdraw that remark . . ."

"I withdraw the remark, Mr. Chairman. Let's say it's a little misleading . . ."

"Misleading is just as bad . . ."

"Misleading is unparliamentary . . ."

"Mr. Chairman, on a point of order . . ."

"Order, order."

"Mr. Chairman, please ask the honourable member to withdraw that statement about my statement being misleading. Does he have any proof of it? I'd like to see documentation of that."

"If I can proceed I'll prove it."

Mr. Chairman: "I would inform the member that the word 'misleading' is unparliamentary and ask him to withdraw the statement."

"I withdraw the remark." Mr. Martel went on for half an hour or more on the experience of giving knowledge to the adoptee and material obtained from the ombudsman on similar acts in England (1975), Scotland (1958), Israel and Finland since 1932. "I want to get to the real person involved in this situation . . ."

"They are all real," insisted the Honourable Harry Parrott, Oxford.

"The real one, the *real* one, the person it's all about . . ."

"You've made a big mistake, they are all real."

"Harry, control yourself"

"Look who's talking."

"Oh, take a sabbatical."

"Order, order"

The democratic process, at times, tended to be a childish affair but the noise relieved the boredom. It wasn't exactly Saturday Night Live, but spontaneous interjections were honed to a fine art and were often more frequent than political oratory.

David Cooke, NDP Windsor-Riverside made an attempt to be heard. "I'm disappointed that the government and the ministry could not accept this amendment and make it part of this positive revision to the Child Welfare Act. In the committee I voiced the opinion that I would be voting in favour of the amendment and that I was disappointed that the amendment had been watered down. If the amendment is defeated tonight we are faced with the unsatisfactory situation prevailing all over the province where one Children's Aid Society is cooperative and easy and another is uncooperative and it's even impossible to get health information. This very small step forward will at least make policy consistent across this province."

"Put the adopted child on top of this triangle for the simple reason we are looking towards and respecting the rights of a person to find his/her background. What about the adopted black child, the native Indian child?" asked Liberal Alf Stong, York Centre. "Those children have the right to go back to determine their ancestry; they ought to be proud of their ancestry."

A Conservative Member sidetracked the issue by suggesting that the amendment created a double standard, two classes of adopted adults; if a biological parent is deceased and cannot be located and no confirmation is forthcoming . . . those adopted adults can never have access.

"Why don't you save our time and just vote no because your back bench won't let you say yes?"

"Back bench? I thought it was the front bench."

"I don't know why you are so hostile when I comment."

"We are not personally hostile."

"You are not personally hostile?"

"No, no"

"Impersonally?"

"We'll be hostile to anybody who gives us such gibberish."

Yes, a day in the House without interjections could be dull.

A Liberal member took the initiative to say something positive. "I support this amendment on the grounds that we are creating an opportunity for disclosure, nothing more, nothing less. Nothing mandatory, nothing compulsory. It is voluntary and represents the opportunity for disclosure. I bow to what has been said from the heart these many days."

Many of the Conservatives were in their seats. Support on the Liberal side was strong and the NDP Members, who had introduced the legislation, were all present. The Speaker recognized the NDP Member for Carleton East, Evelyn Gigantes, who rose and made a perfunctory bow to the Speaker. I prayed she would be taken seriously. I had made a point of introducing myself to her because, when I sat in the visitor's gallery during evening sessions of the House, I admired her perception on this issue and her clarity in delivering unambiguous facts. I had talked to her about my orphaned life.

"Mr. Speaker," she began, "civil adoption has always been part of our cultural tradition, though the nature of the proceedings and its purpose have varied. Adoptive parents carry historical sanction, unmarried mothers who gave up children bear historical stigma and their babies are struck out of existence as the beings they really are and renamed at someone else's initiative. There are an estimated 398,000 adoptees in Canada, 168,000 of those in Ontario. There are no absolute answers to the dilemmas which evolve from the adoption triangle, and the solutions we find to some problems will generate others to be solved. Our duty is to start with an awareness of the rights and needs of all those in the triangle and to study adoption with an openness to change.

"The definitions of illegitimate in any dictionary include *illegal, unlawful, born of parents not married to each other; contrary to law or to rules; (slang) a bastard.* First point. Next, the natural father? He's regarded as a nonentity. A baby has no control over this and it's only humane that on the birth of a child the name of the father be correctly registered in the public records, and that failure to do so should constitute a criminal offense. It should be against the law to destroy, tamper with or give misinformation to an individual. To be given up, as the term goes, is something children have no control over, but to deny an adult the truth about one's heritage is equivalent to slavery—victims of a dominating influence, never given the chance to be free, never given the most basic of human information—birth facts.

"Next point, the desire to know is permanent in many given-up children, it won't go away. It is summoned powerfully in the give and take of life. We need this information; it will make us civil and human. Society needs it too; it needs its citizens to be reconciled with one another. The solution lies in the plain and ancient fact that reconciliation brings something new into the lives of the reconciled. It brings peace and wisdom to those who dare seek. As far as incriminating information hurting birth mothers is concerned, that depends on the maturity of that person. Most would find a sense of fulfillment and relief, satisfied there are no bad feelings harboured against them. The adoptive parents whose children are grown up often are supportive in releasing information to the adoptee. This strengthens their relationship. The government has always ruled in favour of adoptive parents and there should not have been that favoritism in the first place. If we used common sense there'd be no threat to adoptive parents or to any birth parent who wants anonymity.

"So, my proposal is for *controlled* access to information with professional counselling, and the adult adoptee must be the catalyst." The House was quiet, listening. "The law is not immovable and permanent," she went on. "It is living and changeable. The adopted child should have full status and the right to be represented. We are not saying push all persons concerned into new relationships. We are asking that those adults who want and need the truth be given the truth. For most it will end there."

"The thin edge of the wedge," a voice squeaked.

"Foot or wedge," she answered, "let it happen. This government has the facilities and the skilled personnel to deal with this proposal. As it is now, Children's Aid policies in fifty different locations have fifty disparate sets of regulations, tied to local preferences and prejudices." Evelyn fiddled with her notes. She had been speaking for four minutes. It seemed longer.

"This is the United Nations year for Human Rights," she continued. "The trend is towards monumental social rights. A fetus has rights, felons have rights, the government says every person is free. Yet the peculiar and unique rights of the adoptee are cruelly nonexistent compared to the civil rights of others." The House had not grown restless or sarcastic, there was no jocular banter now.

"Each speaker to this amendment to the Child Welfare Act seems to think it relevant to get on the adoptive parents' bandwagon personally. Many Members declared that you had adopted children, or your brother had, or your uncle, or your grandmother. It's inconceivable that any of us, mother or father, would acknowledge having given up a child to adoption or even that we had been adopted. The word illegitimate is still in popular use, especially in our laws. Everyone knows and uses the invective term 'bastard.' There is a woman sitting in the gallery who wrote this to me, Mr. Speaker. I'd like to read it. It's brief."

The Speaker rose and nodded assent. "Thank you. Quote, 'I am illegitimate, I am a bastard. I've not had the security of adoption. I do not have feelings of inferiority but, because I have no surrogate parents, no method or rights to know who I am, I am vulnerable. I've looked in directories and telephone books; I've looked in nursing homes and obit columns for my mother's name. For more than thirty years I've asked my government for help because every day of my life I think about my mother and pray that one day I will stand before the woman who gave me life to let her know that I am worth the pain or shame or whatever she felt for my existence. I have to believe she wants that satisfaction. I believe I have that right.' That's all." Evelyn bowed her head in my direction, I made a slight inclination to acknowledge her words; it was immaterial to me who knew my personal business now. She went on: "Mr. Speaker, I support this amendment because the human rights of adults must be recognized." Evelyn sat down.

She had read my words to an attentive assembly and my relieved heart beat against a wall of silence. It seemed a respectful pause or more like a stunned hush. Then the little nervous coughs started, throats cleared. A man named McNab, sitting in the gallery, suppressed a yawn, cleverly massaging his jaw as if to feel a stubble. *Insensitive bore*, I thought. *He's against any change that will help us and works hard with the government to thwart change.*

The Lady Member for St. Paul again argued that she had evidence that learning the truth was destroying families and people. The NDP social critic insisted again that she table the documentation. He made a point by saying an adopted child should learn in stages information about his or her parents, the same way children find out other things in life. "A good example: our third child was on the way, my wife told our ten-year-old daughter about the happy event, suggesting that the months before the baby arrived were the best time for her to ask questions about babies. A few days later try to imagine what her first concern was? 'How come Johnny looks like Daddy?' The level at which the question occurs is the level at which the answer must be given. It's time for this amendment and more. A search conducted with courage and respect can be very rewarding." Then he surprised me.

"Mr. Chairman, it is very difficult to sit in this Legislature and to hear the words read by the Member for Carleton East and not be touched by them. I've hoisted my flag for the amendment. I've given my reasons." He nodded "I want to say to the Member, I listened, I heard every word you said."

I was grateful.

The amendment was passed by one vote and adoptees' rights were now a serious issue requiring application. Left begging for more resolution certainly but the proverbial stone was rolling. A backlash was possible for already rumors were rife that some M.P.'s wanted all vital records closed to even genealogical researchers and vowed that this would be done. While I understood that reform would come slowly, the cause had gained momentum.

The Toronto newspapers sustained the principle of the debate to a degree, saying there'd been too much 'mealy-mouthed self-righteous rhetoric.' The Toronto Star added fuel to the flame:

> Yesterday's Legislative debate proved more dramatic than the TV soap operas . . . Ontario's Child Welfare Act and the Vital Statistics Act contravene the rights of adoptees. Whatever may have been the rationale for sealed records sixty or seventy years ago, that rationale does not apply today. There are grave psychological penalties to pay. Taking a long view and considering what we have learned, what is plainly needed is the reappearance of the principal to supersede the proxy empowered to act for the adoptee.

Christina called. "I'll be right there. I'm sorry you carried such a burden. You should have told me about it when I asked you."

"I never tell anybody, now it seems I've told the world. It's a relief."

Many editorials and letters to the editor cheered for a better way to deal with the overt wrongs of the system. Adoptees wrote that they felt like misfits needing to be grounded in the human mainstream. The letters from adoptees who had shared their search and reunion with adoptive parents were the best. Existing bonds with their adoptive parents had been strengthened by the sharing.

About this time a letter from Mother Monica surprised me. We had kept in touch for years and sometimes I wondered why I bothered. There was still an immaturity in me, a need for approval, to have a mother figure in my life, I suppose. Who knows? She had moved across the country in recent years and we had lost contact for a while. Now she wrote to say she was visiting not far from Toronto at a farm owned by the sisters. "Maybe we could see each other? Sharon is north of Toronto, phone me and I'll give you directions."

She looked wonderful. I was not prepared to see her wearing the new modern-day habit that came just below her knees, the neat shoes, the strangely feminine dark curls with bits of gray showing all around her short veil. Her skin still had that dewy Maritime look, she was beautiful, dark laughing eyes, her mouth peaceful. I felt that singular force, that spiritual depth that used to attract me, and when Mother Monica held my shoulders and kissed me, I recalled how we were made to believe it would be a sacrilege to touch just a fold of her skirt. Did she consider me different now because I was not of the class of the women in the laundry?

"Do you remember telling me, that day in the parlour, not to worry about you, you'd make me proud?" she smiled.

"I remember. I didn't know how I was going to make you proud. My only thought then was to get away, as quickly as possible." Then I felt very much the prevaricator, for she did not know that Julian and I were separated.

We walked outside in a beautiful country environment of fields, a barn and a cottage that accommodated seven sisters. Of course, there was a chapel. There was also a large outbuilding with cots and kitchen facilities used for group retreats. They called the place Regina Mundi. Mother Monica did a little sidestepping when I wanted to find out what had happened in Saint John. She was enthusiastic about the new residence in Windsor, Ontario.

"Our building was falling down, it was poorly built."

"St. Vincent's was a lot older. It's still in use."

"Yes, St. Vincent's was much older but it was a better building. In Saint John I felt I was working for prison reform. Unfortunately you were unwanted girls and women. We did our best. You should have been in the younger class where you could go to school but you came to us with a reputation, you know."

"I know I did."

"Have you heard that some of the girls are suing us? Bernadette's daughter for one. She's saying terrible things about us in the papers in Halifax and you know it's not true. We're trying to keep it out of the Toronto papers."

"It seems fashionable to sue nowadays. I saw a news article about the Good Shepherd sisters being sued by women in Quebec, saying they'd been locked up, abused, molested and deprived. Now when I think of it I remember your administrator phoned me one day at work, some time ago, and told me about the lawsuit in Saint John. She mentioned needing good witnesses. I was as honest as possible saying I was certainly never molested; I was deprived of education and I thought I was punished unfairly. We spoke pleasantly enough but I knew she wouldn't consider me a good witness."

"There was no such room as those women are talking about; it's a lie."

"Don't you remember St. Peter's Room?"

"Oh, but we didn't use it."

"You did use it. I spent two terrible nights there once, remember?"

"No, we didn't use it."

"There was often someone there, Germaine especially. Recall how we had to beg pardon on our knees in front of the class when we were let out of St. Peter's?"

"That was before my time. Our place in Windsor is now called a Residential Treatment Centre for Adolescents. We have a vast amount of space for thirty-five girls. We are limited to that number. They are school age only, from twelve to sixteen. We have eight classrooms, science labs and a library. The girls live in individual cottages, like private homes. They have private bedrooms. Oh you wouldn't know us now!" She placed her hand on my arm. "There is a male administrator and lay teachers," she said solemnly, evading the issue of St. Peter's Room, which wasn't important now.

"What part do the sisters play, Reverend Mother?"

"We aren't called Mother any more," she whispered. "Sister will do. We play no part in caring for the girls, the staff is government-appointed. The property belongs to us but we don't have enough sisters as some have been giving up the religious life and young women aren't coming in. We are not getting vocations, our youngest sister is forty-six. Before Vatican II in 1963 life in a community was predictable and orderly. Maybe because women religious were more oppressed, when we were given a little edge some went further. Times have certainly changed." She petted a St. Bernard dog she called Brandy as he nosed gently between us. "We have a younger contemplative group, they are called The Magdalens. Now that name is familiar to you." She looked for some reaction.

"Too familiar. Unfortunately I've had too many names and I still don't know who I am." I had always believed that this nun knew nothing about my background. To her I was an incorrigible runaway from St. Vincent's.

"So often I trace my course back, searching for a beginning and I ask myself, the beginning of what? The beginning of memory? The beginning of wondering? The beginning of being alone? There had to be a veritable beginning to me, my self. I want my birth information. I see it as my basic right and I'll continue to fight for it."

"Oh my, you sound unsettled. I thought you were doing so well."

"I am doing well but I'm terribly unsettled because I don't know my biological background and I encounter only people who won't help, who are smug in their own milieu, who treat me like it's not important. But I'll continue the journey, it could be a long trek, maybe as long as my life."

"To know joy one must also accept the ironies and inadequacies of life."

"I do that but there are times when I have a low level of self-worth. The underlying conflicts threaten me but I don't give in. My determination makes me think my parents must have been capable people."

"It's too bad your younger years went the way they did, Molly. Today they don't look at the behaviour, as we did, but the reason behind the behaviour. The girls have court-appointed counselors and psychiatric boards who follow their progress. They are treated with drugs when necessary, psychologists delve into their phobic symptoms and the therapeutic goal is to bring the conflict into the open so that it might be resolved. They are taught anxiety management. Would you believe there could be so many changes?"

"Yes I would," I admitted with a degree of bitterness. "As a mother I know it's only natural that children need something tangible, someone to touch them and make them feel worthwhile. I had no one. The horror of my situation was I didn't need psychiatrists or drugs. I needed love. Instead I suffered displacement and repression and was imbued with anxieties I had to learn to manage myself. It's true, you know." She dropped her head and pursed her mouth then looked at me meekly. "Is strict religious discipline still part of the new method, Mother?"

"Sadly, no. We try to make friends with any who are disposed to be friendly and if they express a desire to go to chapel, that is accommodated. But we have no official contact with the girls."

"Forgive me if I sound resentful, but why were we taught self-denial, to reject the world as if we were nuns, deprived of education, forced to divest ourselves of the most natural thing, friendship? Even little girls love to have a friend, to whisper and giggle with, tell secrets to and depend on, it's natural. Why were we suspected?"

"We made mistakes, the rules were strict and too much was expected of you. I tried more than you know to get help for our girls. A terrible time for me was when Helen went out to work in a doctor's home. She was asked to write a list of the things she needed in the kitchen and she couldn't spell or write. She was forced to go back to the laundry. I was determined I'd do something then. The procurer would not give me money for schoolbooks. Anyway, I went up to the attic and found lots of primers and spellers. They were old but the words were the same. We all lived on what came in from the laundry, you know."

"It was wrong for girls like me to be working in the laundry. The older women, that was another matter."

"Well, we are a community of prayer, but you don't live on air. The balance of prayer and manual work has always been connected to monastic life. You remember when you were allowed time to learn shorthand and typing?"

"Indeed I do, that was my salvation. Your plan gave me the initiative to stay with the books and figure it all out on the sidelines during evening recreation. I learned enough to start my working life in an office with plain typing and Gregg shorthand; then learning office procedure as I worked I found I could always take charge of my situation. Thankfully I didn't have to work in a laundry.

"I sometimes remember words I heard and read: *Holy sisters and fallen angels.* It was annoying that we were dismissed as rejects. I never dwell on this but when things come up, like now, It's hard to forget or forgive."

"That's too bad."

"It is. Something else I think about: why was I subjected to an internal examination when I went to the Good Shepherd? I was thirteen, I didn't know what was happening to me. Some nun in the infirmary stood outside a curtain while a male doctor examined me. Why? To prove or disprove my virginity?"

"Hygiene. It was assumed that most of you were unable to take responsibility. But that was wrong. To be a Christian means to be responsible. To be responsible, one must be master of oneself. If you are not in control of yourself you are nothing." She showed her glowing smile. "Our approach was a conditioning; all created things and their works had to be forgotten, nothing could lie between you and God." She had gained a degree of spiritual compromise. Her conscience was in order. However, as far as I was concerned hers was still a narrow approach to life as it was lived in this world.

She smoothed her short veil back, the same recurrent gesture I remembered and I almost laughed when the nun folded her arms with determination under her short scapular, just as she used to do when I was in trouble.

"We couldn't allow particular friendships because you know very well there were some bad girls in our group. Now there is evidence that promoting the natural process of friendship in adolescents is terribly important for adult social development. I know now that it's right." She loosened her arms and folded the whiteness of her hands and looked sad. "I know you girls needed something we weren't giving you. I felt it then;

remember I was living under a rule too. The time the girls hurt you. I'm still sorry about that. Trying to understand it is important to me. Do you understand?"

The narrow mindedness and inciting of the incident came to mind. Why go into that, I thought. I just answered, "Something was terribly wrong that time but that was the least problem. Lack of a home life, lack of education and incarceration were the worst kind of injustice. Today, in human rights lingo, they go to bat for high security criminals. Some of us were innocent children. They're hard memories, done and over with, but I say that with sadness for I still feel the stigma. Knowing my mother would help me."

"Remember the little silver bell you sent? They listened to it, there was a nice feeling in the class about it because someone cared enough to think about them. My successor discarded it and resurrected the old brass bell. I was disappointed."

The nun spoke about the disestablishment of the laundry business, about economic and social aspects of that time, about new policies in the nuns' lives. Government influence was a delicate issue. The real issue was the phasing out of the order as it used to operate. "Even if people were joining us, our way of life would change because life is change. Our numbers decrease but it's a sign of new life."

Change was a long time coming but changes in consciousness have been driven, I like to think, by a universal force for justice and all sorts of bastions are falling. During our walk around the farm I mentioned my sustained effort to find my mother. "You should write a book about it." Little did she know that I had started long ago.

"My story is far from ended. Do you really believe the world wants my words?"

"Yes."

Maybe my frankness worried her for when I was leaving, Mother Monica coyly added, "I've been thinking of what I said; maybe you shouldn't."

There's no stopping me.

The moon's greygolden meshes make
All night a veil,
The shorelamps in the sleeping lake
Laburnum tendrils trail.
The sly weeds whisper to the night
A name - her name -
And all my soul is a delight,
A swoon of shame.

James Joyce

BENT TREE ➤ THE SEVENTIES

"*I*T ISN'T ETIQUETTE to cut anyone you've been introduced to *(Through the Looking Glass and What Alice Found There),*" so I shook the hand of Benjamin McNab when Ina introduced us and overlooked his stand on sealed adoption records. He was handsome, casual in brown slacks and a beige cashmere sweater. He held a flattened sports cap under his arm and clung to his briefcase as though it had gender.

"Just leaving for the cottage."

Tanned to advantage, he had an outdoor look. He rolled his tongue over a long tooth, giving a mischievous smile. That lop-sided grin had amused and annoyed me in the Visitor's Gallery of the House and at other times. I remembered I had reason to dislike him.

"I'd like to ask you to go to the lake with me some weekend. Ina's welcome too."

I didn't know what to say to him.

"You hesitate with such deliberation."

"I'm not hesitating, this is *so* sudden." *Now why jest with the enemy?* "Where is it?"

"Land O' Lakes area, near the village of Fernleigh. Deep in the woods on Kashwakamak Lake. I call it Bent Tree. I think you'd enjoy it."

"Maybe I would, I'll think about it." *Fat chance!* He kept smoothing his brown hair self-consciously; it had a blondish cast. *All that time he gets to spend in the sun.*

"Come to dinner with me and I'll tell you all about it, then you won't be able to resist."

"I'm not resisting. It's just . . . We've got to go. Glad we've met."

"Well, enjoy your weekend."

"You too, Ben." Others called him Ben. He hadn't used my name at all. Ina drove, I asked, "What do you know about him?"

"Just what everyone else knows, he's formal, keeps to himself. He's friend and adviser to the Minister of Health, who carries the toughest portfolio in the cabinet in such a way that he's seldom under the gun, and I believe McNab has a lot to do with that. There's something about the man that's hard to define; he's an accountant, you know." She hesitated, thinking about what she was about to say, as she always did. "He's a bachelor, and confidentially," she looked away from the highway, "I met McNab outside the lounge and he asked me to introduce him."

"Well, why?"

"Don't know. But let's be realistic. He wanted to meet you, he's aware of you. Why don't you meet the challenge? For fun."

"I'll consider dinner if he calls me, but he must be naive to suggest I'd go to his cottage. Besides, he won't want to know me any better when he gets my opinions firsthand."

I met him at Mr. Tony's, the new place in Yorkville where the waiter, with patrician dignity, recited the menu. Ben directed me to a corner table and I had a crazy notion, *I'd like to find a chink in this man's armour. Apart from politics he's so complaisant.* However, I loved going out so I'd make the most of a date as though we were friends. But we weren't and it was necessary to become acquainted.

"Where did you grow up?" I asked after other formalities were taken care of.

"Plymouth, England, and you?"

"I haven't yet, my kids keep me young. But I come from the Maritimes. Any children?"

"No, never been married. I met your husband once."

"Oh. Was that important?"

"I suppose it was because I wanted to meet you. What happened?"

"Ask me some other time, not tonight."

"You're right, my apologies. Your interest in politics, about Bill 114 for example . . ."

Anxious to talk about something interesting I told him, "You can gather from that episode in the House with Evelyn Gigantes that my life as a child was not the best. There was a specific moment once when I was a little girl and they locked me up for two long nights to punish me. I think it was then I knew I couldn't settle for being less than ordinary . . ."

"I can understand that."

"I didn't have resources to be a professional person, I had children early in my life and I loved motherhood. Then I got the opportunity to be in on some groundwork on this Bill with truly dedicated people so I took it. I'm in awe that the truth can be heard at last. Hopefully change will come. I'll be there for the next round."

"That attitude could end the personal trauma in your life and maybe pave the way for others as well. Think about that."

"I do, often. The width and depth of these issues takes over my thinking. I want action right away. I'm learning the art of compromise too slowly."

"Some things take time. You simply have to wait and see what happens now."

"Look who's talking, you're one of the hurdles. If I have to leap over you, watch out. Kidding aside, my judgment bothers me, not that I ought to be admitting it to you, but what the heck. I'm impressed when someone takes a stand, then the argument develops in another direction and I'm impressed again."

"I'm learning too. I may not be the hurdle you think I am. We all learn the hard way. Stevenson wisely said, 'Politics is the only profession for which no preparation is necessary.' Sadly this stuff is all politics."

"Yes Robert Louie said that," I chided, "but he actually said, 'Politics is *perhaps* the only profession for which no preparation is *thought* necessary.'"

"Right on. You're fun."

"I'm having a good time upstaging a learned man. That's fun."

"Just don't lose your zeal for disclosure. You are right you know."

I was speechless.

"It's true," he said, "until I saw you in the Visitor's Gallery on the day of the vote not many of us were *au courant* with the total issue; we were hard-headed. You've started something and now you have to take responsibility for the aftermath."

"What do you mean, *I* started something?"

"It takes the human touch to make it real. You did it. A simple parallel to the arguments over access goes like this. Building the railroad in England was a bitter fight. There were those who argued—the cows will stop milking and the hens will stop laying and the trees will die. We cannot allow this steel thing to run amok on the countryside. Well, the cows are still milking and the countryside is still lush. I know that every adoptee does not want to know their origin. But since you bared your soul to the House, I recognize there are persons like you who need to know their parents and the nature of their separation."

"Be careful, I'm going to like you."

"It's so fundamental when I think about it. There are few things in this world that are *not* interchangeable, and this is one of them. I would have to question someone who wasn't curious about who they are. We have to take the trouble to grasp this problem."

Unexpected words from a man who had openly worked against Bill 114. "Thank you," I told him. "In time there will be a better way."

"We have to have the truth—good or bad. Let's order dinner."

We talked about growing up. ". . . a handsome, rich father? School in England? Travel? the Granite Club, friends in the government, tell me about you. Was anyone ever mean to you?"

"Do I have to answer that?"

"No. I don't know why I asked."

"Just because I've achieved some success doesn't mean I've had a proper and satisfying childhood. I'll tell you something, confidentially."

"Okay."

"It's a secret." He looked for assurance.

"Cross my heart," I kidded.

"I grew up in an orphanage in England."

I nearly choked. "Really?"

"Really. My mother died when I was five but I was old enough when my father remarried to know he had a mistress on the side. Suddenly he and his bride went away to India and my sister and I were put in homes, separately. She was older than me. Once I was taken to see her. Those in charge meant well but it was an embarrassment. I didn't know her anymore and I was glad when the visit was over. I used to plot going back to Pentyre Street where I was born. When I finally got there, it was such a disappointment. The house was so small, the memory of my mother faded. I knew then I was on my own to make something of my life. I went to study near Dublin but that's another story."

"Were you treated well in your orphanage?"

"Yes, the matron was warm-hearted. We called her Ma'rm. There was disorder but only because there were bullies amongst us. No bad treatment from those in charge."

"How did you learn about life?"

"By trial and error. We were all curious about Ma'rm and we talked about her soft tummy. We wanted to get closer to her to be mothered. We were very young. And how did you learn?"

"Mostly by error. I never thought about sex until I met Julian. The nuns had chosen lifelong chastity and their rule applied to us while we were with them. I must say though, just before I left the convent at seventeen, a nun in charge surreptitiously handed me a book of sex instruction in a brown paper jacket. *Letters to Mary.* Each chapter, a letter from a mother telling of some aspect of life between a man and a woman, had an odor of sanctity, warning and fear. I couldn't understand her motive. I was indifferent to the letters on white slave traffic and venereal disease and unconcerned but a little curious about male physiology."

"No doubt during your time with the sisters some of them projected their aversion to sex on you."

"Certainly, right from the beginning when our mothers were 'girls in trouble' and filled the orphanages with the product of sin. I couldn't take that book seriously and I was frightened she'd expect me to discuss it. If I'd known that when I gave it back she would tell me I was leaving, my approach might have been different. Who knows?"

"It was the Church who defined nuns in sexual terms and it was men enforced their rule to keep them separate. But now most religious orders acknowledge that it's not possible to sublimate natural feelings. It's very different today. No shaved heads or flattened breasts to neutralize women."

"So be it. *Deo gratias.*" I taunted.

The steak was rare, succulent and garlicky. "How was the food?" I asked, changing the discussion from one necessity of life to another.

"Well, no variety. Most days we were served ersatz pie." He shook his head at the memory.

"And we got hash, same thing." I grimaced. "Johnny cake. Jello!"

"Bread pudding! Porridge!"

"With molasses!" I cried.

"Yes, always molasses. In the spring we all got a tonic of sulfur and molasses for ten days."

"We were given Wampole's cod liver oil all winter and castor oil for everything else. No matter what was wrong, out came the bottle of castor oil. Two heaping gruesome tablespoons. Ugh."

"I looked up the meaning of ersatz to see what I was eating," said Ben. It was German, a replacement, a substitute. Whatever they called it, it was greasy and cold and clung to the roof of my mouth."

"Well, I checked too. Hash—a new mixture of old matter, a jumble, a mess. I was never hungry except for sweets."

"I'm very much in favour of foster homes or adoptive homes, not institutions. At the orphanage, as I got older, I wanted to be helpful and whether I was carrying papers down a corridor to an office or helping in some way, I learned early it was important to be useful."

"Me too. But the nuns didn't encourage that. They had this habit of pinching us on the arm to make us conform. That made us reluctant rather than enthusiastic."

"I understand; by comparison we were fortunate. No nuns."

"We were taught fear. We suffered badly from lack of advantage. Some of us were doers and were called brazen, bold, ringleaders if we showed any initiative. I think some nuns thought parenting meant punishing. You'd think they'd see the likeness of the Child Jesus in little children. Wouldn't you?"

"You'd think so."

"Thinking back, I believe I was pushy because I had the semblance of a family, a foster mother, an Aunt Bertha, a cousin or two. I developed the nerve to stick up, as we used to say, for the others. I was stubborn when there was cause to be, but I got away before I lost all determination."

"There was a time in Britain when homeless, abandoned and destitute children of all ages lived on the streets; cold, dirty, barefoot, hungry, and consumptive. They were forced to beg or steal or die. Decent types with a degree of compassion, it seems, opened Refuge homes, some were actually called Ragged Schools and the orphans were called Angels from the Meadow. That marked the beginning of orphanages. I believe they were good homes. Let's relax upstairs. Brandy?"

"I've never been 'Upstairs at Mr. Tony's.' Let's go."

When Ben settled the bill I looked at his hands, large with short fingers, well-defined white tips. They impressed me as strong hands, different from Julian's. *Maybe they'd feel every bit as good. Maybe someone else, at this moment, is wanting Julian's hands.* Upstairs in the muffled softness of the dim room we indulged in an exchange of trivia, *quid pro quo*, as Ben said. I wanted to know about him and found we shared likes and dislikes. He dropped Latin phrases as nimbly as falling leaves and I was able to grasp words due to the preponderance of Latin prayers, vespers and hymns at the Good Shepherd. I was having a good time.

We danced to the smooth tempo of *How Insensitive*. I didn't mean to let go but I trembled in his arms and he merely tightened them around me. He crooned in my ear, "*I know a little bit about a lot of things, but I don't know enough about you.*" Halfway through the dreamy *Meditation* my heart slowed to normal. *If time could be suspended, I would cull this moment for safekeeping but time is a strange dimension, it moves unheeding, leaving only memories, and prejudices return.*

When the dance ended he said, "You are beautiful tonight"

"You can say that again, sir. Hi." It was the drummer speaking to me. I was surprised to see Paul's friend, Dean, smiling enthusiastically.

"Ben, I've known Dean since he was six years old, peeking from the back stairs during his mother's party, looking for goodies. Believe it or not my daughter's future husband, Paul, was with him. I always smile more when I see Dean." Tall and blonde, his flashing smile was contagious.

"Very friendly, isn't he?" He smoothed his hair, it was his habit. Then, dammit, he returned to mundane talk.

"When the government insists it can't change the law for the one percent of adoptees who are searching, it's taking the wrong attitude. And the law doesn't take into consideration people like you. You weren't adopted?"

"No, I wasn't. And that one percent assumption is absurd. There are many afraid to say they want information."

"So you've never had parents, not even surrogate parents?"

"I didn't. Just secretive nuns and an absent foster mom who changed my name."

"God, what has society done to people all these years with its passion for secrecy? We've been trapped by tradition. That's all you're saying. More power to you."

"Your opinion is important to me," I told Ben. "I'm so glad we've talked."

"So am I."

"If I gave you the whole megillah about my orphanages it would take all night There were no sealed records in my case, just keeping me in the dark because a selfish woman fostered me briefly and the nuns accepted me back at the orphanage bearing her name."

"It's hard to imagine that you children mattered to no one."

"It was hard to accept, I couldn't. To think that you grew up in an orphanage; and that you told me your secret. It's safe."

"Just one thing more then. Even though I knew who my parents were, my wrath with the social order is not so different from yours; I also bear the burden of an unnatural childhood. Anyway, my judgment was well-intentioned when I spoke against the amendment. So be it."

"I'm determined to find my mother, Ben. I've always had a single, pure purpose. I never made her a scapegoat. Even if she's someone I couldn't like, I'll take that chance. If my search takes me to a senile old lady or a grave, I'll find her and I'll find some peace."

"I'll help you find her. You can count on me. Keep the child alive in yourself, Molly. I like that about you."

Sincere words. I would always be grateful. He was a nice man and I'd enjoyed being with him.

*I*n the afterglow of a lovely evening I surveyed the panorama from my balcony in the Colonnade. The moon silhouetted the Toronto-Dominion Towers, monolithic, prodigious, darkened to protect migrating birds. So much of my world at my feet. Queen's Park glowed in the dark green oasis leased to the city for nine hundred and ninety-nine years by the University of Toronto. Seventy-four St. Mary Street was gone and in its place was a new residence for university women built by the Loretto Nuns. A monument to my first and only love, standing there in celebration of naked youth, face to face, summer rains, forbidden, immoral, beautiful, life-giving love!

I traced a path to the maple tree where I sat that day the doctor told me I would have a baby. How I needed my mother then. I remembered my determination to never let anyone take my baby from me. Now I didn't want to look towards St. Basil's, the hall where Julian and I had met, the chapel where we were married, but some baneful devil pulled my focus there. It seemed such a short time ago, we'd had so much love for each other and we thought we could foresee the striving and sacrifice. Later this month there'd be a wedding anniversary to bring back memories. The years had a way of romping by. This would be, O God, not twenty-seven years!

I wonder where Julian is tonight?

*C*onversation was relaxed during the three-hour drive on Highway 401, north through Tweed and Northbrook and east to Ben's cottage. We settled into the comfortable redwood building. He put a match to a laid fire and added seasoned oak to the blaze.

"I hope you relax here."

We shared stuffed peppers and salad with a piquant wine. The open concept design of the living space was interesting and large sliding doors led to a deck. Wainscotted walls enhanced the wonderful oak floor and braided rugs. The maple furniture glowed with earthy highlights of green and rust in upholstery and cushions. There were healthy plants in an alcove and I asked how they survived Ben's absence.

"I have an arrangement with a woman who lives near here, just before we turned onto the bush road. If I'm not here on a Saturday she waters the plants and she does other things too, like cleaning. She makes these peppers and freezes them here."

He showed me my bedroom and we stepped out to the deck into the country night and a million stars and the scent of cedar. I held my breath to hear the quiet which emphasized the gentle slurps from the lake below, then the grating *peent* of a nighthawk. A shrill laugh came from a distance. "Voices carry a long way," he said. "Most people stop coming in the fall. It's the best time to be here."

Long, wistful calls of a pair of loons spread through the night. A single tremolo like echoing laughter, then the answer, quavering and resonant. The peaceful commotion and the privacy were surprising.

"Will I see the loons tomorrow?"

"Probably, they're always in the bay. We could start early in the canoe."

"The shift in feeling from the city is remarkable, the night sounds are amazing."

"I thought you'd feel it. One can't describe it."

He switched the light off in the room behind us. We leaned on the deck rail to watch lively clouds form faces around the waning moon. Trees were silhouetted against the bay and the sparkle of a million diamonds rode on tiny wave swells. The far-off hum of an outboard on the lake was comforting because it was distant.

"Is there a Bent Tree?"

"You'll see." He stepped inside, I followed. "Good night now." The door closed and I was alone.

The bed had been warmed and I nestled in the thick duvet and didn't rouse until I heard a series of sharp cracks from a morning fire. I lay there and watched a mystical yellow line on the horizon over a small island become a yellow diamond as the sun lifted between dark-spired pines. I dressed warmly for the canoe.

"It's a perfect day," Ben said as he fastened the fire screen. "When we get back, this fire will feel good."

The morning sun skimmed the variegated leaves on the ground. The loons called, their song less eerie in the dawn. The unique common loon, I mused. The forest smell soothed the senses and the panoramic scene from the dock was startling. The ash trees were a golden orange. Flaming maple, crimson oak, yellow birch and tall green pine vied for space. Lush green cedars lined the shore. The air so fresh it filled me with energy. Ben pointed to the end of the dock where a little brown animal stared at us, a small fish in its jaws.

"It's a mink. He's been around all summer. Don't try to get close to him, he'd bite." Then he pointed along the shore. "There it is, Bent Tree."

An old cedar grew straight out from the bank, skimmed the water for ten to twelve feet then it bent straight up, reaching for the sky, suspended over the water. A veritable bent tree! I felt like an intruder and, at the same time, a chosen sharer.

We paddled quietly, gliding past a turtle sunning itself on a log, and moved through the narrows to the big lake. The morning mist was gone. A cottage with an unfurled Canadian flag, a dock, a boat and white birch trees, all mirrored in the water. Movement! A girl with long red hair wearing a blue robe stooped to put her hand in the water, making ripples in the pure woodland privacy.

Late in the day we tramped through the woods. Earlier he had asked, "Would you mind if I carried a gun? I hunt only small game and don't often shoot. I enjoy putting partridge up just the same."

"Don't mind at all. I know nothing about guns."

"It's important to have some knowledge of guns. Let me show you something." He trotted down the path to the lake, it was plain he was enjoying this. He put a light bulb on a stump, came back to the deck and loaded a .22 rifle. Then he showed me how to hold it and find the bulb in the sights.

"Pull the trigger," he told me.

I surprised myself and shattered the thing. "Beginner's luck," I quipped, but I wondered about his ability to hit anything in flight.

Assuming that hunters made no sound I stepped when he stepped, stopped when he stopped, for branches on the ground snapped and the leaves were dry. I followed him along a ridge that offered a view of islands and lake.

"See that sheer rock on the other shore? I've hunted that ridge and the view from there is indescribable." He pointed at cloven hoof marks. "Fresh tracks. I'm glad there's still some deer left." There was a startling swoosh as the birds left cover and his reflex action was deft as he aimed his shotgun and fired twice.

"You wait here." He went to retrieve the spoils and came back to the clearing empty handed, but grinning. "I got two that time," indicating the big patch pockets on his short denim smock. "It's partridge, ruffed grouse."

"Can't I see them?"

He turned a little to arrange a bird on his hand so that no wound or blood showed. "See the feathered legs and the brownish-gray plumage? That's for easy concealment, and believe me, if they stay still, close to the earth, you couldn't find them."

Kingbirds twittered. Ben looked up with pleasure.

He roasted the partridge for us with wild rice and mushrooms and the most delectable bread sauce. Onions simmered in milk then removed, dry breadcrumbs, heavy cream and plenty of pepper. I watched, bewitched.

Bent Tree was a good place to be.

Big clouds gathered in the evening sky while Ben selected music.

"Tell me about Julian, or if you prefer not to, I understand."

I told him the story of a love affair between a naive girl and an insecure student. Given time, the relationship might have run its course or become solid but they made a baby and got married; how a normal life was never established because they were separated by war and later he was away at school; then married life became difficult and ultimately impossible.

"His way of living and his preoccupation with his problems, real or imaginary, robbed us of any hope of a normal life." He made no comment. "Well, we stayed together for nineteen years. I loved him and I tried to make it work for our children. When I left I felt it was the only thing I could have done."

Talking about Julian was not easy. "This is is an *ex parte* version of the love story. It's a defensible one."

He stirred the fire arranging more logs with a long poker. Little tongues of blue flame licked between them at once.

"I can't give you his version. I was in love, so in love! Julian used to say, when the break was imminent, that I had changed. That's all."

Ben squeezed my shoulder. "I wanted to know. It's sad when people say they've never been in love, but it's sadder when love ends."

"I haven't stopped loving him. He put his addictions before his family. Drinking, gambling and his personal comfort were more important to him than we were and he lost us. But we'll always have one thing in common, we are parents. For that reason we remain friends." The gaiety of Mozart's German dances might have lifted the sadness of Julian's memory and I concentrated on the trumpets and sleighbell effects in the *Sleighride* to no avail. Perhaps Julian believes that I failed him? Well, I refuse to accept guilt for that; I did not neglect him. Ben was quiet. I closed my eyes and heard my voice whisper, "Not guilty." And the music played on, totally uplifting.

"Have you been divorced long?" Ben asked me while he changed the record.

"No, just recently. The new divorce reform legislation with the marriage breakdown rationale made it easier. I was divorced without being there. Julian looked after it. My annulment was of greater significance."

"Your annulment?" he said curiously.

"Yes, it was hard to believe that the Church would invalidate a twenty-four-year marriage intended, as they put it, as an indissoluble bond between two baptized persons. After I took a trip with Julian, I knew we'd never live together again. There was nothing to lose by my petition and I was curious too. Oh, the older children were college age; there was no reason to be connected for their sake. I was married nineteen years, separated for fourteen and divorced recently."

"Am I rude, asking so many questions?"

"No. I'd like to drop the subject just the same. There's nothing more."

It was easy being with Ben. Now the surging passion of the Tristan and Isolde love-death music was building to its overwhelming climax.

Ben said he was sleepy, his announcement like a climactic yawn at the end of a beautiful day.

"I'm sleepy too," I fibbed. "It must be the country air."

*B*en became my friend; Bent Tree became my habit. Before Christ, Diogenes, the cynic, claimed "Habit is a second nature" and I experienced an inner giddiness as I indulged my habit as much as possible until Ben and Bent Tree were second nature to me. Our relationship was grounded in reality and our friendship was dignified. I admired his strength and his gentleness but his natural good manners delighted me. God, I was proud being with him, enjoying all the moments while the threads of intimacy were spun. And my determination to search for my mother grew stronger.

Early one Sunday in the woods we examined areas where the beavers had felled several poplars lying criss-crossed on the ground, forming an intriguing corral, some covered with bracket fungus, others with bright green moss. Huge poplars had been partially chewed through, then abandoned by the beavers.

"Why is that?" I asked.

"They want the branches; they can't climb trees and sometimes they just give up. Sometimes a wind will topple the half-chewed tree and they get what they want."

Ben held saplings and branches aside, now and then offering a hand. I looked for some pressure from his fingers, but he was casual. *A knight in blue denim*, I thought. We hiked along the south side of the bay towards the rocky point we had seen from the other side. Autumn's flamboyant blaze and multiform white birch on the other shore reflected in the water; soft dusks of brindled light on the path behind and the feel of noonday warmth on the open cliff. A runabout emerged from the narrows and made a sweeping white circle of wake in the dark blue water, the lone person in the boat obviously unaware that we watched his carefree celebration of dizzying curves. The craft whirred away over the lake and the air was silent.

I reached for Ben's hand in his pocket. His fingers quivered, then tightened on mine. His mouth was warm when he parted my lips with his. I felt strength and boyishness in that first kiss.

"You are lovely." He hesitated. "But we don't have to make love."

"Why not?" I asked. "I'm relieved to know love is on your mind too."

He put his hand against my cheek and held me in his eyes and asked "You know what this will mean?"

"I want to know how it will feel," and I heard his decorous question, "Here?"

"Oh yes, yes, here!"

The cedar bed was soft and resilient and the smell of the dark earth a provocative aphrodisiac high on the rocky promontory in the woods. His was a quiet frenzy, then an outcry of passion with such pathos I thought he was crying. After, I nestled my face in his chest to prolong the intimacy, utter, complete and thorough, pure peace.

Ben spread his arms to take in the freshness, then pulled me to him. "My Molly, I can't tell you enough how I love you. But I must ask you, right at the beginning. Will you give me the chance to work it out between us?"

I could see no objection to working it out and solemnly pledged my love for Ben.

"And I promise to love you, forever. I'll call this Promise Point. We may never find this exact spot again, but we'll try sometime." He set three small rocks like a miniature teepee. "Our landmark, a little cairn to respect this spot."

"Let me have your knife, Ben. While we're being young and foolish and noisy where no one can hear us, a woman's vow I'll write upon that tree!" I made a few notches then he took the knife and carved our initials. "There you have it, our register."

"There's one thing more," he said when he handed me a clump of Queen Anne's lace, "I'd like to take all your hurt away."

"Take it, I crave tenderness. I'll take all the love you want to give me because you're gentle and I want you."

We walked arm-in-arm through the slanted yellow lights and shadows of the wood aisle in the after-aura of love, sighing alternately. "If you don't have to be back in the city tonight, what do you say we stay and go in early tomorrow?"

"I'd prefer to stay," I said huskily.

"I hoped you would." He helped me over the remnants of an old split rail enclosure which criss-crossed in snake fence fashion and we came upon an abandoned root cellar in the side of a well-preserved knoll with a stone front and sturdy post and lintel doorway of cedar logs. The solid plank door lay on the ground inside. Squared cedar beams and empty bins were still in place.

"Square logs? We didn't see this on the way in. Are we lost?"

"No, just leaving the bush a little further west than where we entered, that's all." The squared cedar, he explained, had been dressed by hand with a heavy tool called an adze. "They would stand over a log and knock chips off until they got the thing squared. And certainly people lived here. This area is full of remnants from earlier days when pioneers put up log shanties and sawmills. They'd bring cattle or pigs, a gun, an axe, sometimes a bride with a dowry of a bed and linens and maybe a heifer. I often follow a spur in the road to find a piece of land that once was a small farm. A clump of rhubarb growing near an old foundation is a good indication, or lilacs, always lilacs."

"But why did they leave?"

"The families tried to cling to their shrinking acres. The family at the farm once owned all the property on this bay. But it's not good farmland, too rocky to cultivate. Then the younger people today go to college and go to work in the cities. City people now buy up the lakefront lots, urbanism spreads, but there is a rural Canada still; it's not entirely gone. You'll find it in my friends in this area."

At dinner I looked at Ben across the candles, raising my glass in a gesture of celebration. "To us," he whispered. "I can't tell you what this means to me, Molly. You're the first woman I've loved."

"Imagine being your first woman!" I was flippant.

"I said the first woman I loved," he chided. "Your eyes are the colour of blueberries tonight; they change you know. I've tried to know you through your eyes, your moods make them different."

"It's only the colour I'm wearing. There's nothing mysterious about it."

"It is mysterious, I'll tell you why. They're smoky when you're amorous. Do you mind if I say that?"

"Mind? This is so natural. Tell me more."

Later, the bay reflected the setting sun, the trees stood in a windless evening and a robin trilled his lovely song to a dying day. In the rural night, a tedious whippoorwill sang. My inner core of being loved Ben and we made our own *Te Deum*, the rest of the world far from our bountiful world of happiness, purpose and joy.

I thought how strange we grow when we're alone,
And how unlike the selves who sit and talk
And blow the candles out and say goodnight.
Alone . . . the word is life endured and known . . .
And all but inmost faith is overthrown.

Siegfried Sassoon

IRELAND ➤

*H*OLIDAYS FROM WORK are earned and deserved. My time had come. With Ben in mind, and mindful of Julian's propensity for the Shakespearean quip, I was in a light-hearted mood. Like a song that goes round in your head and won't go away, I was tempted. *Come woo me, woo me, for now I am in a holiday humour, and like enough to consent.*

Being a sane person I flew to Dublin, a trip expediently planned to remove myself from memories of my wedding day. Not running away from reality, just avoiding the melancholy the conventional anniversary would bring. Optimistically I resolved to initiate a search for my mother's family. I was suffocated with yearning; extreme measures my only hope against hope. I had no idea how I would use any newfound data, whether conjectural or cogent. I was certain of one thing, I would not barge in and embarrass anyone nor would I, unnecessarily, divulge my identity. The probability of locating my mother through her family was feasible. If I had any success in Ireland, further steps could be worked out. Alden Nowlan's *Between Tears and Laughter* lay unopened on my lap. His poem "Sister Mary Cecilia . . . the Sisters of Charity Convent . . . Yo-Yo champion of Saint John, New Brunswick" was a masterpiece of truth and humour for me to study. I had cried at the reality and harshness of his earlier poetic "Britain Street, Saint John, New Brunswick," the street I ran away to in October 1938. I was inside his poem. His Britain Street was "a street at war." Where "gentle words were whispered and harsh words shouted." What is it that makes a certain place weigh so heavily in the imagination after almost forty years?

171

My mind was all on Ben. A vision of his bare, muscular shoulders and the exciting thrust of his hips when he put all his strength into splitting a log teased my memory. I thought about his natural good manners, although he had admitted to me, "I often choose to be an agitator, it brings out the best in people. I take secret pride in it." His formal manner of agitating was potent but now that I loved him I could find no fault with it.

On the way back to Toronto Ben talked about meeting Julian. "I sought him out because I had to understand my feelings for you."

"And?"

"He sickened me. Some younger counsel hung on his every word while he was being dramatically Shakespearean, crassly sentimental, really. Said his marriage was *more honoured in the breach than in the observance*, and he dramatized the line, *Did Heaven look on and would not take their part?* His infidelity in that instance was shocking; he was ridiculing you." Ben reached over and pressed my hand. "I was severe when I worked towards rejection on the motion for access, I knew you were interested. When I saw you in the Gallery I was sorry."

"You, you . . . I thought you yawned at the end of Evelyn's speech and I disliked you more than anyone else in that room at that moment."

"I'm glad you got over that. What do you think of St. Jerome's cut-and-dried philosophy, *Man is paper, Woman fire and the devil a mighty wind?*"

"I'll take St. Augustine's adage over that any day, *Love with care, and then what you will, do.*"

"*Ama et fac quod vis,*" he translated, devilishly.

I found a deep reflective consciousness when I first saw the coast of Ireland through the clouds. *A never but always known place*, I'd read. It's as if I'm going home, coming back to where I've never been. I've always felt Irish; it's in my bones. I've always loved Ireland, it's natural. I felt hope in the sea-hewn cliffs, boglands and expansive greenness, square after square of different hue. From the air, cattle and sheep appeared like little toys bounded within stone fences. *Somewhere, someplace on this small island, my mother has been and my father might be.* On this journey into the past I'd take the search as far as possible, making use of every waking minute.

In the prepossessing lounge of the Shelbourne hotel on St. Stephen's Green, I rang for service and encountered hospitality of the rarest kind. I enjoyed afternoon tea and scones served by caring people and marveled at the friendliness of a smile, a glance or lusty and lyrical voices in conversation. *This is another world, my mother's land.*

At the Custom House on the Quays first thing in the morning I was down in a tomblike room to search among thousands of volumes of registered births. After I paid thirty-five pence each for a ten-year search for the births of Kathleen Shannon and Francis O'Hara, a clerk obligingly set the volumes down on a crude wooden table in a tiny anteroom. There was no chair. From 1903 to 1912 there were eight Kathleen Shannons born in County Cork, two of them love children and two were younger than my mother would have been. Of the remaining four I already had three supporting certificates so I ordered the missing one for a girl born in Clonakilty in August 1906. Her mother's name had been Murphy, she would have been nineteen when I was born, seventy-two now. I took the time to list others born in the Republic of Ireland.

I extended the search for Doctor O'Hara another ten years — from 1885 to 1905 in all, assuming he would be at least twenty years old and possibly forty at the time of their tryst. In all the names investigated there was no mention of Bresak. In the Public Records Office at the Four Courts a scan of the Index of Townlands showed there was a place called Bresagh in County Down. The census for all Ireland was available too, up to 1900. But no O'Hara family lived in Bresagh; a Dr. F. O'Hara was indexed in Tullamore, County Offaly. I entered these facts in my old yellow search book. Matching birth registrations to directory listings was a stumbling block and my request for assistance brought little help.

The Irish Medical Association directed me to Kildare Street where I sought information from the Medical Registration Council, CÓMHDHÁIL NA nDOCHTÚIR LEIGHIS, and was advised to write the General Medical Council in London. I telephoned and learned that the only Mental Health Institution in Ireland in the twenties was Saint Brigid's Hospital at Ballinasloe. On my way there I enjoyed the drive to Tullamore where I stopped at a tiny row house on Chapel Street to see the family O'Hara named in the census. Charming people, they lived in tiny rooms and admitted what I already knew. "There are many O'Haras in Ireland, you do have a task."

At Saint Brigid's I was told that the records dating back that far were scant and many had been destroyed through the years. "We regret there is no trace of Dr. Francis O'Hara here. You could write the Faculty of Medicine at Queen's University, Belfast."

To see as much of Ireland as possible, I drove westward. In the rugged magnificence of Lough Corrib at sunset I felt my mother's presence in the brilliant splendour on the water. In the stillness I spoke to her spirit. In Connemara next morning I felt an eerie peace while I watched wild horses that roamed free on the bleakly beautiful shale and limestone land: great imposing mountains, beyond them loftier mountains like a blue mist fold on fold and then two rainbows in the sky at once. Absolutely breath-taking! Peat smoke drifted upward from low-thatched, whitewashed cottages and here and there a primitive TV aerial guyed to a chimney. I stopped in a village pub in Connemara and was awed by a simple air of greeting. One old man stared intently for a while; his fixed look annoyed me, but when he raised his glass to drink he said with a twinkle, "It's a durty wind." I took a seat on a bench, a low pedestal table at my knee, listening to the Gaelic sound. I wondered if my order for lunch would be understood. A few men in dark clothes and caps leaned against the bar, speaking in soft tones, simply and bluntly. A solemn woman in a kerchief, old sweater and dark dress enjoyed a Guinness alone. I found myself admiring the old Irish faces but then the cigarette smoke and a rank odor wafted by to still my daydreaming. The tender came from the bar and I asked if he spoke English. He was amused. He did of course, beautifully. A man in a maroon sweater sitting near me on the bench, and bending low to eat his plate of chicken, asked if I was looking for picturesque countryside. In my enthusiasm I said, "It's all picturesque seeing it for the first time."

"If you've come for the scenery drive out to Clifden, you'll have wealth enough to satisfy you for a long time. They speak the ancient language."

We talked on. I mentioned the names of my parents and got no reaction. "All the best," he wished. "It's a grand day now." He drove away in a black Mercedes bearing the small Irish tricolour decal in the window. Would this stranger be a writer, an academic, maybe a priest on vacation or a bishop in his maroon pullover? I would never know. I drove out to Clifden remembering Julian on the front porch at St. Mary Street after Young People's dance the night we met, "I think my grandparents came from Connemara." I heard the curlews cry, mindful of Yeats's poem and Julian's love letters.

The roads were quiet, no great convoys of traffic, just now and then a friendly peasant herding cows down a narrow way between high hawthorn hedges or the odd cow blundering past while a little dog nipped and yapped at it; or sheep spread clear across the road. I waited each time and the herder doffed his cap, giving a shy, often toothless grin and a Gaelic greeting. I found a spot from which to watch the surging sea and feel the wind spray on my face and hair. There were miles of gray rock fences, a labyrinth of man-made enclosures, as much a part of the landscape as the donkeys and sheep and sparse wind-bent trees they enclosed. I really wanted to explore those roads, all endlessly inviting, but a more pressing errand urged me on to Cork.

At Ardrahan I sought out Máiri Monahan, sister of my friend Tom, in Toronto. Máiri kept a guesthouse and all manner of Irish hospitality was offered: tea, scones, cheese or sherry. Máiri was in awe of one who had recently seen her brother Tom and was loathe to leave my side before she heard over and over the news from Canada.

"My ancestry is Irish," I told her and inquired again about the two names.

"Oh and be sure there's O'Haras all over, though not so many Shannons. Now there's Shannons in Gort, Thomas Shannon's family."

Next day I hesitated in front of a little shop in Gort, undecided about entering. I had to get on to Cork. A youngish man with laughing eyes was friendly. He doffed his cap. "Who would you be wantin'?"

"I'm curious about anyone named Shannon, my family name. They left Ireland a long time ago, from Cork."

"Aye, 'tis my name. 'Cross the street, fourth door, you'll find my Uncle Fergus Shannon, glad he'll be to see you."

A very tall, shy man in a dark suit coat, old trousers and a white shirt stood outside the door, tweed cap in hand. Laugh lines crinkled around his merry eyes when I introduced myself and I had to wince when he shook my hand, squeezing my fingers with his strong, brown hand. "You are most welcome. Come in," he said. "I have two brothers in New York and Boston. Would you live near them?"

I smiled at that simple assumption so prevalent in this small country. He led the way into the hall with a hewn stone floor and a large bicycle resting against the stairs suggesting raftered mystery above, into a tiny, crude kitchen, warm and pleasant with the smell of an open turf fire. He took two glasses from a dusty shelf and poured straight whiskey. He broke a piece of straw from a broom and lit his cigarette from the fire.

"Do you take a smoke yourself, do you? No? Me own dear sister went to America long ago but I was a gosson then."

He spoke freely, his manner winsome in that way that sets the Irish apart; his dialect hard to understand but I got the gist of it. He had massively strong hands, a thick leathery neck and a weather-beaten face. I asked warily, "Do you write to your sister in America?"

"Oh! if I t'ought I could write a letter, I would. One of her boys come by once, he was in the army. I hope I will meet her again, and me brothers, and have a long chat with them." A donkey brayed impatiently and Fergus Shannon took me beyond a small stone patio outside the kitchen door.

"There's Seamus," he said. "I keep him for the novelty but there was a time when he was a necessity of life. Here, I'll put you in the cart and we'll go round." We sat side by side being jolted over a rough piece of the old sod, Fergus tugging this way and that to make the animal conform. Choosing our steps carefully back to the tiny patio, he showed his pride in an ancient sewing machine and said that his father had been a cobbler and had shod the whole community with this instrument.

"Before Wellies were made, the farmers had to have good boots. My father stitched them mostly by hand. He'd stitch all through the night. His poor fingers wo' be so swollen." He held his big hand up and bent his fingers as if to feel his father's pain. "Then he'd sell them for shillings, aye. 'Tis dismal that none of his sons learned the trade, I being youngest."

Nephew Aidan came in to tell me that I shouldn't leave Gort without a visit to Coole Park or Thoor Ballylee. "I want to show you these sights and everything else." Aidan wouldn't "touch the stuff," but Fergus had another snort of whiskey. "*Uisce beatha,*" he said softly with a heavy breath as we left. I felt privileged as we drove down a peaceful ilex avenue to Coole's Seven Woods immortalized by Yeats, all the while Aidan quoting the poet's words in a lyrical voice. *What's water but the generated soul?* . . .

Before leaving Gort I pressed Aidan for the address of his relatives in the United States. He was vague about that, his philosophy appealing. "My uncles are lenient to the bottle and hard to locate. I don't know what you expect to find in Ireland, I hope you will gain some peace here. Often reality can be banal."

"Your aunt in America, do you know where she lives?"

He looked at me sharply as though he had the advantage. "When I traveled to New York and met my uncles, I had a feeling of journeying into the past, into the unconscious, in a way. I had so much in common with them and meeting them helped me understand my makeup and why I behave as I do. Aye, theirs was a hard life. It's to their credit they remained honest." Tugging at his cap to put it straight took care of his emotion. Though the Irish are warm and loving they sometimes suspect the stranger and will keep her at arm's length if she attempts to pluck at their mystery, so I was touched by Aidan's sincerity when he asked, "Why don't you stay on for the *Fleadh Cheoil*? There'll be singing and dancing and ceili bands, and uillean pipes and lilters, have you heard the lilters then?"

"No I've never heard the lilters or those pipes, and I can't stay on but maybe I'll come back some day."

"Please God, 'tis a shame though for the music fair is the best. Maybe then you'll stop to see the waterfall on your way at Killarney. It's Torc, there's roaring white waters and black shining rocks, there's evergreen trees in their brightest form, there's branches dancing 'round the cascade. You'll not miss it now, the waterfall?" He was breathless in his rapture. "Tis some pull-up to the top, but it lets you feel holy. The woods smell of incense. You will . . ."

"I promise."

"I'll write you if an address can be found for my uncles. In time I intend to expand my consciousness beyond the boundaries of Ireland, so please God, we'll meet again."

*T*he late October gardens through Mallow to Cork were rich with colour. Tubs of roses bloomed and the hedges were bright with fuchsia, rhododendron and holly. I stationed myself in a cell-like room in a guest house at the top of Patrick's Hill in Cork city and started the rounds of presbyteries, shipping lines and the birth registration office. Dismayed at the unhelpful method of recording births in order of date, I had to surmise that any existing birth information on Kathleen Shannon of County Cork had already been found in the Dublin records.

Not everyone in Ireland had a telephone. There was one directory for Dublin and another for the rest of the country. Church people were unwilling to reveal anything to a stranger; though they may be enchantingly friendly at first, they were evasive when I asked direct questions. I had to wonder how many people with spurious ancestry were trying their patience.

Next day at noon I walked down one side of The Grand Parade looking for a drug store, a shoemaker and other places while enjoying the friendly people rushing about. Some were friendlier than others. I crossed to the other side and stopped for a moment by a street lamp, continuing my quest for those commodities.

"Hullo," said a young Irishman. "I've been looking at you. My name is Johnny Walsh. Would ye have a drink with me? I know just the place."

I hedged and made excuses but he persisted in a winsome way.

"Just here, sure 'twon't take long, I'd like to talk to ye."

"Thank you. No. I have these things to do," and without reason told him I was looking for a shoemaker, a drug store and a bottle of vodka.

"Here, we'll go into the chemist right now and later I'll take you to a cobbler and a spirits merchant. Please?"

Sheepishly I let him direct me to a pub where we sat to talk and drink and ask questions. His grandmother's name had been O'Hara! He operated a Celtic book business, wrote poetry and had been acclaimed for writing about the new generation of revolutionaries. Everything he said ended with a question: "Do ye follow?"

"Sure, 'tis a warm and easeful way to let the hours flow, have another." He'd been in love recently, but ". . . she off and married some bloke. The memory is sacred though, not even your lover's behaviour can take it away. Can ye follow then?"

I could.

"Ireland's full of O'Hara's. Me own grandmother and me mother, God rest them, came from Mayo. It's a grand country, big mountains and moors and sea cliffs and inlets which make the coast far grander."

Mayo was a long way from Cork or Bresak, wherever it was, but the O'Hara name was the issue and I listened with purpose.

"Ye'll have another I know. I'd like to pour it for ye m'self. I'll show you me flat and tell ye more about the O'Hara's. C'mon," he coaxed when I responded with a prim squint.

"I'll leave it to yurself to decide then but don't interpret me motion as a prelude to enticement," he added with an expression of pious abstraction, trifling with my curiosity and well aware of it.

"Now Shannon is one of the oldest of Connaught names, common before the tenth century, scattered in the west, Clare, Galway and Mayo. Some in Kerry too. It can be Ó Seann acháin or Seanáin. I have a concordance that'll tell ye all ye want to know. Come and I'll show ye."

Feeling unsure I said, "I'll come for a short while. I have little time and much to do, I mean it." Was I not here to follow any trace, to grasp at any straw?

Johnny Walsh's flat was a large, dusty room, gay with bottles of fresh flowers and bottles of whiskey. *Deutsche Grammophon* record jackets lay about and a bookcase was all askew. A wicker hamper and a boudoir tray holding his brushes and things indicated that he lived in this room. He blew specks of dust from a record, and soon the sorrowful strains of Ravel's *Pavan* filled the room. He poured himself a whiskey, I declined. Around the walls I saw an Irish Blessing, a picture of a boxer flanked by two elderly people and two large posters of the coast of Mayo.

"I was a fighter, ye know; thar's me mother on one side and me father, God rest 'em, and that's the Coraun Peninsula and the mountains of Braoghaun on Achill. It's the highest sea cliff in Europe." He lifted his glass and emptied it. "Ach, 'tis inspirin' and spinechillin'. I hope ye'll see it someday, it's grand altogether."

I agreed it would be grand to one day view the coast of Mayo.

Johnny Walsh went on solemnly about one's sense of mission if one loved Ireland; about his one-time interest in the IRA and the terror of trying to break away. "They're a funny lot, just eatin' each other up. Me mom was always givin' out to me about it. Aye, I've caused many a ruction in me day, but me father would put the manners on me. Christ Jaysus, he cracked the head of me with a pot a time or two."

"The Irish are great talkers," I said. "I enjoy listening."

"Listening is something the Irish are not good at, they prefer expressing rather than absorbing."

He read two of his poems aloud, autographed one and gave it to me. That pleased me but I recognized the improbability of learning anything pertinent to my search and decided to take my leave as courteously as possible.

"But ye've just come, ye musn't go yet," he pleaded and, fastening his arm tight around me, he transferred his whiskey glass to the same hand, reached up and pulled an untidy Murphy bed from the wall. I dodged his grip but he came close again, fondling and wheedling with smooth talk, for he was good at it.

"Now don't be difficult, it's time for me to go, I mean it," I said, but he clutched at me and used his free hand to unbutton his trousers and expose his puffy distress, immediately repugnant.

"Put that away!" I shouted, grabbing my purse and then the doorknob. "Let me remember you as a nice person." He'd have none of that, but whimpered disgustingly, "Hold it, please."

My fleeting thought was of Christina, *if she could see me now!* "Wee cock-a-leekie," she'd say. For all I knew she *could* see me from a tartan throne in the heavens, for sadly Ina had died of a deadly fast cancer. Her memory brought more than a smile as I fled from the ebullient Johnny Walsh.

*L*eaving Dublin airport, I rejoiced for I was on my way back to Ben, longing for a weekend at Kashwakamak Lake, but more than a little woebegone at the elusiveness of the clear facts I still sought. I relived the ten-day trip in half as many hours, then collected my luggage and cleared customs. Ben was there to meet me, distinguished, a lovable smugness written all over him. I caught his eye for those first exquisite moments but turned away from the stare of strangers, saving my emotions to be enjoyed privately. *I love, I am loved, he is here!*

In the car I lamented that my search file was bulging with facts that seemed to take me no further ahead. "I go over it, double-check everything and still there is nothing to tie these disparate facts together. There must be a clue in all of this, one simple thing I'm overlooking. I'm sure I'll find it."

Lines of pleasure crinkled round his eyes; I loved them. Once inside my suite he dropped the luggage and wrapped his strong arms around me while he closed the door with his foot. While we hugged each other, I saw the sight of his strong, handsome back in the hall mirror and I made a good-for-you face at myself.

"I've missed you so," he whispered. "Thank heaven you're home safely." His kisses felt lovely, I was delighted. He leaned back, taking my weight on him. I adored his gentle eyes, his mussed hair, the vigorous communication from his body, his strong hold of me. I thought I must have been dreaming when I heard him say he had to go to Ottawa that day! And I knew I'd cry when he said it was a weekend session.

"The premier wants me along, Molly. It's almost mandatory."

"Don't we have at least a few hours?" I searched his face for agreement in the second before he told me, "Yes, we have time for lunch. You'll be tired this evening, and then you know what will happen."

"What?"

"You'll be up again at four with jet lag. After the weekend you'll be back to normal. Why don't you take your papers to Bent Tree in the morning, sort them out and make that big effort to find the missing link? Being alone could be the best thing while you try to find your next step. I'll only be half as far away from you than if you stay in Toronto and I'll go to Bent Tree from Ottawa. Besides, it's a beautiful drive in the morning, you'll be up very early."

"All right, I guess. But I don't want lunch. I'll see the children for a while later. I'd prefer if you held me now. I've waited too long."

Ben lifted me like a feather, strong and consenting. "You'll wait no longer, my darling."

*I*t was the season of plenty in the Province of Ontario. An early morning drive was a wonderful time to savour the spectacle of nature that transformed woodlots and trees. The hay had been stacked long ago; crows pecked at the stooked sheaves. The sumach bushes with their crimson drupes changed. Little chipmunks, seeming to wait until I was almost too close to miss them, rushed out and raced across the road, their tails straight up, like toys on wheels pulled on a string from the other side, daring me. At daybreak I caught a glimpse of Green Bay Hill and christened it palindrome hill—a protrusion straight down on the west side, around the contour of Green Bay by an enormous rock cut, and again straight up the east side. Ben called the west hill "the road home" to Toronto. Heading to the cottage I felt that way about the road in; the road home to where our love began, the road home to tie up the loose ends, to unravel the knotted hunches in my data. Such thoughts made me impatient. The last bit of road wound round the hillside and just before I turned into the bush road I spied a white-tailed doe and her fawn. I stopped the car. The deer watched me, perceptively sniffing the air for a moment before bounding away to the freedom of the forest.

Bent Tree was different with no one there. I ran down the path to the dock and stopped short, feeling like an intruder in the enveloping stillness. Not a motion, not a sound; then a solitary hawk appeared riding the air currents, gliding and wheeling so leisurely it made me want to dawdle and procrastinate and pay no heed to the wearisome thought of time. But this weekend was an encounter with time.

Impatient to begin, I arranged the pile of papers on Ben's table. The sent pile, the received pile, then the stack of Xeroxed sheets from directories and my yellow book, which now represented more letters to be written and names to be scrutinized. I sifted through the pieces again and again during the day, discarding the positively no-clue pages, the denials, examining what was left, frustrated by tedious phrases from the registrar general in New Brunswick and annoyed by the bureaucratic form letter written by somebody—lmc; signed by somebody—abj, for someone else— rm. So much useless paperwork and no information.

What remained to be considered was child number 583's record from the infant's home and my three letters to the Registry of Vital Records and Statistics at Ashburton Place in Boston with their acknowledgments. The record was the only substantive information I had and the words Cand. or Gord. and Bresak were so vague. In the three letters I had asked that the records be searched for a marriage certificate for Kathleen Shannon, emigrant from Ireland, maybe married in Boston after 1926. A form letter answered: "No search can be made for the record requested without the name, date and the place of the event." Understandable. The same form letter answered my second request, worded differently in hopes that, with luck, a different clerk might take some action. With the third request I had sent a cheque. The reply was slightly different. My name was printed boldly with a thick black pen after the typed *Dear* . . . and my mother's name was written in a blank space in the one sentence making up the body of the letter. "We regret we are unable to assist you in tracing the whereabouts of *Kathleen Shannon* since this office keeps no files designed to show the current addresses (or employments) of living persons." After the signature there were appended questions in black felt pen: "Did Kathleen Shannon ever marry? a) who? b) when? c) where? Your cheque returned." They were asking me precisely what I was asking them. A new group called Parent Finders had suggested when I called that I could go to Boston and search for information. It seemed practical, but how should I begin? The child of my rootless Self will not grow up without help.

Frustrated, I assumed that hope is wiser than despair and the spectre of "mild monastic faces in quiet collegiate cloisters" goaded me to determination. Julian would have aptly paraphrased my frustration, "Desires desperate grown, By desperate appliances are retrieved, Or not at all."

For the journey is done and the summit attained,
And the barriers fall
Though a battle's to fight ere the guerdon be gained,
The reward of it all
I was ever a fighter, so - one fight more,
The best and the last!

Prospice. Robert Browning

TORONTO/BOSTON ＞ 1978

*A*S NEVER BEFORE I was obsessed with finding my mother. She would be over seventy now; yearning and wishing weren't going to bring us together. It was my problem and my responsibility to plot my way out of this blind alley after so many years of self-pity. The subject came up, most often in secondary conversation with Ben, but in the everyday world of family and work and pleasure it happened less often. I was guilty, not of the way I looked at my problem but of the way I didn't look at it. A sublime moment happened at a friend's cottage while I watched a grandmother, over seventy, (visiting from Ireland!) jeans turned up, barefoot, dancing with her baby grandson, Brendan, in her arms. It was said she managed a bakeshop in Dublin and travelled. I whispered to Ben, "If my mother is alive, she's likely younger."

A passive Provincial Registry had been set up by the Legislature whereby an adult adoptee and a birth parent, who had both registered independently, needed the permission of the adopting parents before a meeting could be arranged; balancing two rights: the right to know against the right not to be asked. Giving the natural parent the right to refuse was good and proper but an adult adoptee needing permission to seek was asinine. However, the registry was a good, big step causing a sudden overwhelming outpouring of adoptees' stories in the news; an effusion of articles in leading magazines by informed writers, such as Margaret Mead's In The Best Interests Of The Child . . . and an overflow of information on organizations willing to help adoptees and natural parents search. A revolution was afoot.

I read a well-timed article by Sidney Katz featured in *The Toronto Star* in which he interviewed adults who had been given up. I went to St. Paul's

Church on Bloor Street to attend a Parent Finders meeting. I didn't know what I expected to accomplish in this milieu in a province other than New Brunswick, or Boston or Ireland. I hung back to observe the people. *Perhaps they'll think I'm a social worker, or an interested person.* I didn't want to appear desperate but I was drawn in and became more desperate than anyone there. I had found my element, I was aroused and I could let go.

Parent Finders had been co-founded by Joan Vanstone in Vancouver and quickly spread to Montreal and Toronto. There was a preponderance of women at this meeting; in reality it is women who give up babies, and women who search for parents. The chairwoman and a male lawyer, who were both searching, explained the aims of the group and their policy of allowing a parent the right to refuse contact. Their philosophy was simple and hard-line: that promises of secrecy made by adoption agencies to natural and adoptive parents were invalid to the children who were too young to make promises. Someone called out, "Adoptees' rights should come first whether it's disruptive or not."

"There's a lot of us searching. Twenty years ago ninety percent of unwed mothers gave their babies away. Today ninety to ninety-five percent keep them." Sounds of approval waved around the room. They invited first-time attendees to say hello and state their expectations. The rage at a system that denied human beings their genealogy was pitiful. "Legalized fraud, discrimination against a minority . . ." a woman said. News of reunions since the most recent meeting was invited. A man in his fifties spoke from the podium and he became a little boy as he tearfully told of having spent a day with his real mother in Hamilton. "My mother wrote to the Children's Aid for thirty years asking them about me. We should have known each other when I became an adult . . . The hardest part of searching was the subterfuge; lying to get information, and being treated like a child. The more I wanted information the less available it became. I was robbed of my genetic identity. Curiosity in one's constitution is healthy, isn't it? Well, it's over now, thank God, but we've suffered very much."

I had to find him after the meeting just to speak to this person, older than me, who had found the light in his blind alley. I never saw him after that night but his determination and his pure joy were my goad. I joined Parent Finders that night and my complex search went into high gear. Soon I was editing their newsletter, which kept me in closer contact with people and issues.

Members were urged to write the premier, the minister of community and social services, newspapers, the Law Reform Commission, the Human Rights Commission, the Faculty of Social Work, authors, broadcasters, any one at all, putting signatures on petitions that were prepared by Parent Finders Inc. when unfavourable bills or sections of the Act were in danger of becoming effective. Many polite answers and some concerned letters came to me from the premier, Bill Davis; from party leaders David Peterson and Bob Rae; from the chairman of the Ontario Law Reform Commission, James R. Breithaupt; from Hugh Mackenzie-NDP, Ralph Garber, John Sweeney, Minister of Community and Social Services, and others.

TVOntario's Harry Brown, Host of *Speaking Out*, aired a compelling program "The Geometry of Adoption" with the dean of social work, University of Toronto, Dr. Ralph Garber; Clare Marcus, journalist, author and adoptee, and Dr. Robert Seim, Psychology Department, University of Waterloo, an adopted person and adoptive father. They invited viewers' opinions so I wrote a pronouncement about my particular situation.

> ". . . Who is my mother and what is her name is a question one might find in a Dr. Seuss book. Who am I? is a legitimate question that is in the nature of all human beings, capable of thinking, to ask themselves. So, Who am I? I don't know. I have known no parents and no real name for years. All my life I've wondered, Isn't there anyone on the face of this earth related to me? What can I make of my life? What are my possibilities within the biological framework? What limitations to me or my children are imposed by that framework . . .
> Adoption has filled many lives with love, security and friendship but for many of us there is a negative, underlying effect—our identity is overwhelmed by other issues . . .
> Thousands of us who vote, marry, are licensed to drive and enter into contracts are deprived of the right to know our names, our genetic heritage, the physical, occupational, health, educational or personality characteristics of our parents . . ."

Next program, portions of my letter were read for which I was awarded a copy of Clare Marcus's book, *Who is my Mother?*

Certainly Parent Finders was there to guide those searching locally, but a wealth of factual information was now at my disposal. I joined CUB, Concerned United Birthparents, in Milford, Massachusetts and Lee Campbell led me to Orphan Voyage, a search and support group headquartered in Cedaridge, Colorado. There was an enthusiastic branch in Peabody, Massachusetts. Coordinator Susan Darke put me in touch with a professor in Toronto who was occupied with his own search in the U.S. His fundamental thoroughness lent tremendous impetus to my plans. He was emphatic that I:

> "Write to St. Joseph's hospital and state that you are constructing a family medical history and you want <u>copies</u> of records not a transcribed recap. Send a reasonable sum for Xerox copies."
> *Already tried, three letters and nothing gained but I'll try once more.*

> "Inquire of the orphanage as Kathleen Shannon, your mother. Ask about the fate of your child. This reverse identity strategy has helped many gain information."
> *Why not? I'll try St. Vincent's once more.*

> "Your mother either became a U.S. or a Canadian citizen. Write The National Archives and Records, General Services Administration, Washington, D.C. and the Canadian counterpart."
> *Will do.*

> "If your mother married in Mass. you can obtain a copy of her marriage license by writing to (or visiting) the Registrar of Vital Statistics, Room 107 McCormack Building, Ashburton Place, Boston. Be careful to omit any reference to adoption. Casually request information to construct a family history. The fee is two dollars and always request 'full copy'."
> *This would simplify every other step IF I knew her married name.*

> "As people go through life they pass through similar bottlenecks: birth, hospital, church, school, citizenship, jobs, marriage, property, life insurance, etc., all points where traces are left. Concentrate on these bottlenecks. Assume that changes came to your mother's life ten years after your birth. Concentrate on that."
> *I will*

> "You may do well to inquire again of the good sisters in Saint John. Do not refer to past correspondence. Some change in staff might bring you in contact with a more favorable heart."
> *Unlikely.*

Surprise action came from the American Consular Service at Saint John, New Brunswick; it was Kathleen Shannon's application for immigration visa. My God, it was exciting to hold a piece of paper with her signature and personal information spelled out! On January 10, 1927, she duly swore that her occupation was *Domestic*, she was five foot six, light complexion, reddish-brown hair, green eyes; spoke, read and wrote English. Examined by U.S. Public Health Officer, certified free from disease. Purpose in going to the United States was—*to study*, to remain—*indefinitely*. She had never been in a prison or an almshouse, or an institution for the care and treatment of the insane. She said that neither her mother nor father had ever been in such institutions, that her port of embarkation was Saint John, N.B., passage was paid for by *self*, that she would enter the United States at the port of Vanceboro, Maine, going to Sister's Hospital in Waterville, Maine to work and study nursing. Her mother's name was Mary, her father's Thomas and she was born June 30, 1906 in Gort, Galway. An attached document certified that the within-named immigrant had arrived in the United States on the Canadian Pacific Railway and was inspected on February 1, 1927. Her visa No. 853 stated her nationality—Irish Free State.

This was real, this had happened! I was stunned by these concrete facts. My mother was born in Gort, not Cork. She immigrated to the USA and uncannily her visa number resembled my orphanage record, Child No. 583!

She had worked at nursing in Boston. There were unanswered questions there. Nothing in Saint John, nothing obtainable in Ireland. Parent Finders stressed that one could make use of the Department of Vital Records in Massachusetts by visiting the office. "However, it is better to make no mention of adoption." I had read Betty Jean Lifton's compelling and instructive books, *Twice Born* and *Lost and Found*. She had searched the Vital Records in New York and found her parents' marriage license with a signature she used to trace her mother. I felt bound to go to Boston. I could try Lifton's procedure. There was nothing to lose and suddenly I knew this was the open door I'd hoped for. The drive would be shorter from Bent Tree, just over the Ivy Lea Bridge to the New York Thruway. I had to go!

Ben agreed with me. On Monday morning, November 13, 1978 I was at Boston's McCormack Building when Room 107 opened for business. Wary but adventuresome, I had walked uphill to Ashburton Place from the hotel on Blossom Street. I wondered what this day could possibly bring.

"I'd like to examine some records, please."

"What kind of records?" asked the youthful clerk.

"Marriage and death," I answered with apparent indifference, but my heart was pounding with excitement.

"For what reason?"

"Oh, genealogy." I tried to be casual as though I had done this very thing before when all the while I dreaded refusal. I was not at all certain that even a genealogical search was permitted and willingly risked being thought some kind of fool.

"Sign the book here then and come through that gate."

I wrote my name and could not believe this was happening. I fumbled with the gate, he moved quickly to help me. I went through in a daze.

"Are you familiar with the method to search for documents? Have you been here before?"

"Not to this office, sir."

He was most obliging and showed me the index books of records. "Write down the names and dates you want to examine; you may take seven volumes from the shelf at one time. In the case of marriages and births you cannot examine them until I make sure they are not confidential. If you find what you are looking for we can make you a certified copy for a fee. Enjoy."

To think I had the freedom of these labyrinthine aisles containing millions of records! I stalled to calm down, slowly putting my sunglasses away and lining up pen and paper while I took a surreptitious glance around. A man appeared to have a definite set-up with file folders and papers spread on his brief case; a blonde woman, sitting on a window ledge, pored over index cards. Maybe it was necessary to have an exact plan to work effectively. I started with the five-year index from 1926 to 1930 and found that several young women bearing my mother's name had been married in Massachusetts during that period. Most were either too old or too young and some were native-born Americans, but I officiously entered them on my foolscap pad. I returned that volume at once, having established the first step in the routine. I found my daughter Mary's birth certificate in the births section despite the clearance rule. It contained errors and gave me the feeling that if there was some hidden information not meant for my eyes the rule was lax. Seconds later I studied the death certificate of Doris's second husband.

The next five-year index also showed one K.S. married in 1931 and one in 1932; there were five in 1933, four in '34 and seven in '35. This would take some time to narrow down. I listed the index numbers and chose the marriage volumes out of chronological order. The aspect of chance was intriguing. *Chance favours only the prepared mind,* Pasteur had said; or better still, Charles Nicolle's dictum: *Chance favours only those who know how to court her.* The conceivable hypothesis was, if my mother had not married between 1926 and 1930, perhaps she had not married for a long time. And so I concentrated on the later records and most facts appeared irrelevant. With only two years in the second span to check, my hopes faltered. *Just don't give up now.* Then something happened. Turning the pages in the 1932 volume, I became very excited. It seemed unreal, I was in a daze, but at first glance I was certain and took another look, recognizing in a flash my own mother's marriage certificate. I looked again to be sure I was seeing those names: Kathleen Shannon had married Michael O'Connor in June of 1932; she was twenty-six, he was thirty-two. She a nurse, he a labourer, both from Ireland. No county cited. *Imagine! It seems Mrs. O'Connor was my mother after all!* My heart beat like a drum in the library silence, and when I was able, I asked the clerk for a certified copy.

"Are you ready to search death records now?"

So excited with my find, so out of control about my next move, I could only say, "I'll come back later for that, thank you."

"It's really simpler, there aren't so many. Same routine, the indexes are on the opposite shelf, go ahead."

Thank God for that eager clerk or I would have run from the building clutching the first unequivocal proof that my mother had lived in Boston. Thanking him, I went to the telephone to look for a listing of O'Connors on the street named in their marriage certificate. No O'Connor family was listed on Crescent Street now.

Apprehensive that I might find Kathleen Shannon O'Connor's death certificate, I searched for Michael's first. He would be seventy-eight now. Terribly excited, I worked backward from the present and soon knew that my mother had been widowed nineteen years before. Michael O'Connor of the correct age and address had died of a subarachnoid hemorrhage, thirty-six hours between onset and death. They had been living in the house on Crescent Street up to that time. That his father's given name and his mother's surname were different on the two documents was no deterrent to me. To stall for a short time the fearful task of looking for my mother's death certificate, I ordered a copy of Michael's. Possibly I'd impress the clerk that my business was *legitimate*. Settling down, I researched death information back to the time Kathleen was widowed and the lack of evidence led me to the happy conclusion that she had not died in Massachusetts and was now seventy-two years old.

It occurred to me to look at re-marriages. Access to these things was a stimulus, goading me on with a bold sense of being able to act. It didn't take much time to verify that Mrs. O'Connor had not remarried, at least not in Massachusetts.

I had not signed the register to examine births, but I quickly peeked in one index which showed that there were many O'Connor babies. But I needed calming. Self-possessed, I went to the Boston public library for a change of pace where I could fix on the family name in city directories. When I signed the Out column in the registry the clerk became more attentive asking, "Do you work in Boston?"

"No, I'm a visitor."

"You look nice," he ventured.

"I feel nice," I said happily, but it was not a day to dally with a friendly male.

Outside, I literally skipped down Ashburton Hill, anticipation and an enormous sense of getting closer to my goal surged through me. Downtown at the library, I scanned the phone books again for O'Connor listings and recorded pertinent addresses. In a far corner of the microtext department, with no activity around me, a long table and directories dating back a hundred years, I checked and found that two men were indexed as the present owners of the Crescent Street house. Then I began in 1932. Kathleen and Michael were listed separately, a nurse from Chelsea, a labourer from Brighton. The next year they appeared simply as *O'Connor, Michael Lbr. (Kathleen) hw.* The street directory indicated they owned their home. Subsequent years showed Kathleen, nurse, Michael unemployed until 1952 when Sean, a student, was added. The next year Thomas, fruit handler lived at the same address; in '55 another son Patrick and in '56 Timothy. Kathleen's status now—*nurse Longwood Hosp.* In 1960 she was listed as widowed with yet another son, Michael, a student living at home. Sean now owned a house on the same street. The next year Kathleen's address had changed to Fidelity Way, just nicely between St. Elizabeth's Hospital and St. John of God Hospital, where she worked alternately, it seemed, until her name disappeared from the directory. Maybe she had gone to live with one of her sons; maybe she had left this area; maybe she *was* married, maybe she was in a nursing home; maybe she was dead; maybe, maybe, maybe! I carried the huge tomes, three at a time, through the lobby, past security to the copy machines in the central library, reproducing everything relevant. I looked again at the phone books. No Sean, but several each of Thomas, Patrick and Timothy.

I went to Fidelity Way first and found a vandalized, boarded-up apartment complex, partially occupied, victim of the School Bus Legislation, I was told. The rental office had no records. I visited both hospitals where my mother had worked latterly and the last residence known to them was Fidelity Way. The receptionist at St. Elizabeth's suggested I might leave a note, for if a later address could be found for this nurse, they could not give it to me but they would forward a message to her. So I wrote a few lines stating my name, birth date and place and where I could be reached. It was a poignant moment and I wondered if my mother might ever hold this message in her hand.

Early evening I dashed over to Faulkner Hospital to see Doris. Reluctant to leave my papers and so preoccupied with the search, I had great difficulty visiting. I spent a long hour wheeling her chair up and down the geriatric ward corridor, using up nervous energy, mentioning the night lights along the Jamaica Way. She refused to see the view turning her head away deliberately like a sulky child.

"I hate it here."

Doris was widowed and Anne, her stepdaughter, had cut herself free as early as possible. I had always stayed in touch and saw her a few times a year because she was a human being whose life, through some quirk of fate, had been aligned with mine for three short years. I was sympathetic when, in the midst of men and women who had totally lost it, she'd say "Molly, I'm trapped." It was true, her legs were of no use, but her mind was sharp and there wasn't anyone with whom she could talk sensibly. She suffered with rheumatoid arthritis and had resided in many nursing homes. A difficult resident, when she was hospitalized her bed was often given to another woman. I got to know Boston nursing homes very well during those years of hasty visits and always had an ear cocked for anyone named Kathleen, Shannon or even O'Connor. But I never heard those names.

"This is a beautiful hospital, I'm glad you're comfortable."

"What makes you think I'm comfortable? I hate institutions."

I made a wry face for the irony. "Most of us do," I said and the sarcasm was there for Doris to take or leave. A nurse emerged from a room, gripping the arm of a dazed old lady, and called to the nurse's station, "Guess where I found her. In Mr. Walker's bed. She got lost."

While the nurse tried to maintain her grip, the woman pulled her arm away in a stubborn gesture, hurting herself and making a scene but the nurse held on. Others watched this show of defiance and authority from wheelchairs and walkers in the hallway, an ongoing tale of human life. I said impulsively to the back of Doris' head, "That makes me sad. She's helpless. It makes me wonder if my own mother is alive."

"Your OWN mother," she echoed scornfully.

"Yes, my own mother."

I anchored the chair and leaned against the windowsill at the end of the hallway to face her and use this moment to advantage. "She came to Boston, just as you did, from Saint John they told me. Remember when I was twelve, that O'Connor family wanted to take me? Do you know anything about them?"

She looked at me as though I had stabbed her.

"Do you remember?" I insisted.

"He was in construction, very wealthy," she said with authority. That didn't fit the labourer I was researching.

"Did you know anything about them, then or now?"

"Why?"

"Because it's only natural that I want to know about my mother. Don't you know anything about her, please?"

"I wouldn't know a thing about any of it." That ended the conversation; everything remained vague. I tried another angle though it saddened me to be coercive.

"Mary's baby has a breathing problem. You'll remember I had pneumonia when I was a kid. Knowing something about my background is important; health information is necessary today. Don't you remember anything about this family?"

"No, I can't."

Frustrated, I accepted that.

"What did Mary call her baby?" The pathetic loneliness in her old eyes made me sad. "I never thought I'd live to be a great-grandmother. I hope I can see the baby sometime."

"Her name is Jenny. Her older sister is Julie. I hope you will see them but I have to go now. I've had a long drive today. I'll come again tomorrow."

Sunlight brightened all of Government Center on Tuesday morning. Up the hill from my hotel the McCormack building was resplendent. I would return there later in the day but now there were other priorities. I had slept well despite the excitement. I had checked all the details of my day's work, though I hadn't made phone calls, not having the courage to act yet.

At the post office I learned there was no hope of checking an address change beyond one year. "But you could try the registrar of motor vehicles, if it's important."

At the registry I recorded several relevant addresses, some of the areas familiar—Peabody, Billerica, Burlington; some unfamiliar—Roslindale, Randolph, Pepperell. There was no motor vehicle registration for Sean in Massachusetts. Back at the library in that private corner with time to think, I rechecked the current directory for the owners of the house and telephoned. No answer. No doubt my mother's whereabouts could be established only by speaking to one of her sons. I wrote down what I might say. *My mother used to work with Kathleen O'Connor at the hospital. I promised her I'd look up her friend.* If that worked then I could ask later, *Did your mother come from Ireland?* And then, *Did she live in Canada for a while?* All very casual and friendly. But first I had to settle on the right Thomas, Patrick, Timothy or Michael, or Sean. Above all, I told myself, think straight or nothing can happen.

Unwittingly, I flipped through a small volume, North Suburban Boston, and there in bold print was the name, address and phone number of *a* Sean P. O'Connor of Winchester. This single Sean in the Boston phone books narrowed the possibility that this man was Kathleen's son. I was not surprised when there was no answer, it was eleven in the morning. I collected my papers and returned to Vital Statistics to look at the birth records of Kathleen Shannon O'Connor's children. The incredible truth was that she had given birth to eight sons, the last, Joseph, a month younger than my son Thomas. When I was pregnant, carrying Mary in Beachmont, my own mother was not far away and still having children.

I tried the number again, Sean O'Connor's phone rang busy. Someone was home. Next time he answered.

"Hullo," he said impatiently. I did not allow the voice to intimidate me.

"My name is Molly McBeath, I'm from out of town. I'm inquiring about a Kathleen O'Connor who used to work with my mother at the hospital. Would you know a nurse by that name?" *God help me.*

It seemed an eternity before he said, "Yes my mother's a nurse; she's fine. She had a recent illness. What's your mother's name?"

Oh God, make up something quickly. "My mother's name is Lynch, Doris Lynch."

"That's nice of you to call. My mother lives with Tim, my brother, in Dorchester. Why not give her a call? She'd enjoy talking to you herself. Here's his number, got a pencil?"

"I do, thank you. How old is your mother now?"

"I guess my mother is about seventy-six, maybe seventy-seven."

I thought she should be younger and my preoccupation with this caused me to forget the all-important question, did she live in Canada? Sean was proud to say she was from Ireland. I called Tim right away. An obliging, younger voice answered my initial questions then gave me the sense of certainty I craved by announcing, "Yes, Ma lived in Canada before she came to America. My Ma is seventy-two now."

My head was swimming and my ears were listening to my heart. His voice sounded away off somewhere ". . . but I don't get it, what are you calling for?"

"My mother asked me to look her up while I was in Boston, that's all."

"Ma is fine, come and see her anytime, she loves company. She's right here, do you want to speak to her?"

Oh God, no . . . I need a little more time . . . if I could fly through the telephone wire. What do I say? He said she was seventy-two!

"Thanks Tim, I will come and see her soon." His good nature supported the use of his first name. "I'll tell my mother I spoke to you."

We said goodbye and he added sincerely, "You sound like a nice person, she'd enjoy meeting you, she likes company." That did it!

Possibilities thundered in my head, yet I couldn't consider how this imminent change was going to happen. I walked around to quell my excitement. As much as I wanted to tell someone about my mother, or to have someone tell me what to do next, I knew that this voyage was mine alone. The journey was nearly done. *Think clearly. What do I do next? What do I say when I do whatever I do next?* These thoughts would whirl in my head until I acted. I called Tim back to say I had a change of schedule. Maybe I could behold and observe my mother this very day and find out if she was capable of a reunion with me. There was no possibility of leaving Boston now. I dialed the number quickly before I lost my nerve and heard my mother's voice for the first time.

"Tim works late today. He'll be home after ten tonight."

"Is anyone else there, Mrs. O'Connor?" *Did Tim have a wife?*

"No Mrs., I'm alone, I'm his mother. I'll take a message."

"Thank you, I'll call him at work. Good-bye."

I am his mother! YOU are MY mother! Go immediately. Worry about what to say when you get there.

Excitedly, I pinpointed the street on the map. Going to see my own mother for the first time—I could not believe it. *What will I feel when I see her? Will I be like her in any way? Will she remember? Will she want to know me? There's no possibility I'm mistaken.* I had often fantasized, with Doris in mind, that even if my mother turned out to be insensitive or domineering, I would want to know her, no matter what. *I am ready for this moment. I'll protect her privacy. There is no reason for her to tell anyone about me. This is so amazing, we've never spent a moment together, yet I've spent my life thinking about this moment. We've never done anything natural together, but I guess she held me in the beginning and maybe she nursed me.* All the pent-up cravings of my entire life sustained and directed me. I wanted to but could not think beyond this moment of my critical mission. I laughed out loud and made other happy sounds in the privacy of the small car. Outwardly I was self-possessed as I parked the car and moved up the walk like an ordinary person. I tried to look calm. *I'm not ready . . . I'll never be more ready. How do I handle this? I have nothing to go on . . . I can't stop now. Try not to say anything foolish.* At an entrance to the side of the house I saw remnants of a garden, tomato plants and the cages that held them. A coiled hose, an untidy garden shed. I attempted to knock and some force slowed my fist. I had heard my mother's voice. I could see her approaching through the lace curtain on the door. It was an old face. In a split second the thought struck me—I had knowingly brought about the circumstances unfolding so quickly before me; how unaware she is by comparison. I would be careful. I would not hurt my mother with the buried past if that was how it had to be.

The door opened. Each moment was in slow motion. In a glance I saw a tidy woman, taller than myself, wearing a short-sleeved blue shirt and neat navy slacks, stylish blue-rimmed glasses, and I peered into the same blue-gray-green eyes as my own. I saw wrinkles, lots of wrinkles, a lovely long hand on the doorframe, mousy coloured hair, not gray, and a beautiful smile! She looked older than her years. I saw so much of my mother in that split second on her doorstep; I loved her immediately and wanted to grab her.

"Mrs. O'Connor?"

"Yes?" She smiled, eager for company.

"I'm Molly McBeath, I spoke with Tim earlier. I spoke briefly with you, too. It's a lovely fall day, isn't it?"

"It is of course. Do come in, you are most welcome."

Still Irish to the core, I thought, as I stepped over my mother's threshold. My feet moved forward, my arms yearned to reach out, my mouth wanted to cry out, but outwardly I moved without effort knowing full well I was climbing a mountain, the colossal, significant first step into my mother's life.

Afternoon sunshine flooded the small room cheerful with plants and photographs, portentous symbols that this woman belonged to and was loved by many others. A large black and white cat lay curled up on a yellow cushioned rocking chair; a green carpet; French doors and white woodwork brightened the room that also contained a terribly drab sofa and chair. The woman made a polite attempt to establish who I might be.

"Should I know you from the hospital?"

"No."

"Should I know you from Staten Island then, Michael's?"

"No, not there." I spoke again of the lovely November day, stalling, while I sat down, wanting to evaluate my mother's state of mind and body. I remarked on the sunny room, the pictures, and the cat. "That's Charlie Brown," she said. I also mentioned Tim working late. That gave me more time.

"We've met before; I wish I could place you."

Her healthy curiosity assured me that she had her wits about her. I feared my first name might cause suspicion but it seemed not to.

"Do I look that familiar?" I finally ventured, not pleased with my question.

"No," she said, taking a serious look.

Being studied by my mother, who admired my fall suit and commented on my hair, was lovely. I had never given thought to what I would wear the day I found my mother, but my traveling suit, a deep green French model with a paler green cashmere sweater, was cheerful enough for this unprecedented time. There was no stopping now.

"How about Saint John, New Brunswick?" I said it hesitantly and was given another welcome delay.

"Were you in training with me?"

"No, I wasn't."

"Of course not, you're too young." Her grasp of logical things gave me more courage.

"Do I look like you?" I dared.

"Oh, you're young," she smiled.

I loved her smile. I wanted to see beauty and I saw it. I moved to sit on the edge of the sofa beside my mother, to be close, to see every expression, hear every nuance. Mrs. O'Connor leaned back, perhaps to see me better, perhaps a little wary of a stranger playing guessing games and moving too close.

"My name used to be Molly Shannon," I spoke deliberately, "I'm fifty-three years old, I was born in May in Saint John, New Brunswick."

Her slender fingers flew to her face. She stared at me for a long moment then gasped in amazement, "St. Vincent's and the Sisters?"

"Yes, yes," I cried and we were in each others arms, crying and hugging, questioning and affirming. I kissed my mother, tears streaming down my face. I leaned back to realize more fully what was happening and touched her cheek. Her words tumbled out.

"I can't believe you're here!" She literally looked me over. Her smile was radiant, bright with joy.

"My mother! I've waited all my life to say that. My mother!" I held her again.

"I blame myself for not finding you . . . Have you had a good life?"

"Yes, a good life; I have a wonderful family, you'll meet them."

"I should have found you! The Sisters were heartless, in a way. After I left the home I'd try every excuse to see you and they'd say 'If you don't have a home for this baby, leave her alone.' You were such a good baby." She held my hand then reached up and touched my face, questioning. "Aren't you full of resentment for all the trouble I've caused you?"

"No, no resentment, never. Just longing and curiosity and now, relief."

We smiled and caught our breath. There was a lifetime of stories to tell and my mother was as plain speaking and unhurried as though she knew this would happen someday. I wanted to hear every word she had to say and left my own story for later, except that some things came tumbling out, especially about my children.

"When I left Saint John that woman had you and I was satisfied you had a home." She looked off then raised a finger. "We tried to take you from the orphanage, my husband and I."

"Yes, I know. That's the reason I was able to find you today. I had nothing to go on for most of my life, not even a name. They gave me her name, you know."

"My husband, Michael, I'm widowed you know. He's the only person I told about you, I couldn't have married him if I hadn't. He used to say if we could get you no one would know you weren't ours."

"When did you know I was taken back to St. Vincent's?"

"I can't remember how I found out. When I wrote to the sisters I didn't say who I was. They made us feel guilty, you know. I gave them my married name and said I had a home and other children. I never heard back from them."

"Do you remember getting a letter from me then?"

"No, I never got a letter; we didn't hear back at all, I gave up. It wasn't easy being far away.

It was clear now that Sister Juda, on that occasion, let Doris McGlyn have the final word and I remained the chattel, so to speak, of a distant and unofficial foster mother who had changed my name and who was mistress of the situation.

"Your father, his name was Francis O'Hara, he was a good man."

My heart missed a beat at the mention of the name on my orphanage document.

"He never knew anything about you after I left Ireland. My mother didn't know I was pregnant. That part was difficult. It wouldn't have been easy to tell her, just that now it seems I should have." She became thoughtful. I waited. "We broke the rules but did they have to make us feel so unworthy of being mothers? We had to hide our problems when it's natural to share a baby with its father. It was a struggle to keep a proper self-respect." Her face lit up and she rested her hand on my arm. "But I met a grand priest on the boat coming over, Father Savage; he had lovely white hair. I told him I was in trouble and he took me to the Sisters."

Another name giving absolute proof of what I already knew, *This is my mother!* To please her I pulled Child Number 583's record from my briefcase with the names Francis O'Hara and Father Savage in black and white. My mother barely looked at it, actually dismissed it with a gentle wave of her hand, not questioning my identity at all. I imagined Kathleen as she sat before the nun or the official who wrote those names on this piece of paper. My mother was watchful for she pointed to O'Hara's name, becoming pensive for a moment. She laughed.

"He called me Katie, I remember. I had long red hair and I loved to ride his bicycle down the hill, my hair flying. Some said I was a tomboy; I suppose they were right."

"That's funny. My first son had red hair when he was born and I didn't know why. Tell me about your sons!" I asked eagerly.

"I had eight boys . . ."

"I found out in the last few days that you had many. You even had a baby after I had two. My son Tom was born a month before your last." We didn't stop talking for a second. There were two lifetimes to align.

"Shall I make us a cup of tea, Katie?" I asked with a gaiety so prevalent in the reunion. That delighted her, her humour was fine. I saw my reflection as I filled the chrome kettle and shivered with a surge of love. I looked myself in the eye animated, gratified; my head full of a million lively thoughts of me causing this to happen; of my children, of Ben, of love of life, love of love. I felt a prayer without words. Sister Rosa? Sister Juda? *Ha! you two, look at me now. My mother is real flesh and blood. I made her laugh. She's in this room with me, I made her laugh and it's a good feeling*. I thought about telling Mary and Ben and everyone else; even Julian should be happy for me, especially Julian. *I love her, it's only natural that I do. I've loved a missing person all my life and here we are.*

"There's muffins I made this morning. I never dreamed we'd be sharing them!"

We talked about everything essential and frivolous in our attempt to know all we could about each other. She was afraid I might not come back after this first meeting, and I, deep down, feared that my half-brothers might resent or impede a close relationship with their mother. Sean had phoned soon after our revelations to each other and my mother had motioned to me to answer the phone.

"Is my mother there?" he asked. I had this weird feeling, knowing I had spoken to him once already. My mother was still in a state of emotion and choked up when she took the phone.

"Sean, I have a visitor," she began. I put a finger to my lips. "Shh." My mother took control of herself. He did not question her quivering voice or the presence of a woman and later I surmised that she was given to weeping because of inactivity, maybe loneliness and that a social worker called in regularly. Sean was not surprised that his mother was not alone.

I made no assumptions about what would happen after today. My mother would decide that. I had found my mother; nothing could change that. These first hours were precious and I would go away sustained no matter what followed. We had tea in her Belleek china and my mother fussed about until she found a gift to give me to remember this unique day—a Connemara marble salt and pepper set. I hugged her and she touched me affectionately every time I was near her. Once we stopped in front of a long mirror to look at the image. "We are alike," I said, but my mother was taller.

I wouldn't have recognized her as my mother, she appeared elderly, anybody's mother. Our hands seemed the same but when we put them palm to palm, my mother's fingers were half an inch longer. We compared fingernails and shoe size, even weight. So many things had been revealed before my mother mentioned her home. "We lived in a place called Gort. My father was the village shoemaker."

I caught my breath at this inconceivable coincidence but did not interrupt.

"I had four brothers and a tiny sister when I left Ireland."

"Fergus Shannon of Gort!" I blurted out.

"God in heaven!" she shouted in amazement, "Fergus was a tot when I left Ireland and Norah was a baby. You don't know him?"

"I passed through Gort last year and met Fergus quite by chance, and his nephew, Aidan. They didn't know who I was, nor I them. I was attempting to meet any Shannons in Ireland though I concentrated on Cork. The Infant's Home record says you were from Cork. Now I remember, your immigration paper said you were born in Gort. I'd never heard of the place and my mind was dead set on your hometown being Cork."

"We were from Gort, that's in Galway. When school was out I left home, twelve miles away, to work in a pub, a shop and at housekeeping. Girls in service they called us. Your father came to the pub."

She mentioned the name of her employer; surprisingly it was O'Hara. More surprising it was, of all names, Francis O'Hara, the name on my orphanage record. Impulsively, not thinking, I asked, "Was the man you worked for my father?"

"Heavens no. They had the same name. They were friends, that's all. Your father was good looking."

"Where would you go when you wanted to be alone together?" Why not ask? She answered with a sparkle.

"Out in the country. He took me on his bicycle. It was grand altogether."

A good question. I was entitled to visualize my mother, my parents, lying together in a lush field in Erin. The far-off memory brought a gleam to Kathleen's eye, even now, but I knew the fear she must have suffered in the aftermath.

"This record indicates he was a mental doctor."

"I don't remember him being a doctor. He was much older than me. He made me feel important." She raised a slender finger to emphasize the truth. "He wouldn't be alive now."

Her gestures and expressions were honest. Her statement was plain; it was obvious she didn't want me to look for my father. He had been dead to her for a long time and I admired her simplicity in recounting a daunting time in her young life and her willingness to try and lay it there for me to know about. If he had not really been a doctor, she might have said that to impress the nun taking her information. I visualized her with the nuns, nervous, saying *Gort* with a brogue. Maybe the nun misunderstood, or maybe it was a deliberate error as so much identifying information had been with the Children's Aid Society. Maybe my mother *had* said Cork to steer the record away from her family and the man who had loved her, at least physically. *Was it her employer?*

"I'm a nurse, you know. I still have my certificate. Recently I've been working weekends in a retirement home. That pace is better for me now. When I became pregnant I knew that abortions were possible in Europe. Also, there were books for a few pence, though I'll never know how they got into Ireland, explaining how any woman could use a uterine syringe."

To me, her words reflected what she had learned as a nurse, certainly not conditions in Ireland when she became pregnant in the twenties. She put her hand on mine and turned the ring on my finger.

"At least I didn't have an abortion. More than once I've wept at abortions in the hospital and more than once a doctor threw a towel at me saying, 'Dry your tears O'Connor, you'll get used to it.' They didn't know why I cried.

"God is so good," she kept repeating, "God is so good," she said sadly and I saw it as something she wanted to believe. I wondered if my mother had been given a chance to feel love, to be loved or was it just sex forced on her? Maybe she had shared true love eventually because she carried many babies after me. I asked her why so many. She was sincere when she said she was happy having babies.

"The hardest part was they behaved as though signing away my rights to you was the only choice I had, that I would simply sign away my feelings of responsibility and love, you know. But it wasn't that way. It was like signing a death certificate. There were so many of us ashamed of being mothers, being told of the hardships of keeping a baby. They didn't say we'd suffer forever when we let our babies go. All these years I looked at faces in crowds, not that I expected to find you in a crowd, it was an irresistible thing that took hold of me. Oh the looking and looking." She gripped my hand. "I've prayed every day you'd come, though I'd given up recently. I thought it was too late."

"Well, I'm here now and it's not too late. I would have been here twenty-five years ago if my baptismal certificate had read Gort instead of Cork." I held her close. "My life is a gift from you and I've made good use of it. I'm glad you took that bicycle ride, Katie."

"God is so good," she repeated. Somehow I couldn't see His goodness in our years of yearning and my lost childhood. I visualized a home with so many brothers. It might have been hectic, it might have been fun, it might have been hell, but at least I would have belonged somewhere. I'd always maintain anything would have been better than St. Vincent's and the Good Shepherd. It occurred to me then to tell my mother just how close we had lived in 1944 when Mary was born at Chelsea Memorial Hospital, fifteen minutes from each other in the Boston suburbs. Our paths might have crossed.

"I worked at the Chelsea Hospital. I could check the dates."

"Yes, we can do that sometime."

We looked at some of the names I had amassed in Ireland and Boston. My mother was on the Dublin list of many Kathleen Shannons, the one born June 30, 1906 in County Galway. She had grandchildren and when I told her about Julie and Jenny, and Tom's baby, Thomas, making her a great-grandmother on the spot, my mother gave the reunion a crowning touch saying, "Just this afternoon you've gone from being a baby to a woman, a wife, a mother and a grandmother. God bless you for coming, Darling."

"I'll come back tomorrow for another day with you. I'll stay in Boston until Thursday. My boss will understand. It's not a critical time at the office; it's not the new season or playoffs or training camp or the entry draft for that matter. My friend Dorothy is covering for me now. We've worked together for years and she's willing."

"You'll not go away," she said emphatically. "There's room here and I'd like you to stay."

"But there's no need to tell Tim tonight or your other sons about me, not until you get used to the idea. I'll meet them in time. Don't do something you might regret."

"I'll sleep here." She patted the sofa.

"No, that isn't necessary. I have a hotel room."

"Please listen," she said with the determination I would expect of myself. "I want you to stay. I'll not sleep at all if you go, how could I?"

I wondered how I could sleep, except from emotional exhaustion.

"I've always wanted to tell my sons they had a sister. But Michael said it wasn't necessary. I've been very close to telling Sean. I've thought about it this afternoon, we'll tell Tim first. I'll tell the others in my own good time. I'll sleep here, you take my bed."

"No, no, I'll sleep out here then." I really didn't want to go.

"You'll not, you need your rest if you're traveling."

"We'll share your bed then, how's that?"

"That will be best."

"I'll phone Mary in a moment and tell my family. They know I've been searching, but all their lives I've been quiet about my obsession to find you."

It didn't surprise me that Mary's reaction was, "Are you sure, Mom?" Logical Mary! Or that Jenny's over-the-phone greeting to me was "Congratulations Grandma!"

Suddenly I remembered Doris and explained to my mother, that I had to hurry to the Faulkner Hospital for a visit, then we would have our first dinner together to celebrate this day of days.

"I'd like to go to the hospital with you. Could I meet this woman?"

"She wouldn't understand our joy, honest she wouldn't. She'd be unhappy and then, when I'm gone, she'll have endless hours sitting alone in a wheelchair. She'd resent it. If her circumstances were better or if I lived in Boston, we could work it in gradually. You come with me for the ride and wait in the parlour. I won't visit long."

It was hard to believe my own mother was in the car beside me. I found it difficult to visit Doris; what could I say? I visualized my mother walking into Doris' room and saying, "I'm Molly's mother." I wished it could be that easy to do but it was impossible. I talked to Doris about my children and their accomplishments and filled in much of the time with news about Mary's children, Julie and Jenny. Then I ran back to my wise little mother in the waiting room asking myself, *Is she still there? Is this really true?*

When I heard Tim's key in the lock around ten o'clock, I went to the door anxiously. *The next step!* I told myself and gave him my name.

"I spoke to you on the phone this morning, but when I called back you had left. I'm sorry to surprise you in your home at this hour. We can explain." What else could I say at this juncture? We sat down cautiously, our mother in her rocking chair, ready now for this eventuality.

"Tell him," she said.

I hadn't thought about being the one to break the news but I did it quickly with a few words.

"Tim, I've never known my mother. She was a young girl who came from Ireland and when I was born she had to leave me with the Sisters for adoption. I've tried to find her for over thirty years, and, well, I finally have."

Kathleen O'Connor did not look up. I sensed her waiting trust and Tim's reaction. He stared, blinked, he pointed to himself and to me and asked loudly. "Are you telling me that my ma is your ma?"

"Yes, it's true Tim," my mother said and she went limp with relief when Tim let out a boyish shout, "You're my sistah?" in his distinctive Boston twang. "What took you so long? Why didn't you come before?"

"I've tried so hard, Tim. You'll never know how hard I've tried."

He slapped his thigh with some alacrity, laughing loudly. "Wait 'till Sean finds out he's not number one!"

"That won't matter," our mother said coolly, obviously the tension was cut. "Sean will understand."

Tim had red hair, fine and straight and the pale complexion that went with it, and my mother's eyes. He was stocky and strong and just then he threw his arm around my shoulder and pulled me to him, rough in a way that any brother might be.

"This is great! What do you know," he cried. "I'm not number four now! Let's celebrate, Molly. I like your name. Do you take a drink?"

"Of course I do. I was hoping you'd ask. I brought Canadian Club with me. It's in the car."

"That was good thinking. I'll get it."

Tim and I drank to a significant day, a milestone in our lives, a link with Kathleen's obscure past, to this big step that freed me to be myself. Kathleen did not take a drink.

"I am home," I raised my glass and held my mother's hand with infinite love. "I'll go home to my own children changed, knowing who I am and where I came from. A toast to us!"

In all of us there is a hunger marrow deep, to know our heritage.
To know who we are and where we have come from.
Without this enriching knowledge there is a hollow yearning.
No matter what our attainments in life there is the most
disquieting ~ ~ ~
~ ~ ~ loneliness.

Alex Haley

AND THEN... ➤

AN AWESTRUCK CHILD on cloud nine, I drove home to Toronto trying to understand what had happened to me. Leaving was difficult. I wanted the wonder to go on, to know everything, feel everything in this new animated existence. I wanted to tell my mother about my desperation all those years, how much I had yearned to know her. A childlike voice insisted, *That's over. Be happy.* But it was not right then and nothing could make it right now. Intangible arguments with myself helped pass the hours on the New York Thruway. I could not forgive and forget but exhilaration won the day.

I wanted to say to my mother, *Let me tell you what I'm like.* But what am I like? I can't tell her. My mother will know a person made happy by finding her, a person who will fill her days with letters and phone calls and occasional visits, a happy person. She'll never know the real me. I mean, given time we'll discover each other's habits, learn each other's dreams and goals; talk about being pregnant, young and insecure, not ready for that important issue; about the war, about being working mothers, raising children, about women in the world today; ask each other if this reunion will change us? In what way? We'll form opinions but we'll never know what living together would have been like. We'll be friends.

I phoned my mother the moment I cleared customs at Lewiston. Sean was with her. He spoke to me like a little boy. "Ma's been telling me about you. I think I'm glad I have a sister."

I think I'm glad . . . H'm. Give him time, this is no small matter.

"Ma has been a tormented person. I believe your coming into her life will bring her peace."

He telephoned on the weekend and we talked for an hour. About acquaintance, feelings, opinions and impressions. I liked him, he was abrupt, got to the point like me.

"My mother was a troubled woman," he said. "I often felt it and there was no opening, no way to reach her. If she wanted to talk about you, as she now says she did, it was not easy for her to do so. Obviously, the loss of her first child was on her mind and in her heart always. I believe she was guilt-ridden."

"Maybe my visit will change that, Sean."

"We O'Connors are a funny bunch, some of us have warts on our noses, some are bald, we all have wild Irish tempers, but we are close. We're all delighted with the turn of events. Even Patrick, who's petrified of flying, wanted to know how long it would take to drive to meet you."

"I'll anticipate meeting you all sometime soon."

The summit of all my dreams came a month later when Tim brought my mother to Toronto for Christmas. To say that Christmas Day 1978 was the brightest time of my life would only begin to do justice to the peace and love overflowing around me that day. All my special people were at their finest. Had this Christmas reunion been stage-managed it could not have been better.

Driving to the airport on Christmas Eve to collect my mother and Tim, I thought how often I had traveled this road, hoping, hopeless. Now they were here, with gifts: a key to my mother's apartment in Tim's house for me, souvenir tree ornaments marked with the year, 1978, for me and each of my children and Canadian Club for Julian. Sean had sent a gold number one pendant on a chain for me. Tim actually brought a frozen turkey through customs.

I calmly told my mother, "Julian doesn't live here. We are friends, you'll meet him tomorrow at Christmas dinner."

With a dismissive wave of her hand, she declared in no uncertain terms that reminded me of myself, "I knew it. I knew right away. Don't you have a friend?"

"Yes, a good friend, Ben."

"Well, where is he?"

"You'll meet him, he's impatient to meet you too. I wanted to go to the airport alone. I couldn't believe you were coming. Ben gave me so much support in my search; I'll never forget it. I'll call him to come over."

"Good."

For all his good traits of being proper and polite, Ben had a way of being completely rapt in an act of love or kindness. His eyes and smile, even his touch, reflected the gentleness he felt. I thought, as I watched him meet my mother, only four hundred and fifty years ago St. Francis de Sales actually said what I was watching—*There is nothing so strong as gentleness and nothing so gentle as real strength.*

Katie said, "I like that man."

"I do too, Katie. It would be hard *not* to like *that* man."

On Christmas morning we indulged in a champagne breakfast at my home, long, easy and relaxed. Ben was with us and I invited Dorothy, my co-worker, for it was important to share this triumph with those who'd been privy to my quest.

As the kinship circle unfolded that day at Mary and Paul's home, I saw my mother's emotion when she met her grandchildren and three great-grandchildren. Tom's comic greeting set the tone. He hugged her and said, "Hello Grandma, long time no see, " and introduced his son Tommy who gave Katie a Hummell cherub wheeling a baby carriage. Her laughter was spontaneous, like the music of childhood, the rhythm of motherhood, the harmony of maturity.

Julian gave her a book about Ireland and I watched their heads together as she showed him the beautiful pictures of her homeland. She asked Julian to inscribe the book and said to me, again, with emphasis, "I like that man."

"I do too, Katie," remembering it was hard *not* to love *him* in the beginning.

There were spontaneous toasts and Christmas gaiety; compliments for Mary's turkey and trimmings. Potatoes roasted round the turkey were plentiful, everyone's favourite, particularly Julian's as he took his fair share then quizzically watched the bowl as we all helped ourselves.

"Just tell me you've got more potatoes, Mary. I have a terrifying certainty this might be all." He said that every year when I cooked them the way Mary had learned from me.

There were Mary's special pies and a gingerbread house Julie and Jenny had trimmed. They joyfully picked at the elaborate ornamentation, eating the chocolate balls, M&Ms, little sugar snowmen, fences, stars and gable ends from the masterpiece. Imagine me sitting next to my mother at this Christmas table! With all my children, their spouses and children, Molly Ann's friend, John, Paul's mother, Jeanette. Julian was there, with his children. Ben was not with me. Two days later I roasted Tim's gift turkey and we celebrated with Ben and my good friend Dorothy. We had worked together for many years and Dorothy had shared many frustrations in my search for my mother. We were kindred spirits, more so because her older baby sister was buried on the day I was born. Many mistook our voices on the phone, people often greeted us with the others' name. "See," she'd say, "you must by my reincarnated sister."

Ben took us to dinner at Villa Borghese, elegant dining enhanced by the friendly host, Ezio, who had his (he said) Romanian gypsy pianist tinkle the keyboard with Irish tunes. My mother's face was like a cherub's when he played "Galway Bay." The Villa was Paul's preferred restaurant for celebrating and it had become Ben's of late. Paul always left the choice of wine to Ezio, who went to his private cellar for a discerning selection. Ben also treated us to the revolving CN Tower dining room. My mother and Tim rode the outside elevator with floor-to-ceiling windows at which some visitors cringe. Not them. They pressed their noses to the glass during the ride up 1,136 feet in 58 seconds; fast enough to be exciting. Ben kidded he'd take the stairs, all 2,570 of them, and my mother thought he meant it.

Brien and his wife, Pauline, were living with me at that time. My mother was sharing my bedroom in Toronto. On her way from the bathroom during the night she made a wrong turn and crawled into bed next to Brien who didn't know what to do in his naked state. My mother snuggled into the queen-sized bed and cooed with pleasure and actually said. "It's so warm." I may have dozed for seconds, then realized she hadn't come back. I looked in the bathroom, behind the shower curtain, downstairs. No mother. I went to the basement, I dashed into Tim's room waking him rudely, saying, "I can't find my mother!" Except for the seriousness of it, my words were comical. He slipped his trousers on, looked under my bed, in the closet then ran downstairs and opened the front door.

"She wouldn't go outside? It's December." I was horrified.

"You never know." He went to the basement then back to my room. In desperation I opened my son's door quietly hoping not to disturb them. Pauline had to be on duty at Sick Children's at seven in the morning. She was on the other side of Brien and from the night light in the hall I saw her pointing vigorously and silently over him. Relieved, I whispered to my mother, "Wrong bed."

"Oh, my goodness!" and we slipped back to my room laughing to ourselves. Poor Tim. I tried to go back to sleep without talking to her. But every so often I felt her body shake with laughter.

She didn't mention it next day and I wondered if she knew or thought it was a dream. Not a word until four o'clock when Pauline returned from the hospital and joined us for a cup of tea in the kitchen. Her appearance in the doorway caused my mother to laugh out loud. She pointed and said, "I got into the wrong bed. Oh my." On subsequent nights I was aware of her stopping at my door and bending low to check the colour of the carpet before returning to bed.

Tim and my mother left Toronto after five of the happiest days of my life.

*I*n March I flew to Boston for the St. Patrick's day weekend. The camaraderie of meeting new brothers at the airport, vying for recognition from their "sistah," was funny. Five of them, Tom, Patrick, Tim, Francis and Danny laughed and hugged me, smiled and shook their heads in disbelief and we all went off to a restaurant to celebrate. The waitress actually said, "You guys are happy, I like it."

"That's my sistah," Danny said.

"So?"

"It's the first time I've seen her," he said boyishly.

"Oh, stop. You're gonna make me cry."

They took me to my mother. She was a vision affirmed. We embraced, she was real, warm and lively. Tim was annoyed that Sean hadn't come to the airport, but early next day he arrived at our mother's and we met. So different from Tim. He was taller, had Irish black hair and fair skin, our mother's eyes. He was attractive and emotional. I saw tears in his eyes and this handsome brother put his head on my shoulder and wept quietly.

"I couldn't go to a public place."

"I understand." I hugged him and he hugged me back. I watched my mother over Sean's shoulder, *God is so good!* written all over her face.

Leaving my mother we went to Patrick's home for a round table get-acquainted session. Three wives were present, Sean and Tim were single. They asked questions and expected me to explain how I had dropped into their lives, just like that! I did my best but my life was a complicated story and I may have caused more questions than provided answers. In an impulsive moment I asked, "This is St. Patrick's Day, don't you Irish guys enjoy a drink?"

There was a sustained shift to the bar and the emotional mood grew lighter and brighter as we sipped the afternoon away. A funny, and telling, thing happened when I asked Patrick's wife, "Are you always this quiet?"

"We were told not to say nothing," was her telling retort. I was not judgmental of their wariness.

One would think life had become a series of celebratory dinners as Sean invited all the family to a restaurant to commemorate St. Patrick and to honour me. The good humour was unrestrained and I wasn't trying to impress when I said to the Italian waiter, "The Gigli tape that is playing is beautiful."

"Ah, you know, signorina?"

"Beniamino Gigli is my favourite tenor. I've heard him sing at Massey Hall in Toronto in1951. In person, twice."

"Ah, bello, bello. Eccellente."

Sean said he was impressed. I did not intend to draw attention to myself, but using Gigli's full name was, perhaps, braggadocio. The high spirits continued next day, Sunday, for Sean invited us all to dinner at his home. Then *I* was impressed! He cooked a wonderful quiche and served an imposing salad in a gigantic bowl. The merry mood went on as they posed for pictures, all taking turns sitting next to me. My mother looked on. They paid little attention to her in their party mood. I could see she was content watching us. God knows what was going through her mind. She smiled knowingly when we posed for pictures. Tom sitting on my right with Sean on my left raised his beer glass in a salute and said, "Look what you've done for us, Molly. I've never been in this guy's house before. Haven't spoken to him for three years."

Sean agreed it was good. My mother looked smug.

Tom took me to the airport very early Monday morning, I feeling the worse for wear while he stopped to buy cigarettes, saying he was having a nicotine fit. After that visit Sean wrote to me:

> My sister Molly, I want to take a few moments to share with you how I feel about your arrival in our lives. It's tough for me to encapsulate emotions and true feelings in a letter. I need to sit down and talk with someone, preferably with a bit of the gargle in front of me. As you can gather, all the O'Connor clan have strong emotions when it comes to our mother. I for one still have not got them all sorted out.
>
> When I first spoke with you on the phone I experienced a curious admixture of astonishment, curiosity, joy and bitterness. Your visit has put the focus on joy and nurtured that instinct for happiness which we all possess. As you saw, we all welcomed you with pleasure.

All of the O'Connors know what our youth was like. What was right about it and what was wrong. We were not alone, you were. I tried to think and feel what your childhood was like but I guess I have nothing in my experience to help me understand what you must have gone through. It must have been lonely and confusing.

I am amazed that you reached your goal with a remarkable lack of bitterness. It appears you are kinder and easier on Ma than any of her sons. When we were all together you stroked Ma's arm and comforted her in a way that we would like to do but are unable to.

Well Molly, the point of my letter is: I was skeptical before I met you. But you make me very proud to have you for a sister. I wish you had grown up with us but I believe you are God's gift to our mother in her old age and I look forward to knowing you better during the balance of our lives.

Your brother, Sean.

*T*he ensuing months were happy but restricted by my job. I took a week's holiday in June and another week in August and spent them in Boston. I loved the freedom of taking Katie to lunch at *The Blarney Stone* and to *Blinstrub's* for dinner, places she enjoyed. When I visited Doris, my mother went along for the ride and still wanted to know her. I couldn't see the humanity in that and said so, gently.

Sean took me to lunch at his club, a tour of the financial district and a visit to the stock exchange, which struck me as uproar and confusion. I could make nothing of the changing prices flickering across the wall or the traders dropping paper on the floor. Wasn't any of that paper important? There was too much confusion for anything significant to be going on. I could easily read the news of the world racing by on the bulletin board above and tried to show interest. Sean laughed at my bemusement. When we left, he rudely said, "Good day, Madame LaFarge," to a receptionist.

"Why did you say that?"

"She gave me a hard time because you weren't wearing a badge."

Perhaps he thought my comment that rules are necessary was inane. He grew impatient. Later, in his office, he demonstrated the new Data General Computer hardware he had just purchased and explained he was a registered broker-dealer. His corporation was a member of the National Association of Securities Dealers and the Boston Stock Exchange. He currently had a sales force of 170 registered representatives in thirty states and D.C. pinpointed on a large wall map with pinhead-sized blue lights. Sean was the sole stockholder in the company. Not that I could remember all he told me; he was pleased to provide a printout about his business, Linsco Corporation.

We went to a bistro and we talked non-stop. Everyone knew Sean. He was keen to say when he introduced me, "This is the sister we didn't know we had." I accepted that but at times thought it flippant. However, I enjoyed being with him; it was a bonding. Among other things, I learned that Sean had been in the seminary. Every Irish mother's dream to have a son who is a priest! He left the seminary before ordination but he had obviously put the advantage of higher education to good use. He inferred that some of his brothers showed resentment, ". . . because they didn't have the sense to stay in school. Did you know that Tom passed his course and he will be fire chief at some time?"

"Yes. He called me about it when he was studying. And when he passed, too."

"You favour Tim, don't you?"

"I wouldn't say 'favour.' I do like him; he's easy to be with. I happen to contact him more, Ma lives with him, you know."

"Ma is not well. I hesitate to say cancer is suspected."

It was a blow and I can't say how I reacted, except to beg that it was minor, early stage, not a threat. I asked to be taken back to her and chided myself for being away too long. She showed annoyance at being left alone and complained that Tim should be home more than he was. She didn't tell me and next day I asked casually about her health. She said, "They want me to have a hysterectomy. Would you if you were me? At my age?"

"I can't say. But if you do, come and stay with me after. I have more holiday time. I'll come and get you, you'd be comfortable."

"We'll see."

I understood her preoccupation. She was a nurse and used to giving care, not receiving it. It must have been a huge shock to her psyche.

"You know Brien and Pauline live with me, she's a nurse. We'd have time together, we've missed a lot."

"Thank you, dear. Maybe next year," was all she said. I took her in my arms. We wept, the first time we'd cried since our reunion.

Home again, I phoned my mother's social worker. She arranged for a doctor at the Massachusetts General hospital to call me.

"The principal diagnosis is endometrial carcinoma, stage two. Your mother has noted an increasing abdominal girth over the past two weeks," she said. "Being an RN she understands a hysterectomy is inevitable. Examination shows her to be well developed, well nourished and in minimal distress for her age."

I haven't any idea what I said to the doctor. Maybe just "thank you." Sean insisted I stay home, maybe I could help her later. I believed him and waited. On August twenty-sixth he called to say the doctor reported Ma "withstood the procedure well." She was now in the recovery room in stable condition. "It's the usual cancer report," he told me grudgingly. "You know, they're sure they got it all . . ."

I spoke with my mother daily. Her recovery was normal. I longed to be with her, but I sensed they were all satisfied the worst was over and no one said I was needed or could make a difference—and I had to work. However, I flew to Boston in September for a long weekend. I found my mother strong and determined, looking trim after her surgery. I didn't move from her side. We had a quiet dinner out on Saturday; she enjoyed going out. Somebody, we'll never know who, sent champagne to our table.

On the fourteenth of November I phoned morning, noon, and night to celebrate our reunion, first birthday we called it. We could afford to be silly now. I promised I'd see her before Christmas. Later Tim called me. He was pessimistic about her condition. He mentioned weight loss and depression. She hadn't seemed depressed on the phone.

Doris McGlyn passed away on the ninth of December. I couldn't get away but was able to arrange a Mass and burial through a young priest I had met with Doris. Father Tim Murphy of St. Angela's on Blue Hill Avenue said he would say a memorial Mass when I visited Boston later in December. I arrived at my mother's Friday, the twenty-first, on a late flight after work. I was free of the office until the twenty-seventh. Tom was at the airport but he had to hurry to the firehall and dropped me at Talbot Street. It was dusk. My mother was sitting alone in the dark, waiting. A grim foreboding plunged through me. She said she couldn't eat and refused any morsel of food or water. She wanted to retire, now that I had arrived, so I prepared her bed.

Shock and questions surrounded me. I kept my fears to myself. Fortunately Sean and Tim arrived, as she said they would, with food and a

Christmas tree which we decorated. She did not eat. The Christmas airs we put on were superficial for I couldn't talk to them about her. Katie lay in bed just beyond the open French doors and laughed at us now and then and sided with me when Sean insisted the tree lights I was arranging on the tree branches wouldn't work. I plugged them in, there was instant colour and brilliance and a charming little chuckle from the bedroom gave me the feeling of what it must be like growing up with brothers. I hope it made her happy to listen to our banter.

During the night I was horrified to find out that even a spoonful of water caused her to heave blood, a most frightening situation that continued all next day even when she asked for a few drops to moisten her mouth. Sean came. In desperation I insisted she should go to the hospital.

"I am *not* going to the hospital," she said vehemently. Her insistence and strength shocked me and I could see she had some power over her sons. While Sean was with her, I dashed over to Forest Hills Nursing Home to release Doris' belongings. I left her clothing and afghans to be used by other ladies, rummaged through papers and pictures and took a small suitcase with some things and a bankbook showing a small balance. I actually searched for the I.O.D.E. book she had borrowed from me in 1942. It was gone.

Pat, Danny and Francis came in the evening. They were a somber lot. Sean called the parish priest and asked him to visit. He came next morning and said he would like to give my mother the Last Rites of the Church. Eschewing the thought of death I asked, "Will she know what you're doing or can it be like a blessing?"

"Don't worry, it's different today than it used to be."

"Please don't give her Holy Communion, she isn't able to take anything."

"Just a tiny particle will be all right." He was gentle.

A nurse appeared at the door. Sean had sent her. There was little anyone could do if my mother insisted on staying home in her own bed. She refused medication. I could understand that for she couldn't swallow anything without an eruption. I prayed she would put herself in the hands of professionals who could help. I wanted so much to stay with her but on Christmas Eve she became agitated each time I approached saying, "You ought to be home for Christmas." I don't know where her strength came from when she gave orders. It must have been from those years of rearing eight boys and nursing.

"You should be home with your family. Take her to the airport," she said to anyone in the room.

"I've had over thirty Christmases with my family and only one with you. I want to stay." Maybe the memory of last Christmas with my family caused her to send me home. I left her bedside, unable to cope. I sat with Tom for a while but when I went to my mother again she cried out, "You *go* home."

At that Tom said, "Let's go."

In hindsight it's easy to think that with a little tact I might have stayed. But she was adamant that I go home and she would not go to the hospital. I didn't know what to do. I was in unfamiliar territory; I had no authority to make decisions. I went home.

My brothers phoned on Christmas morning. Ben was moved by their regard for me. First it was Tom; fifteen minutes later Patrick and Danny. Michael called from Staten Island, then Sean and Tim. There was no change in my mother's condition, or attitude.

Christmas Day at Mary's was as it should be, a unique tree, Christmas stockings, excited children, happy parents, music, everyone hungry for the feast. Julian was there; Ben was beside me, fitting in naturally. My children loved him.

My brother Michael arrived in Boston on the twenty-sixth of December and I was told he just said, "Come on Ma, I'm taking you to the hospital." She went. I was also told she was peaceful, a good patient. Sean's calls to me were hopeful.

My mother Katie died on January 3, 1980.

I knew her thirteen months, I had seen her six times, we had been together nineteen days.

Her death did not devastate me as a mother's death normally would. The innermost part of me felt the triumph of victory for having found and known My Mother.

It took me nearly thirty years to find my father . . .
If it takes me yet another thirty years I intend to have a hand
in changing the laws anywhere and everywhere that deny people the
right to know about themselves, where they came from —
so they can understand where it is they are going.
I am not alone. There are thousands, maybe even millions of
people willing to help.

Rod McKuen

. . . AFTER THAT ⤬

I WAS NOT inclined to appear at my mother's wake where her friends, Sean's friends and others would learn of my status in the family. She had been a well-known head nurse for many years. In addition, private home nursing was her second job and she had nursed some special people. Tim told me she had nursed Cardinal Cushing in his last illness. I would pay homage to her memory in my own way, at home. My heart was broken for the lost years that could never be found. I wept for her sickness, not for her death. When Sean heard I didn't intend to be at my mother's funeral he said abruptly, "Get up here where you belong."

I went because I wanted to be there, to see my mother for the last time. Michael introduced himself at the funeral home asking, "Are you Molly?" I smiled assent. He took me by the hand into a vacant parlour. He didn't speak a word, but held me close for what seemed like a long time. In a touching eulogy Sean made sensitive reference to Kathleen Shannon O'Connor's children, naming me first on the long list. My mother's youngest son, Joseph, did not come from Florida. Sean, in his way, muttered some critical words. Tim came back to Toronto with me and stayed a week to rest. I knew satisfaction and triumph, my search had gone the distance, this was the end. Surely my experience will encourage other sons and daughters to continue to search for their personal information; some could find healing and satisfaction; some birth parents could be relieved of their life-long angst and fulfill their need to know about their relinquished children; some adoptive parents could admit there is a place for the natural mother in the concept of adoption and, in doing so, reinforce their own positions. Then again, things may be the same a hundred years from now. For my part, I gave the devil his due and found complete happiness in knowing my mother, though it was for so short a time.

During the next four years I enjoyed an easy kinship with my half-brothers. I visited Boston on NHL business three times and managed to see some of them. Sean was always eager to take me about and I slept at his home in Winchester. He owned a custom built boat from Ireland, had even tried his hand at salmon fishing on the Shannon. In the summertime he fished the St. Lawrence River with a friend in the Thousand Islands. He told me not to be surprised if he arrived at Ben's cottage with his fishing gear one day. I suggested he give me a days' notice or he'd find no one there. Tom and Marie's children invited me to a surprise silver wedding anniversary for their parents, a grand party to which every one came except Joseph. More than one of his colleagues from the Fire Department told me at the party just how much it meant to Tom to know his sister. I slept at Tom's home that trip. It was as if they had always known me; a pure friendship, benevolent, gentle and fun. At the party I was taking a picture of all my brothers and their wives at Tom's table when Sean grabbed the camera from my hands, gave it to a passing woman and pulled me into the centre of the group. Could anyone imagine that that priceless picture would eventually come back to haunt them?

Five years after my mother's death, Sean suffered a massive heart attack that killed him. Sadly, he had planned to be married on Christmas Eve. We had talked it over and I assured him I would be there. That promise made me think seriously about a commitment I had made to Mary. She had gall bladder surgery scheduled December first and I was to do Christmas dinner at her home. I was determined to do both even if it meant travelling during the night. Happily Sean had called on the eighth to say he and his betrothed had changed their date to December twenty-ninth. "Will that day suit you?"

"Oh perfectly! I'm delighted. Now I'll be able to come to your wedding without running home before I've had time to celebrate with you."

Instead, I went to his funeral.

Patrick's wife called me early Sunday morning, "Your brother died an hour ago. Sean had a heart attack. Can't tell you anything else about it now but I'll call tomorrow about the funeral."

In Boston I met Alana, Sean's fiancée, her children and her father. Lovely people. To my amazement she wasn't awarded a place of respect in the church or a seat in the limousines provided for Sean's family. I waited at the foot of the church steps to speak to her, only briefly, for my brother, Patrick, was urging me into the limousine. When Alana wasn't with us later at the post-funeral get-together I supposed she was grieving with her own family. Still I wanted to speak to her again. I searched for her phone number and rang her home from the airport, to no avail. I wrote a note when I returned home. She answered with a touching sense of friendship.

> Molly, thanks for your gracious letter. . . . The days have dragged on with little contact from the important people in Sean's life. We enjoyed meeting you because your name came up frequently in Sean's conversation. He thought you were quite a lady. My life will never be the same. I have accepted his death but my heart aches. We were two solitudes who found each other. . . . I realize we have a distance problem, however, if and when you touch down in Boston, I would love to see you. Please stay in touch.

On Christmas Eve, Tom phoned. I urged him not to be sad. A few minutes later Patrick called. I urged him to be happy with his family. Innocently I asked, "How is Alana?"

"Alana who?"

"Sean's fiancée," I said, surprised at the tone of his voice.

"Oh, her. She tried to steal three thousand dollars from the estate."

I changed the subject.

Michael called from Staten Island. Ben was impressed again that my brothers were attentive. I told Michael, naively, that I had just spoken to Tom and Patrick.

"Did you phone them?"

"Oh no, they called me."

"That's strange. You want my advice? Get yourself a lawyer. About the estate."

"I don't need a lawyer, Michael."

He let it go at that. I had no interest in Sean's estate. Some young businessmen owe more than they own today, but that wasn't my thinking. In no way did I conceive any notion or opinion that I would share in Sean's estate.

Michael called again on January eighth and the twenty-first. He was serious. I felt he might not be privy to what his brothers were doing, maybe he thought I knew what was happening in Boston. When he said that Tom and Patrick had removed my name from the list of heirs at law and next of kin presented to the court on the application to appoint themselves administrators, I wondered.

"I'll send you a copy of their application today. Someone ran a black felt pen through your name and address with no thought to what is morally, legally or ethically proper."

"Surely Alana is Sean's heir?"

"Molly, Sean died intestate. Alana has filed an affidavit that they were engaged to be married within days of his death; that Sean told her he had created a will and she was the sole beneficiary of his estate; that he had made her a gift of his real estate in Winchester and a new home for her in Osterville; that he made a gift of securities, stocks and bonds. She expected his will was with his papers at his home. No lawyer has come forward with a copy, maybe he executed it himself, maybe it wasn't signed. Who knows? I have her Complaint and Affidavit in my hand. Let's see, let me read: ". . . for Breach of Express Contract, for Breach of Implied Contract, one million, five hundred thousand dollars . . . replevin for his home in Winchester and replevin for a $250,000.00 property bought in Osterville where he had made a deposit, entering into a purchase and sale agreement . . ."

"It goes on and on, legal words. I'm just giving you the titles, I'll send you a copy. The point is, you're not on the court's list or a lawyer's list to get these documents. I'm obligated to let you know. Just how far you think you'd pursue this is your business. I'll say it once again, get a lawyer."

"Michael, Alana has every right . . ."

"We know that."

"What did Patrick mean when he said she tried to steal three thousand dollars?"

"Sean had given her a rare emerald gem stone, $25,000 she states in her claim. He was having it set for an engagement ring. The setting cost three thousand dollars. She tried to claim her ring from the jeweler, he couldn't release an estate item. As simple as that."

"Where does this contemptible attitude come from? I can't understand it and I won't accept it."

"Off the record Molly, I believe it could be Patrick's wife. Your brothers have never rejected you. She loves controversy in the family. After Sean's funeral, when you left for the airport, Jane solemnly told all present, 'She's not Sean O'Connor's sister.' The estate lawyer called a family meeting in Boston. When he said that you had equal rights, Patrick complained, 'No one proved to me she was my sister. She has one hell of a nerve trying to get money.' They are so crass their lawyer gave them a lecture on handling people. There you have it."

"How vulgar. Me trying to get money? Is he insane? I had no idea this was going on, Michael. If it wasn't so brutal it would be funny. If that's the way they feel though, they've got a battle on their hands. No one on the face of this earth will tell *Me* I am not my mother's daughter."

"Like I said, get a lawyer."

Finding my mother was my life's dream. My identity was proven, unmistakable, priceless, everlasting and personal. Having come this far I'd fight her sons if they dared to discredit me. I had no choice.

*M*ichael called next to report that a *new* estate lawyer had gone to court with a petition for disbursement emphasizing that "All legal heirs had agreed to disbursement . . ."

"We are NOT in agreement, Teresa and me. We gave it to them in writing. A copy of my letter is on its way to you. Also, we're not sending you information because we've chosen sides, Molly. We mean it because it's right. It's a full-blown fiasco now. You should have seen us in the lawyer's boardroom, we came in large numbers. Even Joe, who didn't come to Ma's funeral or Sean's, was there. We looked like the odd-balls. Tom is mad and annoyed but he has a little heart somewhere. Patrick is mad and will go to his grave getting what he wants."

"Michael, I was married with a child before I knew my name and a grandmother before I was able to hold my mother in my arms while we both cried for the inhumanity of uncaring people. They won't get away with discrediting me."

"It's incredible that you persevered. It's a beautiful story that still chokes me up whenever I think of you meeting Ma. That's why I'm saying get a lawyer."

With the lawyer who had closed Doris McGlyn's bank account for me, I appeared in probate court on an Equity Complaint for Injunctive Relief, seeking a Temporary Restraining Order on distribution. It was granted judiciously by an old Irish judge named Sullivan with one terse statement. "The administrators shall maintain assets in the estate of Sean O'Connor of at least two hundred thousand dollars as a reserve to satisfy the one-eighth potential share of the plaintiff." My lawyer wrote out the judge's dictum and Judge Sullivan signed it. Maybe he foresaw the stupidity of expending thousands of dollars on a lawsuit the cost of which would far surpass my share, for he asked, "What is the problem here?" My lawyer spoke to him and he quite humanely answered, "They will put aside her share and do what they want with the balance." The fight for my identity started all over again.

Each time I had to be in Boston, Paul, Mary's husband, was by my side. He was there for the initial interview with my lawyer, he sat with me when I gave my deposition to my half-brothers' lawyer; he was there when I begged a restraining order, he was with me at a pretrial hearing and he was beside me now in Middlesex Family Court in Cambridge. His constancy gave me strength. Two years and nine months to the day of Sean's death, September 9, 1987, the case came to trial before His Honour, Judge Vincent Leahy.

I gave testimony and was cross-examined for two days. It was not difficult, except in the beginning, when I faced the fear of not knowing what would happen and how much the outcome depended on me. I believed I was right. If I stayed with the truth, I could not make a mistake. In recounting my story to the court I was inclined to say, my mother said this, or Tim said that. Their counsel jumped to his feet repeatedly shouting, "Hearsay." It worked for a while and I tried to be more selective with tense. He continued to be disruptive and the judge finally told him, "We have to know the story, neither the mother nor the brother can be here, continue." I thought the judge believed me. I sensed a rapport with him and began to enjoy the drama, keeping in mind that one could be lured into presumption and trust that might boomerang.

I saw red when their counsel produced a copy of Particulars of Registration of my Birth, waving it about in a victorious manner. I had been specifically denied that copy six times by the Registrar General in my own country, twice since this case had come to trial. My final appeal to the Privacy Commissioner of Canada resulted in more so-called red tape. "The information that you are seeking was received in confidence from the Province of New Brunswick. Therefore, your complaint is not justified."

For God's sake, I had found my mother by my own determination, loved her, buried her. Where were these shining-faced do-gooders when I was deprived of my own name at Doris McGlyn's whim? Prevented from going to a family when I was twelve—so she might have an arms-length daughter to look after her? By what law should I have been called Molly McGlyn all my life? When a Human Rights Office wrote me that the information I requested, even for evidence in court, was beyond the scope of the Canadian Human Rights Act, I was tempted to ask him: Should I appeal to the Society for the Prevention of Cruelty to Animals?

These days in court were crucial; they had to confirm the validity of my lifelong search for my mother and the brief joy of reunion and acceptance. Sadly my erstwhile loving brothers could shatter that truth ruthlessly. Those who were dear to me knew I was right, so I'd bear up while the defendants' lawyer tried to reduce me to a nonentity, an insignificant whiffet, a cowering nobody. Life was like that growing up alone. Incredibly this outrageous dismissal was being inflicted on me by my own family. They'd find out, like their mother, I was a woman to be reckoned with.

The white-haired judge appeared annoyed by the continuing unpleasantness. "The hostility you are creating has nothing to do with the simple question—Is the petitioner the mother's daughter? Continue now."

After the judge's caution all eyes in the courtroom were on the defense attorney. He rearranged papers with apparently cool indifference. Making me out to be a money-grubber, insinuating that I "took" money from Harry McGlyn's estate, was a waste of time because it wasn't true. He emphasized that I derived benefit from Doris McGlyn's bank account for I was *her* legal daughter. I flatly informed him the nineteen hundred dollars therein fell short of her funeral cost and the lawyer's fee. Defying the judge, he stooped lower, "You said in your deposition that Harry McGlyn gave you fifty cents every time you saw him when you were a child. Isn't that the reason you went to see him?"

"No. Maybe."

"Let me read what you said. 'Whenever I could slip away from the orphanage and not be missed I would go to his shop. Or if I was sent on an errand or to the doctor I always went to see him because he gave me a fifty-cent piece. I liked to think he kept one ready for me in his pocket.' Wasn't that a lot of money then?"

"Yes, it was. I was a child and I've never forgotten it. But there was something else besides the money. He cared about me, against all odds he cared, that's why I went to see him. He planned to have that half-dollar for me because he always had it in the same little vest pocket. It was an act of love when I saw his hand go there. Sadly, I was too young to express my feelings for him, so I'd grab that shiny fifty-cent piece with the head of King George V on it and run happily on my way. I always looked back and waved. He made me happy when he stopped his work to watch me go and I made him happy. I could see it. How can you twist that childhood memory into something selfish?"

My brothers Tom, Patrick, Danny and Joseph were on the other side of the courtroom, exuding antagonism and resolve. Tim was too ill to be in court. My brother Michael and his wife were beside me. Paul, my strength during these long days, was unswerving in his devotion.

I looked across the court room and wondered how anyone with vision could dispute the gray-green eyes on every sibling face, some warm and some cold, but all with that unique shade our mother had passed on to us. These brothers had become closer to me in six years than most siblings would after growing up together. Maybe that was the crux of it, we didn't grow up together. Sean had said earnestly more than once, "I want to know you better." I felt the same way about him and told him so after our mother's funeral, sensing we were alike, stubborn, sensitive, susceptible and stable. Now he was dead of cardiac arrest at forty-nine, intestate. We would never know each other any better. But I was getting to know my other brothers too well.

Tom, a year younger than Sean, always said when he had phoned, "It's your favourite brother calling." He called often for moral support when he was doing exams for a major promotion, happy that a distant sister cared about his struggle. Then when he got the promotion, the phone calls were joyous with enthusiasm for that extra relationship that meant so much to him. Still, on the witness stand he swore he never told his children I was their aunt. Insipidly he repeated, "I have five children. How could I tell them their grandmother had a baby?" Even after the exhibits of cards and letters addressed "Dear Aunt Molly" and signed, "Your niece . . ." Tom swore again, "I told them maybe, maybe she could be, but I never believed it myself. She never proved it to me." He actually blundered once, looking at his lawyer, "Oh, you told me not to say that."

I found Patrick quiet. I don't think he resented the sister he never knew, for he found extra moments to see me. Once, at six in the morning, in a driving Boston rain, he picked me up from our mother's home for breakfast at a pancake house. Conversation was not easy with him but he didn't seem to resent me. Another time, with his family he took me to the airport and sent me off with a foot-tall Little Drummer Boy statue who beat a drum and played the tune, and photographs of his exquisite little girl and teenage son. He'd say with pride to someone nearby at the St. Patrick's Day parade or in a bar, "That's my sistah." When Sean took us all to dinner, Patrick signed the menu, *To the best sister a man could wish for.* And then he swore on the witness stand that he never drove me to the airport, never gave me pictures, never believed I was his sister because I didn't prove it to him.

Red-headed Tim, next by age, had from the outset been happiest about my appearance in their lives; happiest because five times that first year I travelled to Boston to visit my mother in his home. Because I brought a new dimension to our mother's life it relieved him of the everyday association with her. Tim was emotional when he told me, "You've brought Ma more happiness in a year than any of us could in a lifetime." Tim also denied our relationship in a typed letter read in court stating he had gone to Toronto because he was curious. That surprised my son-in-law, Paul, recalling that Christmas Day at his home in Toronto when my whole family took to Tim. It was obvious he believed in me then. He was deathly ill at the time of the trial, so because of my declarations under oath and pictures and cards he had sent to me, his letter of testimony was deemed tainted by undue influence and struck from the record. Just the same, his suggested turnabout made me sad. He died within the year.

Dark-haired like Sean and Tom, and me, Michael was genuine and honest, I sensed. When he heard about the mother-daughter reunion on his birthday, he had written from his home in Staten Island, "I can't think of a better birthday gift than to have a new sister even though this gift comes to me at the age of thirty-six." He was mature enough to consider with me the pain our mother must have suffered. It was natural for him to say, "I knew there was something, I often felt she wanted to tell me something. She was always sad on Mother's Day and sometimes she seemed so alone, days when we couldn't get through her mood." I wasn't surprised that Michael and his wife remained faithful to her memory and to me.

I had never met Joseph, another redhead like Danny and Francis. The youngest, he was not at Sean's funeral, or his mother's for that matter, for at those times it seemed his family in Boston did not have contact with him. Yet, with his brother's estate the issue, Joe was there in court, small and dandy, so blatant about issues in his mother's life which were obscure to him, perjuring himself if it suited him to do so. He expounded on his mother's ill health, her senility, her inability to know him, after having introduced into evidence for the handwriting expert an intelligent letter written to him by his mother during the time of her "terrible illness." A month younger than my son, Tom, he stood in the witness box, choked up, suggesting that my claim to be their sister implied ". . . that my mother, I repeat, my mother, not hers, was a . . ., a . . . I can't say the word." After I found my mother, Joseph had telephoned me at least twice. Friendly, inquisitive calls. He said, "I have to explain myself." I hastened to tell him I would do the explaining. Yet he swore on the Bible in court that he had never spoken to me.

I wondered what caused families to act this way when a family member died. Mere greed? That was senseless and venal for over the three-year argument attorney's fees had drained much of the estate away. I felt it all started with Patrick and his wife deciding there'd be no complications if they crossed my name off the list of siblings, that nothing would come of it; after all I lived in another country. But they didn't know me well enough. No inheritance could compensate for denying my identity and the intimacy of being my mother's daughter. No, they did not know me well enough but they should have known that our mother would have been outraged and insulted. And I knew my mother would defend her rights and would expect me to do the same, at any cost. However bad my brothers' feelings towards me, nothing, no one, could spoil the absolute satisfaction of knowing who I was, knowing my mother and her knowing me. Why wouldn't they let her rest in peace!

Sean's fiancée, Alana, took the stand on my behalf. It must have been painful for her to recount her love for Sean in this hostile milieu. He had said to her, she testified, "You'll like my sister; she's a lady. I hope you'll see each other often." She also told the court that Sean had kept a diary documenting his personal reaction and surprise on learning about me. There was a tape, too, she said, recordings of conversations Sean had with his mother in which they talked about me. I wondered if Katie knew she was being taped. But the tape and diaries were missing and no one made an issue of it. She also testified that Sean had executed a new will, making her his heir. But no will was found. Nothing was said at the trial about the purported break-in at Sean's home the night of the wake. Nothing had been stolen—not the art pieces, gold items, computer equipment, liquor, stereo system, or cameras. The TV sitting invitingly on the kitchen counter had been ignored, yet his files were messed up and papers strewn around. Nobody mentioned this and, unfortunately, Alana's lawyers must have been unable to prove there was a will because she did not succeed with her lawsuit.

My attorney, Geoff Stall, had been dramatic and daring, undismayed by the high-handed maneuvers foisted on the court by the defense. He was tall and fair with a pleasant, easy manner. He utterly demolished Joseph O'Connor's credibility, making him admit repeatedly that what he had said was not the truth. Still trying to get the upper hand, Joseph had the swaggering courage to say, "Molly McBeath insults my intelligence and my belief in common decency. You don't just knock on the door of a elderly and feeble woman and announce 'I'm the daughter you never admitted to having.'" He was cautioned for contempt. Dropping my head I winced and took a furtive glance while Mr. Stall continued to attack and incite Joseph, making me nervous and giddy enough to fear laughing out loud at this young lawyer defending my identity with every bone of his body.

He handled the blood test documentation with remarkable insight, proving that my brother Michael and I were ninety-nine times more apt to be related than any other person walking around the courthouse or down the street. "The Kinship Index for Molly McBeath is 1046 indicating she is that many times more likely than the random Caucasian to have genes in common with Michael O'Connor," he read from the report. "The attached phenotypes and calculations are strong evidence of kinship." He gave emphasis to the importance of just one additional brother giving blood samples for this test, but none would. In preparation for the trial, Michael's wife, a nurse, had suggested that my brother and I have blood drawn on the same day through the same laboratory. "Genetic fingerprinting should be invaluable to the proceedings." She had been right. My lawyers had used the results to advantage. The expert from the Center for Blood Research had been convincing on the stand, her credentials impressive. Without attempting to explain the scientific basis for the test, her testimony established that, of fourteen markers examined, there was a kinship match in twelve. The probability of kinship was determined to be ninety-nine percent. We had a common parent. Judge Leahy questioned the expert as she flipped the pages on the easel to explain the result of each marker; the mean, the norm and her findings. I wanted to cheer her on. Her bold assertions of the high probability of kinship were music to my ears. Of course the defense wanted to throw the evidence out, strike it from the record. Such tests were admissible only to determine paternity, he argued. But the judge disallowed the motion and, with the intensity of a student, questioned the expert witness.

The handwriting presentation was extreme. Called by the defense the expert undertook to prove that the handwriting on my registration of birth was not the handwriting of the nurse Kathleen Shannon, or of the immigrant writer of a postcard from Halifax mailed home to Ireland soon after disembarkation in 1925. Four enlarged signatures appeared to be clearly the writing of two different people. The signatures on a nursing document and a passport slanted to the left, while that on the registration of birth slanted to the right. But the signature on the postcard also slanted to the right and bringing it into evidence proved imprudent on their part. Geoff Stall cross-examined the expert mercilessly on three common characteristics, the initial stroke in forming capital K; the unusual crossing of the letter 't' with the bar to the right of the downward stroke, and pen-lifts occurring between the same letters of all the signatures. I had pointed out this phenomenon to my attorney. My mother's signatures always separated *Shann on*. In court, signatures I had not seen before carried this same conspicuous characteristic.

In spite of the pen-lifts, the handwriting expert defended her opinions. She had to concede many points, but not gracefully. "There are similarities," she would say, "but they are not conclusive." Her attestation was weak. I watched her leave the courtroom, carrying the samples of my mother's writing, like a pup with its tail between its legs, the magnified signatures useless.

The trial had taken four long days. I prayed that the lawyers would summarize briefly this morning. My Irish brothers were ripe for a fight in the corridors of the Boston courthouse. Certainly Tom had tried to cause one, meeting Michael on the stairs to the restroom on the second day and giving him a hefty punch to the shoulder as they passed. Mike didn't punch back, but shouted to draw attention. Maybe it had been a fraternal punch and Mike took it the wrong way. Then, after the third day, while Paul and I waited for a taxi outside the courthouse, Patrick paced up and down the street, ominous, challenging, staring us down while we tried to ignore him. God knows what he intended. Each walkpast he came closer to us and I began to fear he might be armed. I decided to alert security. He followed me and reached the door before I did, turned around and came so close we brushed arms. I thought he was going to tell me, "You lying bitch, you'll get it, just wait." That seemed to be the prevailing position of my brothers. I was ready. He simply said, "Hello Molly." I didn't respond though my heart was wrung as I choked on the lump in my throat. Poor Pat, swallowed up in this vendetta, a stooge for the lawyers.

Too often when Patrick or Tom was on the stand, I had the urge to deny their statements or raise my hand for permission to expose an outright lie. However, court protocol and common sense restrained me, though both Patrick and Tom indulged in simple outbursts from time to time when I, or Mike or Alana, were on the witness stand. Judge Leahy overlooked their rawness and the clerk of the court admonished them.

It was difficult to hear the defense attorney. He spoke directly to the Judge but I caught mention of the name of a lawyer named Snare, a claim for seventy thousand dollars, Alana Cronin's name, Gillis and McGloan, Canadian attorneys, other references and my name. I thought he was trying to emphasize just how many claims existed against the estate and treat my case as one of them. Patrick surveyed the list and agreed. "When we sold the business we undertook responsibility for all claims. This is one of them." The defense lawyer concurred, adding coyly, almost whispering "*e pluribus unum.*"

Someone should remind them this trial was about identity, not about money. But Judge Leahy had stressed that argument more than once. No use protesting.

My lawyer had questioned Tom on the stand. Did he tell his friends at work and his family that Molly McBeath was his sister?

Tom replied with an emphatic NO.

"Are you sure?" the lawyer asked.

"I never said yes she was, I said maybe."

"You gave Molly McBeath's name to the newspapers as Sean's sister?"

"Yes sir."

"You gave the same information to the attorneys for the estate and it was included in the application for administrators?"

"I made a mistake, I was nervous."

"You're not nervous today?"

"Yes, I am."

Stall brought forward the picture taken at Tom's twenty-fifth anniversary party. "You are all together in this family picture, you all look happy."

"That's not a family picture. It was a party."

"Can you identify the people in the picture?"

"Yes sir." He named Pat, Tim, Mike, Fran, Danny, and the wives of four of them, with Sean and Tom standing behind the group each with an arm around me. Tom did not name me.

"Molly McBeath is in this picture."

"She's not family."

Stall let that rest. He then produced a picture taken my first Christmas with my mother, in Toronto. I took selfish advantage of the moment when Judge Leahy said it was a nice picture. ". . . these are happy people, but they're very young. Who are they?"

Proudly I explained. "It's a four-generation picture, Your Honour. Something I never thought would happen in my life. My granddaughter Julie is thirteen, her mother Mary is thirty-four, I'm fifty-three and my mother is seventy-two. It was the happiest of days." I was beaming in the picture, I never looked better because I never felt better and I could say the same about my mother. At that point I thought Paul looked contentedly competent, in another word, smug. He told me later the lump of pride in his throat at the mention of his wife and daughter made him cry.

Then with Patrick on the stand, Stall produced pictures taken at Sean and Patrick's homes, and asked Patrick to identify the people in the pictures. "Look at this, you have your arm round her. You're smiling, you are happy to be sitting next to Molly McBeath at that time."

"I always smile in pictures."

"Here's another one. Who is that sitting in the middle?"

"Her," Patrick said grudgingly.

"You have your arm around Molly McBeath again, you are smiling again."

"I smile in all pictures. I'm not by her in that one," he indicated.

"No, because Sean wanted to sit next to her, right?"

Patrick had to insist right then that Sean did not call me to confirm his wedding date. "Sean phoned all his brothers from my house the night before he died to tell them he changed his wedding date. He wasn't going to get married on Christmas Eve because our families didn't want that date. He did not call Molly McBeath. We have the phone bills right here to prove that Sean did not call her."

It wasn't an issue at this point but Stall was vigilant. And oh, how well I remembered Sean's call. It had come around nine o'clock, during the hockey game. I teased him that the Toronto Leafs were giving the Boston Bruins problems. I didn't know where he called from. And then the devastating call at five in the morning, from Patrick's wife no less. "Your brother died an hour ago. Sean had a heart attack." She promised to call me the next day with funeral details.

Stall asked for the phone receipts and Patrick spent some hurried moments rummaging in his wife's purse. His attitude was typical, characteristic of a know-it-all. My lawyer studied the phone statement and maybe Sean hadn't called me from Patrick's phone but he had called me.

"But, look here," Stall said artfully, "at 4:17 a.m. on December ninth you phoned Florida. Who did you call?"

"I was trying to get Joseph."

"At 4:35 a.m. you called New York. Who did you call?"

"Michael."

"At 4:50 you called Toronto. Who did you call?"

"It might have been her." A guarded reply.

"Now here," Geoff Stall continued, disregarding the impact of Patrick's answer, "at 1:46 p.m. you called Florida again."

"Yes, that was Joseph," Patrick said smartly as though the questions were routine and he knew all the answers.

"And at 2:23 you called New York. Was that Michael?"

"Yes sir."

"At 2:50 p.m. you called Toronto. You called Molly McBeath because you were calling family members."

"We called some friends, too."

"At four or five in the morning? You were calling your sister," he charged.

Patrick yelled, "She's not my sister! She never was and she never will be."

Stall yelled his questions as well and the judge warned him. Then he asked quietly, "If this court tells you she is your sister, would you accept that?"

"NO! In my heart I respect that robe and the man in it, but she is not my sister."

This final morning we were in a smaller courtroom, Judge Leahy's usual room, I was told. The wainscoting, the railing, the benches, the high ceiling, old long windows, so like the orphanage chapel, evoked penurious memories, for I had been poor in every sense of the word. These were feelings I could handle nonetheless, for no matter what the outcome, what was said to me or about me, no one, nothing, could shatter the satisfaction, the comfort, the joy of having found my mother; being able to put a face now, in my mind's eye, to that wellspring that is every child's indubitable right. Though appearing calm and assured, sitting tall on the church-like bench, my pulse rate counted a hundred and twenty by the white-faced clock on the wall and my sciatic nerve was rebelling from too many days on the hard wooden bench. Now in this smaller courtroom, Tom and Patrick, the administrators of Sean's estate, just a little to my left, were too close for comfort. Joseph huddled nearby. They went to the water cooler, after a while to the washroom. The court reporter set up her transcriber, the clerk of the court busied herself with the orderly conduct of the morning and I waited. I thought about my life. It all seemed so bizarre. Who'd believe half of it? The deprivation and cruelty, the hopes and determination, the inconceivable joy of knowing my mother, talking to her on the phone, sending her a dress, taking her to dinner in my car, cooking dinner for her, sleeping in her bed, talking about us both getting pregnant and not being ready for that complication; standing before a mirror with her and comparing our likenesses, or putting our palms together, saying our hands were alike, but finding her fingers much longer than mine. And now, after searching all my life, this denial.

"Please stand. Oyez, oyez, oyez . . . this court is now in session." The moving and shuffling brought a moment of sanity. I just had to endure these hours. They were crucial. I must defend my rights and the joyful memory of that highest possible point of perfection when I first spoke to my mother— or maybe it was when she met my children and I watched her with them.

The defense attorney pronounced, "An illegitimate daughter of an Irish girl is inconsistent with everything we've heard about Mrs. O'Connor. This is an obsession. There is so much wishful thinking in Molly McBeath's conduct, it's really a life-long pre-occupation with wishful thinking. The name O'Connor suggested to her by a nun when she was twelve or thirteen made her search one of wishful thinking. Thomas O'Connor never picked Molly McBeath up at the airport, Patrick O'Connor was not present at Schroeder's restaurant and he did not give her gifts and pictures. There is a large element of wishful thinking in this case. Mrs. McBeath just happened to connect up with *this* Kathleen O'Connor. And Mrs. O'Connor was too senile, her memory too far gone. The brothers had to wait, they couldn't stop the relationship because it might upset her and it wouldn't do any harm to let Molly McBeath's wishful thinking go on." Hemming and hawing, he insisted I lived in a world that I wanted to be true, rejecting reality. He wasn't convincing and during the last few days in court I began to get the feeling he believed in my cause. "As for the blood evidence Your Honor, this procedure is fairly new and has been used so far only in paternity actions. It may suggest kinship, certainly not sibship. Furthermore, Michael is type O and the claimant is type B." He dashed off more extemporaneous argument that I was an impostor. "Whether or not Mrs. McBeath was adopted is another possibility. If so, that cuts off any inheritance rights. First, you'd ask, were there adoption papers? We don't have them. After all we are dealing with New Brunswick in Canada. The state of records is bad in New Brunswick."

His ignoble slander of the state of the records was shocking. Paul whispered, "Not smart." I thought the lawyer was offhand, he had lost interest in a losing battle. However this was all part of the drama and altogether intriguing to hear this Judge, these lawyers go on and on about who I was or might not be when for fifty years or more no one cared, no one knew and no one helped. Now, because of money, it was damned important that hordes of people spend a lot more money trying to disprove my identity. The defense summation was a sentence in a letter from the Catholic Welfare Society in Saint John: "We know nothing about your parents except they were from Ireland."

Geoff Stall took a firm stand, questioning the credibility of the witnesses.

"Your Honor, you have to listen to what Thomas and Patrick say today and what they said and did between 1978 and 1984. It's not enough to muse that Mrs. McBeath wanted these two forces to come together; that the rest of the family stood back and said 'Okay, let it happen.' If the O'Connors cared as much as they seem to care today about the blight on their mother's good name, why did they report to the outside world in the newspapers on two occasions, in two obituaries, that this woman was their sister?"

Stall was emphatic that the blood test evidence was solid scientific support. The Judge was watchful and interested. "Then, in the third category of evidence," he went on, "is not the presence of Kathleen Shannon in Saint John at the time of Molly McBeath's birth significant? And is it not relevant that her 1927 immigration papers were processed from Saint John? They have attacked Michael because he recognized Molly McBeath as his sister; they have attacked the testimony of Sean's fiancée, Alana Cronin because she supported the defendant. AND WHO ELSE SUPPORTED MOLLY McBEATH?" he shouted. "The decedent, Sean O'Connor did! Listen to some of the words he wrote to his sister:"

> When first I spoke with you on the phone I experienced a
> curious admixture of astonishment, curiosity, joy and
> bitterness. Your visit has put the focus on joy . . . I am
> amazed that you reached your goal with a remarkable

lack of bitterness . . . The point of my letter is this. I was
skeptical before I met you, but I wish you had grown up
with us . . . I believe you are God's gift to our mother in
her old age, and I look forward to knowing you better
during the balance of our lives.

This is signed "Your BROTHER, Sean."

While Geoff Stall read I looked peripherally at Tom. He was doing the
same. I turned my head to look him in the eye, not to sneer or gloat, just to
show him how much I believed Sean's words. The angry child in me saw his
hate. I wanted to taunt them, fight them, but just now I was obliged to do
it the so-called civilized way, the only way open to me. A flood of anger and
distress overwhelmed me, I wanted to cry. Tom became uneasy and turned
to Patrick for support but I turned my back to them. Hiding my emotions
to avoid a scene in court was all that could be done, but oh, how I would
like to have it out with them and just ask *What gives? You were my brothers
before all this. Are you really feeble-minded or just greedy? Why can't you see the
truth in Sean's letter?* Blinkered against common sense, too stupid to give in
to their gut feelings, it was certain we would never again enjoy the
consanguinity we had found. Malice and bitterness had taken over, truth
converted to lies and rationalization.

Judge Leahy said he would write his judgement on the weekend and quite
simply, Court was adjourned.

Paul and I rode to the airport. A significant fall rain pinged against the
taxicab windows. I felt satisfied and relieved. As in the psalm, *I am poured out
like water,* I will inhabit the shape of what comes towards me now. I had
defended my presence in my mother's world. I was victorious. What was
left? Judge Leahy's decision. If a human decision ruled against me, so be it.

Crystal clear water trails criss-crossed the cab windows, singing happily
with me for I loved the noise of water, a powerful symbol of regeneration of
what had become dried up and polluted; an image of atonement making my
life free of extraneous matter. The beauty of truth is all I need. I do have my
place, my existence is important.

I know my mother—I know myself. *As water is in water*, I am complete.

Geoff Stall telephoned from Boston ten days after my return to Toronto.

"Judge Leahy delivered his Decision today. I'm reading it now, we'll
courier a copy to you right away, but I want to tell you it's fair and

exciting. You've won, Molly, and he awarded you costs. Now you can let the world know, you are who you are!" He went on to read some good passages.

When you know you've done your best and the decision is up to someone else, no matter how right you are or how hard you've tried, it is indeed gratifying to hear, "You've won." The opposite would be devastating and you'd have no control at all. I can think of my mother now, see an image and say "my mother" with conviction, never to be cowed again. Never again would anybody deny me the basic claim to ownership of my name and my particular persona. How cruel that the O'Connors had actually tried that tactic, disrupting lives, generating burdens for guiltless individuals, strangling good will, dissipating a valuable estate, wasting the courts, and destroying relationships.

Mary called the family together for a reading so they'd all share the judgement. The Judge's comments were lengthy and rather personal for a legal document but they were sweet. I read the Decision loud and clear in the secure circle of my own close and personal family:

> This is a petition filed by Molly McBeath to amend the petition for administration in the estate of Sean O'Connor by adding her name as an heir to the decedent. The issue in the case is whether Molly McBeath is the daughter of Kathleen Shannon O'Connor and half-sister of Sean O'Connor. Testimony was received from Molly McBeath (the petitioner), Michael O'Connor, Debra Kozak, an expert from the Center for Blood Research, Alana Cronin, Susan Sullivan, a handwriting expert, Joseph O'Connor, Thomas O'Connor, Patrick O'Connor and Marie O'Connor. Sixty-two documentary exhibits were introduced. The defendants are Thomas and Patrick O'Connor, the duly appointed administrators of Sean O'Connor's estate. The petition also contains a prayer to remove them as administrators.

> At the outset, I wish to make a few observations. There were conflicts in the testimony among the witnesses, some of them minor and some significant. To the extent that any of my findings are in conflict with any of the evidence, I choose to disbelieve such evidence.

> Secondly, much of the evidence had no direct bearing on the simple issue whether the petitioner was the daughter of the

mother. However, much of it bore on the motives and good faith of the defendants in contesting this claim and to that extent it was relevant. Other evidence was not relevant enough, in my judgment, to warrant any comments or findings, and to the extent that such evidence is not mentioned, such omission is deliberate. Finally, although it is customary to merely make findings as opposed to a recitation of the credible evidence, I will make detailed findings on the central issue of the case.

Judge Leahy took a lengthy journey through my life narrating what he had learned in the courtroom. Then he wrote:

I realize that I have been reciting the evidence in detail, instead of merely finding ultimate facts based upon such evidence. I felt it was necessary to do so in order to get the whole picture of what happened. From now on, however, my findings will be somewhat more general.

They were general indeed and covered many aspects of my mother's life and the sixty-two exhibits presented to the court. I continued to read:

Various pictures and cards attested to their happy reunion (Exhibits 8, 9, 10 and 12). Some show the petitioner with three or four of her half-brothers, all smiling with the arm of one or two of them around her. Exhibit 9 is a Valentine with the printing, "For a Daughter who's Especially Dear." It is signed, 'Molly, is it too late to say I love you? Ma.'

Exhibit 14 is a letter from Sean, dated April 10, 1979, sharing his emotions of the traumatic event of a new sister coming into his life. Exhibits 15, 16, 17 and 18 all are cards, which illustrate the love and affection the mother and sons had for the petitioner . . . Meanwhile, the mother grew ill with cancer during 1979, and the petitioner visited her. She died on January 3rd, 1980. Sean notified the funeral home that the petitioner was one of her children, and she was so listed in the newspaper death notices. She was also mentioned as one of the children in a eulogy delivered at the funeral.

After the mother's death, and up until the death of Sean, contact between the petitioner and the children was less frequent, but it always remained friendly—and there was no mention during any of this time that the petitioner was not a member of the family, or that the mother was senile.

Thus far my findings have dealt with the petitioner, her life and her efforts to find her mother. To complete the other side of this saga, the mother's life must be told.

Judge Leahy chronicled her life and my brothers' attitudes with uncanny accuracy and shrewdness to 1984. My family were eager to hear every word he had written. I read it all, twenty-two pages of findings and judgement.

Sean died on December 9, 1984 from a sudden, unexpected heart attack. He had been a bachelor all his life but was engaged to marry Alana Cronin just twenty days after he died. The petitioner was invited to the wedding. Sean was in the process of drawing a will and leaving his estate to his fiancée. He died before he could complete the transaction. Ms. Cronin sued his estate for 1.5 million dollars, but the case was settled by a payment of $10,000.00 to Boston College, Sean's alma mater, for scholarships, and by giving Ms. Cronin a few articles she desired.

Sean was financially the most successful member of the family. He was the only college graduate and had his own brokerage firm. The inventory filed in Court lists his real estate at $515,521 and his personal estate at $1,865,000. He died intestate, leaving his siblings as his only heirs and next-of-kin.

Sean's death triggered an immediate change of attitude toward the petitioner. Love and friendship turned to hostility on behalf of some of the brothers. And yet Thomas had informed the funeral home that the petitioner was Sean's sister and obituaries in both the *Globe* and *Herald* named her as such.

Only an hour after the funeral, steps were taken to administer Sean's estate. It was decided that Thomas and Patrick would be co-administrators. . . . On December 12th they went to the office of Attorney J.M. Johnston in Boston where a petition for administration was drawn and included the petitioner's name as a next-of-kin (Exhibit 38). It was signed by Thomas and Patrick. It was never filed in Court, however. The petitioner's name was crossed out, and a new petition for administration was filed without listing her as next of kin. That action resulted in the filing of the petition now before me.

From what I have written above, it is clear what my decision
will be, namely to allow the petition. However, there are other
important portions of the evidence that require comment. The
first is the result of a human leukocyte antigen test
administered to the petitioner and Michael. Michael has
supported the petitioner's position at all times, and he was the
only member of the family to volunteer to take this test. He
also testified on her behalf at the trial. The admissibility of such
tests was established by *Commonwealth v. Beausoleil, 397 Mass.
206, 490 N.E. 2d, 788 (1986):* The probability of kinship was
determined to be 99.9%. Such a result speaks for itself.

A principal defense presented in this case involved the health of
the mother . . . there is no question that the mother was frail
and had poor eyesight . . . hospital records were introduced
into evidence. I have examined these records, and based upon
them, I find there was no credible evidence to establish the
allegation that the mother suffered from any mental weakness
as to affect her judgment in this matter. The overwhelming
evidence is that she knew exactly what was going on in all
aspects of this drama and was overjoyed by these totally
unexpected events in her later years. Indeed, even after Sean's
death when some of the family turned against the petitioner,
Tim wrote to all of his siblings: (Exhibit 40) "On a personal
note, the meeting of Molly our sister—it made all the work of
putting a home together for Ma worthwhile, to have her find
Ma in a nice place. And I saw Ma so happy to be reunited with
her daughter after so many years . . . and I am glad to be a part
of it. I am shocked how some of the family react, because of
Sean's estate, to Molly . . ." He tried to account for the
mother's money while she lived with him, telling a harrowing
account of how he took the mother, after discharge from the
hospital, from brother to brother looking for lodging for two
weeks while he finished drywall and alterations in a place he
was preparing for her. I do not find any merit in the
preposterous theory that this whole episode was a cruel hoax
perpetrated by the petitioner, and that the mother was the
gullible victim thereof.

Insofar as the birth certificate of the petitioner was concerned, it
was perhaps the only bit of evidence that the defendants could
argue about. It is marked Exhibit 2 and is a document which

purports to be signed by a Kathleen Shannon. It states the petitioner's mother was born in Cork, Ireland, whereas Kathleen Shannon (O'Connor) was born in County Galway, not County Cork. The main argument, however, is that the handwriting on the document is not that of the mother. An expert so testified. Samples of the mother's genuine handwriting were offered in evidence and were compared to that on the birth certificate. At first blush they appeared to be clearly the writing of two different people. However, after a lengthy and skillful cross-examination of the expert by Attorney Stall, my inexpert and quickly-arrived-at opinion that the writings were those of two people, was badly shaken . . . the most enlightening, was the offering in evidence of a postcard sent by Kathleen Shannon to her mother on which her handwriting slanted to the right (Exhibit 57). The year, of course, was the same year that the birth certificate was signed. While the expert did not change her opinion on the basis of the postcard, the cross-examination cast serious doubts in my mind of the correctness of her conclusions. It is possible that someone else filled out the birth certificate on the mother's behalf in response to her oral answers. If so, that might explain the discrepancy between "Gort" and "Cork" since both words are so phonetically similar, particularly if pronounced with an Irish brogue. It defies credulity to believe the facts which are known are merely coincidences: namely, that a woman named Kathleen Shannon gave birth to an illegitimate child in New Brunswick, Canada in 1925 and that somehow this Kathleen Shannon is not the same person as Kathleen Shannon who just happened to be the same age and living in the same place at that time. Furthermore, it is totally inconceivable that an Irish woman would admit to having an illegitimate child if, in fact, she never had one.

The motive is clear to me in suddenly making the petitioner *persona non grata* in the O'Connor family. Money, the root of all evil, is the answer. With Sean's unfortunate death and his large estate to be divided among his siblings, some members of the family decided that the petitioner was no longer their sister. As we so often see in this Court, greed took over, and truth was replaced with resentment and rationalizations. It is tragic to see families torn apart by such uncharitable conduct. The scars that are left from these battles are seldom healed, and in years to come they often are the source for guilt and remorse.

At the outset of this opinion I mentioned credibility. Before ending, I wish to comment on the credibility of the principal witnesses. I found the petitioner a most credible witness. She answered all questions in a straightforward manner and did not evade or equivocate. Her answers, even when against her own interest, were made without explanations, arguments, hostility or rationalizations. I was very much impressed by her in all respects. She was intelligent, articulate, natural, unaffected and convincing. She was a lady in every sense of the word.

The testimony of Joseph, Thomas and Patrick was, on the other hand, very suspect. None made a good witness. Some of their answers defied common sense, while others were, in my opinion, just lies. Joseph, for example, testified that his mother did not trust Michael. Yet she gave Michael a power-of-attorney to manage her affairs when she sold her home. Patrick testified that a picture of all of the children, including the petitioner, and their spouses, was not "a family picture." Pictures of him smiling with his arm around the petitioner did not indicate any affection for her. Thomas contradicted his deposition testimony and claimed he did not tell attorney Johnston that the petitioner was a member of the family. In his deposition, he admitted he had done so. He now says he was nervous when his deposition was taken, and he was not telling the truth. There is no question in my mind as to who was telling the truth in this case.

Finally, the petitioner's attorney has filed a motion for attorney's fees which I am going to allow. I am convinced that the defendants were acting in bad faith, and their defense was frivolous. Not all of the O'Connor family should be held to account for this however. I charge Thomas and Patrick, as co-administrators, with bad faith in asserting the frivolous defense of this case. The defendants have the legal responsibility for what has happened here, and they must bear the burden of that responsibility. Because of what I have found, the legal fees of the petitioner's attorney shall come solely from the shares of Thomas and Patrick, so that the shares of the petitioner, and the others, shall be paid in full.

Thereafter the judge cited his Conclusions of Law naming precedents and declared, "The petition is allowed." I told my smiling family, "This marvelous decision is signed, Vincent F. Leahy, Justice, October 8, 1987."

When all was read and done in a loving family setting everyone started talking together. Julian, the legal expert, cleared his throat for attention, touched the ends of his fingers together and suggested, "There's just one thing missing in that decision." We waited for his wise words. I was glad he volunteered to say anything at all.

"The judge should have added to that, 'P.S. I love you.'"

Everyone laughed with Julian. Ben winked at me, glanced quickly around the room and mouthed *I* love *you*. Mary poured champagne and the party was on.

Is it so small a thing
To have enjoyed the sun,
To have lived light in the spring,
To have loved, to have thought, to have done.
To have advanced true friends, and beat down baffling foes?
Matthew Arnold

AFTERWORD...

*I*T WASN'T UNTIL October 1991 that Sean's estate was settled. Profoundly thoughtful of the implication of this legacy I used it for a down-payment on my first home, a small condo-loft with large windows facing the sunrise and a dramatically thrilling view of Humber Park, Lake Ontario and the Toronto skyline. My mother and Sean would have approved.

Able and willing, I continued to work for the National Hockey League for another five years; there was satisfaction in belonging to a good company. I thrived on the responsibility of my office. Hockey was made up of magnificent ingredients: skill, speed, danger and competition, the most exciting of sports spectacles. Alas, the game was changing; it had become entertainment and big business, getting bigger day by day and losing some of its appeal for me. I travelled as an assistant to the general manager's meetings, privileged trips to Palm Beach, Vancouver and particularly La Quinta, California where my desk, placed just inside the massive wooden doors of the Golf and Tennis Club, was wide open to the warmth and brilliance of the desert sun, in an oasis of green-green lawns and orange-laden trees. I enjoyed trips to the Entry Draft and the All-Star game each year; the Hockey Hall of Fame induction and Annual Awards, travelling to the most exciting NHL cities. Life was full and interesting.

*J*ulian opted for early retirement on grounds of illness. His peers applauded, honoured and celebrated his career, "his ready wit, his great understanding of and compassion for people, his humour, erudition, forensic abilities, negotiation through cajoling, avoidance of confrontation, fairness, honesty, justice, his impromptu allusions to Shakespeare . . ." He deserved the homage but the side he showed to me was different. Frightened of attention, intolerant of people, paranoid. He was terrified someone was going to write an article about him, expose him in some way, and take away his right to a pension. He'd rub the tips of his fingers as though they were numb, pressing one, then another, then all together, over and over. I couldn't convince him that nobody was giving his shortcomings, real or imaginary, a thought.

Molly Ann found the ideal retirement home for him near her home in Toronto, Mary undertook his power of attorney and liaison with doctors and medical staff, responsibilities taken on with cheerful readiness. He was apprehensive but agreed to the move. Ben and I (yes, Ben) spent time packing his essentials and disposing of clothes and hundreds of books. Julian "held court" as I showed him each suit or pair of trousers and he ruled: "I'll take that," or "Get rid of that." The wads of money extricated from old pockets grew into an amazing pile of crumpled bills; some folded, some bearing a George VI image, now an interesting heap on his coffee table.

"How much is there?" he asked.

"Three thousand at least," I guessed but any attempt to stack or count it irritated him. "Do you have to take that long?" he asked bluntly. "Just leave it then."

With apprehension I bagged several kinds of prescription medicine and took it to the drug store for disposal. He said he would keep the Lorazepam, a controlled drug. Maybe that somewhat explained his worsened agitation, suspicion, and other demands—and his story about the hospital where he lay on the floor in the night, unable to get up, talking to a man who wasn't there who wouldn't help him.

When he was ready I went to Niagara to drive him to Toronto. It was a traumatic end to life as he had lived it. It was hard to act as if what I was doing was normal, impersonal, because it was not. Still, he made me smile when he was leaving his apartment for the last time. "Well, the famous law enforcer is leaving town and does anybody care?"

"Maybe I should call the mayor?" I teased.

"Yes, I'd like a parade," he said sarcastically, but there was a hint of humour.

With rules of dress and hours for the dining room, it didn't take Julian long to say he preferred his breakfast in his room at noon. Wonderful people, they obliged. We catered to his demands for whipping cream for his cereal, keeping it in an ice bucket in his room, replenishing cream and ice daily. Soon he asked if they would serve him dinner in his room. They obliged, opening the blinds to let in some light. "Je-sus, what are you doing?" he cried, giving his customary sharp intake of air through clenched teeth. He made demands, they were met and I was afraid we'd be asked to move him to a nursing home. Instead they kindly suggested that he move to the main floor next to the nursing station and that he rent a hospital bed for the convenience of the caregivers. Molly Ann and her children saw him often, but he said the children irritated him, "Tell her not to bring them here." Mary visited on Friday, the day the doctor came. The boys were faithful. Tom trimmed his hair and shaved him when Julian would allow it, and Brien Patrick often afforded a rhetorical challenge. His CD player and Gigli discs were stacked nearby but he didn't listen to music or read. He preferred the curtain closed, making visiting dreary. Oh how can I talk about such a futile existence? He'd ask for help with his personal needs and I would say, "I am not a nurse." Was that his way of testing or demeaning me? Years before it would have been a labour of love to look after and comfort him, but *love grown faint and fretful, with lips but half regretful, sighs.* Was my young love so innocent it was immortal? I don't know. I did feel relief that Julian's pension would keep him in care forever if necessary.

One Friday when the doctor made his rounds, I undertook to leave the room. "Stay," he said. "It's okay," agreed Julian. He asked the doctor to increase his medicine. "I can't sleep, I need something else."

"You can't sleep because you're in bed all day, not working as you used to, no exercise."

"I'm shaky when I try to walk, I can't walk alone."

"Your stance and gait are bound to be unsteady, that's a side effect of the drug. You can't walk alone because you're not getting exercise. I can't increase your Ativan. You're at the limit. We won't take it away from you but we can't increase your dose." There was no alternative. Seldom did Julian fail to get his way. His pained acquiescence was ironic.

Filling the gap in conversation I told him of my impending retirement from the NHL office, not expecting a reaction, not caring if there was one.

"Christ, why would you quit a job you can do standing on your head?"

"My head gets tired. Besides retirement is overdue, I'm quitting the first of April."

"You're crazy. You can't give up a good job like that."

"I have. Don't forget, you retired early."

"Yes but I didn't have a mansion by the lake to maintain."

"You're terribly funny. My 'mansion by the lake' is tiny and the management of it is under control. Besides, you had a profession. I'm leaving a servile job after thirty-five years."

On April first, a Saturday, Mary said, "Come for late lunch, Mom. Julie will be here." I loved sitting at Mary's round kitchen table; conversation was refreshing, her family loving, and she hummed her way through the lovely preparations. Besides I loved seeing Julie who was expecting her second baby soon. Loved, loving, lovely, all lovesome words for a lovable family merely five minutes from my home. I dressed for lunch because I felt like it. A philosophy to suit my new life.

Ben drove me to Mary's home and we made plans to be together later to celebrate. There was one utterly pure instant when I saw certain cars parked and knew there was a party and it was for me. Thirty-five of my most wonderful people had come. Ben had secretly rummaged in my albums, circa 1943, for pictures which were now enlarged posters plastering the walls of the entry hall. *Our Working Woman!* signs were abundant. Much joy, glorious tributes, clever speeches, significant poems sung and spoken, another litany of my work history, beginning with the laundress in the ironing room and again dissecting my twenty jobs before the twenty-four years with the National Hockey League. Only Tom could pull off those subtle quips about being motherless until one was a grandmother.

Paul presented me with an antique iron, a grotesque type that encased live coals. His lengthy poem, narrating my days in the laundry, saying that he now understood where the coal I used to put in his Christmas stocking had come from, was clever and witty. I treasure it. The "late lunch" happened at seven o'clock because we were too busy with laughter, emotion and love.

On Monday morning, the first workday of retirement life I settled at Julian's bedside with Mary Gordon's *The Rest of Life*, meditations by three women on love, sex and death. I was content and happy.

"I'll just sit here unless you want to talk. I don't have to be anywhere today."

Julian looked through half-closed lids. Maybe I sounded condescending. The blue watery slits appeared judgmental.

"Come here." He took my hands in his, old blue eyes serious and intent. "For the rest of my life" he said, "I'm going to pay you the respect you deserve." He pulled my hand to his lips. I put my cheek on his small gray head and visualized the thick curly hair I used to adore and I inhaled the oily scalp odor and that acne lotion smell that had been peculiar to Julian all his life. He slept after that, his face peaceful and old. Had his words freed him of as much or as little as he needed? Did he need forgiveness? I ached with forgiveness but I thrived on being responsible, not noble. Did he regret our loss of love, of belief in each other; of the formal agreement of marriage to house, feed, clothe and educate one's children?

A peaceful death came to Julian nine days after I retired. The nurse found him ". . . just sleeping, but then I found no pulse," she said. The Niagara paper wrote, "He was an intellectual man with a great wit, well known for his sense of humour and colorful oratories in the courtroom . . . an unassuming man, a distinguished member of the legal profession."

Ten days later. Julie and Tim's new baby, Liam, was born in his mother and father's bed. I held him and trembled at this little life, a cosmos unto himself.

Our life is closed, our life begins, sang Whitman. Life goes on!

New beginnings and the sounds of innocence brought to the world by my grandchildren have been the ultimate contentment. Brennan was born ten years after Tommy, a special arrival to Mary and Paul. Then beautiful Katie arrived to Tom and Donna. I had private hopes that I would live long enough to see Molly Ann and Michael's children. She was studying intently, no apparent plan for a baby. To my delight, Marion Malone arrived before the Ph.D. thesis. Four years later Jack Malone was born. Six months later Julie and Tim's golden-haired, amazing blue-eyed Geneviève, arrived—and I was a great-grandmother. Then her brother Liam was born.

I brag about accomplished students of piano and flute; the chorister with the Toronto Children's Choir, about the little hockey player who races for the puck and scores hat tricks like a pro, and the big hockey player who tells me, when I say I don't much like fighting and body contact, "Grandma, it feels so good." I brag about the newest tiny hockey player whose first word was "hock-eee"; about the little girl soccer players, the Russian/Italian major at U of T and especially about the midwife who was in the first class to study midwifery when it became legal in Ontario. Having spent several years preparing for the event, Julie graduated with honours and has a thriving practice in St. Jacob's. I have many reasons to boast and be proud, and time to enjoy my grandchildren's accomplishments and performances. I drive the busiest highway in this country with élan and pleasure, keeping pace with all they do. Funny thing about retirement: there's never a day off.

Yes, I share my good life. Today I went to visit Sister Monica on her ninety-sixth birthday, a survivor of more than eighty years of the Halifax explosion in 1917. I'd been seeing her at fixed intervals for years and then took my grandchildren, who delighted in singing and performing skits for the half-dozen nuns in residence at Regina Mundi. Julie and Jenny whispered and schemed, wore hats and draped scarves, played the piano and were the brightest stars while the older nuns delighted in them. "I was one of Sister Monica's girls," I told her sisters. Before long she'd gather us to herself and tell the other nuns, "You may go now, sisters," and then tell me, "You don't have to say that."
"Say what?"
"That you were one of the girls."
So, for some, there was still shame about my youth.

Fifty years ago—I can't believe it was fifty years ago that I was invited to join an elite group of young mothers in Niagara. Elite? Looking back we agree we were, collectively, as choice a bunch of young, new mothers as you'd find anywhere. We took turns hosting in each other's homes and we made and sold things, giving our profit to causes or to families who had less than we had. Twenty of us knitted baby clothes, made dozens of aprons and felt Christmas stockings and hand-painted Maxwell House coffee cans filled with newly rooted plants. We had eighty babies and we are still friends. Some strong singular friendships go back to primary school. To this day we have lunch together in Niagara every month and our laughter is civilized music. In literature there are few accounts portraying the pleasures of this time in life but Cicero did hint that nature had aptly planned other aspects of life's drama and it wasn't likely she had neglected the final years as if she were a careless playwright.

Sixty years ago today I ran away from St. Vincent's. Fifty-three years ago I walked to the hospital on a sunny November morning to have my second baby. I was twenty, the war was over, I loved life, I loved the way my body could walk a mile in celebration of this child's birth. I loved Tom best, for when he was conceived I was disappointed only because it was too soon, I had an eight-month-old baby girl and was so afraid of the war. Soon I was waiting for him, imagining him, loving my condition so he'd never know the feeling that was in my heart briefly. During bad times I used to think, if I have to leave Julian and can't have all my children, I'll take Tom first. He was a good child with few demands, cleverly apt with a comic sense of fun, a little sport, so easy to love.

Oh, I loved pregnancy—the months in my life when I felt creative, powerful, important. Such an extreme experience that I could create life in me, a beguiling time to dwell upon my condition while it lasted. It was beautiful to know babies would live all their lives because I carried them while they developed. I loved Mary best; she was the fulfillment of young love. To me she was a miracle. She still is. But then I had to love Brien best, don't ask me why except that he was the first baby I'd really planned to have. When Tom was four I wanted a baby again to snuggle, to feel my lips against his baby hair, to hum a lullaby and say a prayer for what he would become. I walked the hospital corridor for two long days in labour thinking Blake: *My mother groaned! my father wept. Into the dangerous world I leapt: Helpless, naked, piping loud; Like a fiend hid in a cloud.* Eventually he was born, a perfect baby, so content that I looked forward to his wakening and he became such a friendly little neighbour on our street, knocking on doors to see if grandfathers could come out to play. When he was four I found myself in a pregnant state once again and I yearned for a baby girl. Only a girl I said, it must be a girl. I wore pink, I bought pink baby things while I carried her and I knew I would be a mother for the last time. So I had to love Molly Ann best. There was more happiness when Mary wanted to bathe the new baby, rock and wheel her too; the beautiful aspect of little Brien retrieving his special new toy, a large St. Bernard dog, bringing it to the baby's basket and dumping it on top of her, wide-eyed and trusting, telling me, "It's for her." I experienced life through my children. I was as simple as a child myself having these masterpieces to share my days and I fashioned my life through what involved them.

All my life I've been drawn to Ireland and now the bond is firm. I've just come home from my latest visit and I'm inclined to say it was the best trip, yet when I look back I can indulge the memories of fourteen best trips to Ireland, twelve after I found my mother. The year she died I went that summer and met her remaining family. Then I went again and again for my cousin Eileen wrote with affection, "You are always welcome here, your room is ready." I saw Fergus Shannon again and, with keys hanging in the locks of their front doors, he asked, "Have you been below?" and when I went two doors away to an aunt's, the question was, "Have you been above?" I got to cherish Fergus as we drove to the fields to see his cattle. He was a bachelor, he didn't drive, yet one day on an early visit he wanted to show me the sea. We didn't find the sea that day in my rental car but he'd say, "Keep driving, Molly dear. We'll come out somewhere then. Fancy me drivin' round with me niece."

The children of my mother's third brother became very dear to me. I cherish their friendship, I admire their lives and nurture the privilege of family visits. On subsequent travels via England I met my mother's brother Joe and his wife, their son Peter and his wife, Mary. They are the greatest people, loving and giving, saying it is something special to have a cousin from "across the pond." Joe dressed like a prince and carried an umbrella like a nobleman when we walked together to the river where he took crumbs to feed a family of swans. He'd squeeze my hand and call me by my mother's name. He was fourteen when she left for Canada and he readily laid open his memories of her for me to take to my heart. He is gone now, as is Fergus.

Last year Marion Malone turned thirteen. I took her to Ireland and we laughed our way across Dublin to Cork to Galway. Posing for pictures beside the larger-than-life bronze statue of Molly Malone near Grafton Street in Dublin gave Marion so much delight and happiness knowing she'd present the pictures to her mom, Molly Malone at home. We dressed up in our long silk skirts to see Shaw's Joan of Arc at the Abbey Theatre. Afterwards, feeling grandly incognita, we braved Bachelor's Walk and Marion peered with wonder into the Liffey from Ha'penny Bridge, for she is a dreamer of significance. We stayed a first night at the Shelbourne Hotel where her mother and I had stopped many years earlier. We squirreled away terribly dry bread from afternoon tea sandwiches and also hoarded toast from the dining room in the morning and then spent hours on St. Stephen's Green discovering the foliage and vegetation, Marion feeding the ducks, chasing a turkey and watching the many children with nannies. We moved next day to a Trinity College student residence, the freedom of the campus, the wonder of an early morning convocation while we mingled to see the camaraderie of graduates and families on the cobbled square. A happy anonymity can't be planned but it's there to take and savour, which we did. I watched her flit like a butterfly and now and then she would catch my eye and smile knowingly and beautifully, implying she had heard or seen something lovely or private.

On leaving Ireland Marion told me, "I didn't know there was so many ways to say 'It's no bother.' They're wonderful family. And Nana, this trip has been the best gift. I don't have to find a place to put it; it's a memory."

I wanted a family but never imagined the situation could be so sublime in Ireland and so ridiculous in Boston. Long before these disclosures there had been the son and daughter of Harry McGlyn. I had kept in touch with Elinore McGlyn and heard from her each Christmas. On a motor trip to New Brunswick with Ben last year I went to Halifax to visit her. She was eighty-five then and it was interesting to see her and to hear personal things about her brother and her dad. She died soon after my visit so it was a positive bond in the loose ends of my life.

*T*here is a secret in this epic of the orphan who found a family. Known only to the initiated few, it is something I'm proud of having done. In 1982 I called on old Mrs. O'Hara at the same residence in Athenry where my mother had worked in the twenties. I learned she was the second wife which made it easier for me to become acquainted with her.

"My mother worked in this house and shop and tended the O'Hara children. I'm on a short visit and it's a privilege for me to be able to sit here with you."

"Take a look for yourself. I don't run the business any more, I'm too old."

I stood behind a counter, where my mother, no doubt, had toiled; I flicked beer mugs on hooks, they swayed from side to side. I sat on a barstool. I slid my hand over the old bar surface and tears welled. I wrote in the dust *Molly was here!* It was satisfying.

We had a marvelous visit in the kitchen where my mother had once been. "Stay for tea," Mrs. O'Hara said. Such an intriguing possibility as I savored the odor from the pot on the stove but I had to decline. I was expected in Gort. As is the wont of the older Irish, Mrs. O'Hara produced a box of photographs. There I was, sifting through wonderful pictures of the man I felt certain was my parent and pictures of his children, of weddings and events that happened, making them very real to me, especially nominally as the eldest was called Molly!

Just as I was about to ask she told me, "Francis passed away ten years ago."

"What age was he?"

"Seventy-five. His girls live not far away; you should call on them. Here, take any pictures you would want to have then, there's far too many for me."

I selected carefully and went away with a choice collection. Mrs. O'Hara told me there was a brother and I learned that his name was Sean. It was curious that my mother had called her first two children by the names of the first O'Hara children.

In the next few years I imagined what it would be like to meet and talk with just one of these women, my half-sisters I was certain. In 1987 I went back to see Mrs. O'Hara, ninety now.

"You've just missed them, they were all here and just now left. They're visiting Louise in Galway, planning her daughter's wedding. Call on them, they'd be delighted to see you for a wee while, I know."

I drove away not so sure that I would have the nerve to knock on the door of women who might read between the lines. I passed the house twice and the next time I parked. *What is there to lose?*

They were divine, I was ecstatic and had to appear an ordinary visitor.

"We had many girls in service but I remember your mother, she was tall and had strong red hair. I was seven or eight when she left us." The eldest, Molly, speaking. "Do you have sisters?"

"My mother had eight sons after me." *Terrible thought!* their expressions said.

"Was your father Irish?" *Be careful, don't let the sherry loosen you tongue.*

"He was from Ireland, they met in Boston." *Half-truths. Fair enough.*

With great determination they located the camera while I, the guest, sat on a chair, Louise and Eileen stood behind and Molly perched on the arm. Louise's daughter snapped us. The pictures were good, they sent copies to me and I'm glad to have them. Molly and I exchange Christmas notes each year.

How large my longed-for family had become.

"I loved my father," Molly O'Hara had said. "Daddy and I had a special rapport."

And so the secret sits in my heart forevermore. It is not a burden.

I live for the moment now and the most satisfying part of life is dialogue with my progeny and their spouses. I play it to the hilt, sometimes covertly, inclined to be proud that I'm included so thoroughly with Mary, the senior scientist, epidemiologist and associate professor; Tom, programmer and computer specialist; Brien a graphic arts expert and now high school teacher, and Molly Ann, child psychologist. Add to that the profound pleasure of conversation with Paul, professor, biostatistician, great human being, a loving and lovable man as are Michael and Tim. Sharon, Tom's first wife is as dear to me as a daughter. Donna, his present wife and mother of Katie, compliments our family with her truth and beauty. Sharon and Donna are friends. The same goes for Ben and Julian. They were friendly because of me. There are those who have found this unusual and say so. They should be so lucky! Life is too serious now and little moments of goofiness are necessary for me. I'm not sitting on the sidelines, rocking my way to oblivion. I'm into overtime and the best part comes from all the ongoing activity with my grandchildren, valiant souls of the next generation.

I've gotten used to depending on Ben; he makes me happy. When I want him, we are together; when I prefer, I am alone though that is seldom, for there is comfort in a shared life. We haven't transcended romance yet, we live for each day and the best part is going back to Bent Tree, for it's a haven where there's freedom to love and a sense of longevity after twenty-something years. For all his dignity and propriety I love him most at Bent Tree in his old plaid shirt and denim overalls, hunched with his chain saw or swinging an axe. He's happiest there with his hands in the earth or fixing some greasy thing. He'd be surprised to know that I see him with wonder and approval when he thinks I'm apt to be telling him to wash up.

Ben is a leaf on my tree of life as are all the others. Luxuriant, living foliage, whereas I'm the fall maple leaf, strong, many faceted and colourful. "She's our own dare-devil," Marion said to her mom recently. I take that as a compliment from a modern teenager.

Life, while we have it, is an opportunity to do something that would not have been done by anyone else. An uncertain voyage undoubtedly with heartaches, disappointment, failure and even tragedy, but it's the striving to live life fully with what we've been handed that makes life infinitely rich and beautiful.

It can't be better than this!

About the Author . . .

The author grew up at St. Vincent's orphanage
and The Good Shepherd Convent in Saint John,
New Brunswick and has been a resident of
Toronto for forty years. Her greatest blessing—
her children and their families live close at hand
in Toronto.

A member of the Canadian Authors Association,
Mary's short stories have been published in the
CAA's anthology, Wordscape.

Since retiring from her career with the National
Hockey League, she has dedicated herself,
wholly and earnestly, to this, her first book.